the ROCK SAYS...

the ROCK
WITH JOE LAYDEN

CollinsWillow
An Imprint of HarperCollinsPublishers

First published in the United States in 2000
by HarperCollins*Publishers*
10 East 53rd Street
New York, NY 10022

This edition published in 2000
by CollinsWillow
an imprint of HarperCollins*Publishers*
London

1 3 5 7 9 8 6 4 2

The HarperCollins website address is:
www.fireandwater.com

A CIP catalogue record for this book is
available from the British Library

ISBN 0 00 710737 4

Printed and bound in Great Britain by Omnia Books Limited, Glasgow

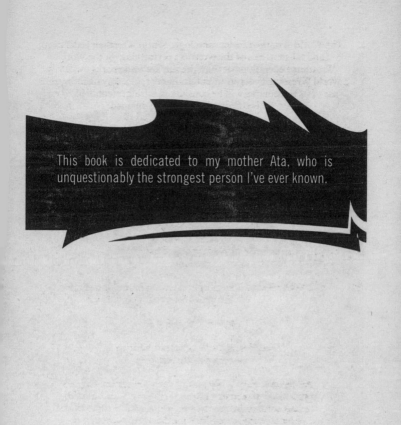

This book is dedicated to my mother Ata, who is unquestionably the strongest person I've ever known.

"Be not afraid of greatness: some are born great, some achieve greatness and some have greatness thrust upon them."

William Shakespeare

"I have never gone so wrong as for telling lies to you. What you've seen is what I've been. There is nothing that I can hide from you. You see me better than I can."

Willie Nelson, "'Til I Gain Control Again"

the ROCK SAYS...

CONTENTS

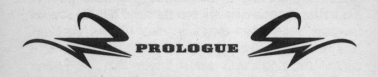 PROLOGUE

March 28, 1999 (Philadelphia, Pa)—The Rock says he can hear them out there, 21,000 strong…21,000 screaming, rabid fans, the best damn fans in the world. They're chanting his name, over and over, with so much fire and passion that the First Union Center is shaking and shimmying. Philly feels like Frisco in 1906. We're at the epicenter of a quake here, and The Rock is the reason why. Adrenaline rushes through his powerful body like a rain-swollen river, feeding his muscles…his nerves…with fuel for the fight. As he stands behind the curtain, waiting for his cue, The Rock knows this is his moment…the moment he's worked for, sacrificed for…the moment so many have dreamt about, and so few have ever experienced…the moment he deserves.

The Rock stands ready—poised, primed, primped, and pumped—for the biggest event in sports-entertainment: *WrestleMania!*

The music hits— *"DO YOU SMELL WHAT THE ROCK IS COOKING?"*—and 21,000 Rock fans, along with the millions… *and the millions*…of the Rock's fans watching at home, leap to attention. The noise is deafening as the crowd salutes the most electrifying man in sports-entertainment. The Rock splits the curtain to a blinding strobe show, a shifting, shimmering sea of flashbulbs. Everyone wants a piece of The Rock! A five-by-seven reminder of the night The Great One made history. Who can blame them? There's never been anyone like The Rock, and there never will be again.

Looking like the Federation Champion that he is, The Rock strolls confidently down the aisle, walking as only The Rock can walk, a big old chip on one shoulder, the World Wrestling Federation Championship belt over the other. With his sculpted physique, honey-brown complexion, razor-trimmed sideburns, and piercing gaze, The Rock looks like a million bucks—which is appropriate, since that's almost exactly what The People's Champion will earn for his evening's labor. To a normal man that might seem like a lot of money, but to The Rock...it's chump change. The Rock is a bargain at this price. And he knows it. There's a reason that this event, *WrestleMania XV*, will be remembered as the greatest night in the history of professional wrestling. There's a reason it will shatter box office records. There's a reason many will call it the single most enthralling, captivating, mesmerizing match in the annals of *WrestleMania*. There's a reason...and the reason is clear.

The Rock! The World Wrestling Federation Champion...The People's Champion...the best damn champion there ever was.

The Rock enters the ring to an ear-splitting roar. With malice in his heart and malevolence on his mind, he turns to face the curtain. His opponent appears. The Rock's eyes are locked on his. At this moment The Rock's intensity is second to none. Within minutes the battle will be joined, and The Rock will commence laying the smack down on this man...this jabroni. His name is Stone Cold Steve Austin, and his candy ass belongs to The Rock!

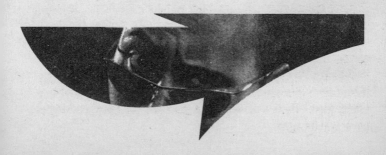

the ROCK SAYS...

chapter 1

ROYAL RUMBLER

I WAS EIGHT YEARS old when my family moved to the island of Hawaii. This really wasn't all that big a deal to me, since I was accustomed to being uprooted on a regular basis. My father, Rocky Johnson, was a professional wrestler, and life in "the business" in those days was nomadic, to say the least. Professional wrestling in my dad's era—he started in the mid-1960s—was not the well-oiled international entertainment machine that it is today. There was no dominant organization, like the World Wrestling Federation, watching over the game and its participants. There were no multimillion-dollar television contracts or Pay-Per-View specials. There was little or no merchandising to fatten the wallets of the wrestlers

themselves—no video games or action figures or
lunch boxes. Instead, professional wrestling was a
gloriously gritty and splintered business consisting of
dozens of self-sufficient, and self-governing, territories:
Florida, Tennessee, North Carolina, and Georgia, just
to name a few. Generally, at that time, guys would
work a territory for six months to a year, two years at
the most. They'd move in, get acclimated, make a
name for themselves, and before long they'd wear out
their welcome and have to move on. That's just the
way it worked. Everyone who wrestled accepted the
life—in fact, most loved it.

I was raised in this environment. It was all I knew,
all I can remember. There was never a time when
wrestling wasn't part of my life. And so, like a child
of the circus, I was a road warrior from the very
beginning, bouncing from one part of the country to
another, from one apartment to another. By the time
I started kindergarten I had already lived in five states.
I don't recall ever being bothered by the constant
movement—to tell you the truth, I found it exciting.
And I sure as hell never lacked for attention or love. I
went to shows with my mother, Ata, and together we
cheered every one of Rocky's sensational, athletic
moves. My mom was the real rock of the family.

Having grown up in the business, she understood the sacrifices that were necessary for success. And so she did what she had to do to keep the family together. When it was time to pack up the van and move to another town, she made it feel like an adventure.

It was in Hawaii that I got to know my grandparents real well, and I think that's part of the reason I fell in love with the place, and why I still consider it my home away from home. It represents so much of my heritage and my past and all that's important to me. My grandfather, Peter Maivia, was a legend in this business, and not just because he was a terrific wrestler, although he certainly was that: heavyweight champion of Texas and U.S. Tag Team champion were just two of the titles he held. Peter Maivia was known for being one of the toughest guys around. Not in a mean or antagonistic or showy way, but in an honest way. He was just a tough son of a bitch, and if you were smart, you didn't mess with him.

Other wrestlers sometimes discovered this characteristic the hard way. Then, as now, the boys in the business sometimes hung out together when they traveled. And one night, in a hotel restaurant, another wrestler began making fun of my grandfather. Peter Maivia was Samoan and, as was the custom of his people, he often liked to eat with his hands. We call it *fa-a-Samoan*—the Samoan way or custom. To this other wrestler, though, it was not a custom. It was something to mock. So the boys were all sitting at a table, surrounded by food, and he was really giving it to my grandfather, insulting him, trying to get a laugh out of something that was actually quite honorable. Eventually, my grandfather, who was a very dignified man, told him to back off and show a little respect.

"Don't make fun of me," he said. "This is my culture."

The other wrestler just laughed and kept at it. Eventually my grandfather stood up, grabbed him by the collar, and dragged him into the lobby and proceeded to beat the living crap out of him. My grandfather was an immense man—about five foot ten, 320 pounds—and so the fight, if you could call it that, didn't last long. It ended when my grandfather lifted the other guy off his feet and tossed him through a window. Then, after his point had been clearly made, my grandfather walked over, helped him up, and said, "You okay?" The man nodded and my grandfather smiled. "Good," he said. "Now . . . just don't make fun of me anymore."

That was just one of the stories I had heard about Peter Maivia. But I had heard other stories, too, and I came to see that they were largely true. Even though my grandfather was the toughest man alive, he was also the sweetest guy you'd ever want to meet. He was gentle and kind, especially to my mother and me. If he was capable of knocking the piss out of you, he was also capable of charming you with a song or a smile. He and my grandmother, Leah, loved each other intensely, but they fought all the time. They bickered constantly, and sometimes their arguments erupted into violence. My grandmother would flail away at my grandfather, and he'd stand there absorbing every blow with his massive arms and chest, until she grew so tired that she'd collapse into him, completely spent. Then they'd kiss and make up, and my grandfather would serenade her with a song on his ukulele. Their relationship was wonderful and crazy and full of passion: *fa-a-Samoan!* It made for some interesting family gatherings, I'll tell you that.

FAMILY FEUD

Wrestling is in my blood. I'm a third-generation worker and part of one of the most famous wrestling families in the business. Interestingly enough, though, it was wrestling that nearly tore my family apart.

In the early 1970s my grandfather was wrestling on the West Coast. Peter Maivia and Rocky Johnson knew of each other back then but they weren't exactly friends. Their paths crossed periodically, and they even teamed up for tag-team matches on a couple of occasions. Well, one night Rocky flew in from Japan to take part in a show and found out that his partner was Peter Maivia. Afterward, exhausted and suffering from jet lag, Rocky started to walk out the door in search of a hotel. Peter, gentleman that he was, intercepted Rocky.

"You're only in town for one night," he said. "Why not come back and stay with us?"

Rocky accepted the invitation, and within a few hours had been introduced to the woman who would become his wife and my mother, Ata Maivia. My mom didn't like Rocky at first. Oh, he was sharp looking and all, very chiseled and athletic and handsome, but he was also a big-time chewer and snuff-dipper, which completely disgusted my mother. She had never seen anything like that before. But Rocky could be a charmer, and it wasn't long before he and my mother fell in love and decided to get married.

There was just one small problem: Peter Maivia was vehemently opposed to his daughter marrying Rocky Johnson. And so was my grandmother. Now, you might think this had something to do with the fact that Rocky is African American. But it didn't. Hell, Samoans are people of color, too. If the KKK comes to visit, they're as likely to go after me as they are my dad. (Incidentally, there is nothing The Rock finds more offensive than racism . . . but more on that later.) Ironically, the reason Peter and Leah Maivia wanted to shield their daughter from Rocky Johnson had nothing to do with his ethnicity and everything to do with his chosen profession. They disapproved of my dad because he was in the business, and my grandparents—especially my grandfather—knew all about the demons of the business. He understood a few things that my mother did not, like the fact that . . . *the boys are the boys.* He knew from personal experience the lifestyle that was typical of an entertainer, of a professional athlete or showman, of anyone who travels for a living. He knew the temptations of the road, and the way that separation had of making the heart grow colder and sadder rather than fonder. And he didn't want that lifestyle for his daughter. Who could blame him? Not that he had heard bad stories about Rocky or anything, but the mere fact that Rocky was a professional wrestler was sufficient reason for my grandfather to disapprove of the union. His daughter may have been born into that world, but she didn't have to *marry* into it as well.

Ultimately, there was nothing they could do to stop Rocky and Ata, of course. When the young couple failed to receive the blessing of Ata's parents, they ran off together and got married, and for a time the family was fractured. Fortunately, my grandparents weren't unreasonable people, and they eventually came to accept the relationship. For them, it came down to a simple choice: *We have one daughter and one daughter only, and either we shelter her right out of our lives, or we say, Hey, if she's happy, then we'll be happy for her.* This development didn't occur overnight, obviously. It evolved over the course of a year and became concrete with the announcement that a baby was on the way. That child was me, Dwayne Johnson.

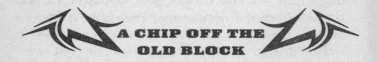

A CHIP OFF THE OLD BLOCK

I was born May 2, 1972, in Hayward, California. My earliest memories are of wrestling—going to shows with my mom, watching my dad fly off the top rope, practicing my dropkicks in the living room when no one was watching. I was always kept extremely close to the business by my parents. They never tried to shield me from it, never pretended that it was something it wasn't. My dad was a gifted athlete and showman, and he made a very good living as a wrestler. He was proud of his accomplishments, and he wanted his son to be proud of them, too.

Rocky Johnson was different from most black wrestlers in the '60s and '70s. First of all, his athletic credentials were impeccable. He was an accomplished boxer who worked for a while as a sparring partner with George Foreman. He was a good swimmer and a natural gymnast. That he wound up in wrestling was mostly a matter of luck. When he was about eighteen years old, while training at a gym in Halifax, Nova Scotia (where he grew up), my dad was approached by a wrestling promoter. At first Rocky wasn't interested, but soon he changed his mind. He began training. Because of his athleticism, he caught on quickly. And because he had a nice look to him—

he was a handsome guy with sharp features and well-defined muscles—his career took off. At a time when this country was still reluctant to embrace strong black men, my father was a groundbreaker. He was the first African-American champion in both Georgia and Texas. He won tag-team titles in Canada and in the National Wrestling Alliance. Near the end of his career, in the early 1980s, he became the first African American to win the World Wrestling Federation Intercontinental title. He also teamed up with Tony Atlas to become the first black tag-team champions in Federation history.

In other words, my dad was one hell of a wrestler, and while he understood the simple truth about his business—that it was indeed a *business*, and that you had to give the people a damn good show—he managed to succeed on his own terms. When my dad broke in, all of the top black wrestlers—not to knock them or anything—but they were all jive-talking caricatures. They'd come out to cut their promos and you'd swear they'd just stepped off the set of *Shaft* or *Superfly*. It would be like, "Hey, brother, I'm gonna kick me some *serious* ass tonight." They'd eat watermelon on camera and do all sorts of degrading things, because that's what was expected of them. My father wouldn't do that. He was the first black wrestler to insist on being very intelligent in front of the camera. When he cut his promos, there would be no jive in his voice. He took pride in cutting promos that were clean and articulate, promos that were *smart!* And when he stepped through the ropes, there was no bullshit funky strut or anything like that. Rocky Johnson was one of the first guys in our business to have a complete package: a great, muscular body, tremendous athleticism, real wrestling talent, and a strong personality. When people saw him perform, it was an awakening. He was a fearless man, a man who welcomed the chance to break down barriers.

I loved watching my dad wrestle. I loved playing with his championship belts. That was a big thing for me, to hold his belt over my head, or to strap it around my chest. But I also understood from a very early age that wrestling was hard work. Did I know whether the carnage on display was "real" or not? That's hard to say. I remember sitting in the front row at the Tampa Armory when I was about five years old, wolfing down fistfuls of popcorn as my father entered the ring. I remember seeing him getting pummeled and feeling, instinctively, that I should jump into the ring to help him: *Who is this man, and why is he trying to hurt my father?!* But my father would do little things to reassure me. And so would my mom. If my father was on the mat, grimacing in pain, really *selling*, my mom would say, "Look, Dwayne, Daddy's smiling at you."

It wasn't like it is now. We'd usually sit in the first seats next to the aisle, and when my father walked down the aisle as he approached the ring, he'd grab my hand, kiss my mom, wave to the crowd. Try that today and the crowd will boo the hell out of you. It's a sign of weakness. I understand that, too, because I always liked the bad guys, the heels, when I was growing up. Bad guys are more fun. One of my favorite television shows was *The Little Rascals*, and I always liked Butch, the kid who would break up the party and start trouble. The mean kid. The kid nobody wanted around. I loved him, even though he was a big pain in the ass. I guess that's because I was a pain-in-the-ass little kid, too, or so my parents have told me. I was the kind of baby you couldn't take to a restaurant because I would always be dumping the food on my head. I was always climbing out of my crib and running around the house. When I started going to wrestling shows with my mom, I'd try to sneak away and explore the armory. I'd run all over the place. When my mother would finally find me, she'd be furious and relieved at the same time. Mom handled the discipline in our family, and I felt her belt across my backside on more than one occasion. Deserved it, too.

My father provided a nice living for our family. He made good money because he was on top almost everywhere he went. Regardless of the territory, Rocky Johnson would quickly become a top contender or challenger and one of the most popular guys in the business. He was different, which obviously made him marketable. He was an African-American wrestler with great fire and emotion, more charismatic than most babyfaces. And my dad *was* a babyface—a good guy—his entire career, which spanned more than twenty years. He had tremendous ambition, as well as great ring psychology. And he was always good to the people, to the paying customer, the backbone of the industry. Endorsements were virtually nonexistent back then, but he still made good money. He'd get a percentage of the house every night, and since people liked to watch Rocky Johnson wrestle, he could always count on a respectable paycheck.

I was fascinated by the business. I loved everything about it: the violence, the theatricality, the athleticism, the volume ... *everything!* By the time I was six years old I was practicing dropkicks and head locks on our dog. By the time I was eight I was trying to have serious discussions about the business with my father. For the most part he reacted like any parent would: *Aw, he's just a kid, rough-housing, dreaming, having a good time. He'll grow out of it.* But he was wrong. I never did grow out of it. And I'm not sure I ever will.

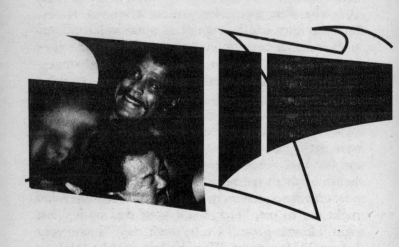

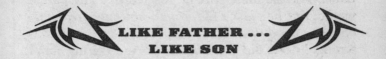

LIKE FATHER ...
LIKE SON

In every territory, the wrestlers enjoyed a healthy dose of celebrity. Barnstorming was an important part of their contractual obligation, so they performed all over the region, usually three or four times a week. They also were featured on weekly television shows. Each territory had its own show specifically tailored to its audience and region so that people could follow the story lines. As a result, everywhere we went—Tennessee, Georgia, Florida, California . . . it didn't matter—people got to know my father pretty quickly. And, subsequently, they got to know me. I was one of those kids you either liked or didn't like. There was no in between. I was too outgoing and confident (and big) to simply blend into the scenery. I always sensed that my father's fame affected the way people treated me. Sometimes positively, sometimes negatively. A kid might say to me, "Hey, I saw your dad on TV last night. He was great." Or, he might say, "I saw your dad on TV last night. Who the hell does he think he is, anyway?!" It could work either way.

I do know that I was about eight years old when I started to defend professional wrestling. This business, from the early 1900s up until at least the mid-1980s, was shrouded in secrecy. There was a code

that bound everyone in the business to uphold the image of legitimacy. This was sacred. If a fan asked a wrestler, "Is this real?" the wrestler would say, without hesitation, "Yes, it is. In fact, I want to go out there and hurt that guy. I want to kill him!" So, at the time, it was important to me to protect the business. Sure, I protect it now, too, but at the same time I would never play anybody for being a fool. I don't want to insult our fans or pull the wool over anybody's eyes. I think my mom and dad almost died the first time they heard me say in an interview, "Oh, yeah, things are predetermined. We have scripts and everything." But when my dad was wrestling, things were a lot different, so when some kid said to me, "That stuff is all fake, it's all bullshit!" my reply would always be, "Is wrestling fake? Well, I can show you better than I can tell you."

"Oh, really? How?"

"Like this!" *WHAM!* Right cross!

I was constantly getting into fights, which wasn't a good thing because I was almost always the biggest kid in the class. I specifically remember being eleven years old, in fifth grade, sitting in gym class in Hamden, Connecticut, waiting for the teacher to arrive. By this time my dad was in the World Wrestling Federation, competing against guys like Sergeant Slaughter, Don Muraco, and Roddy Piper when the whole business was starting to go national. Vince McMahon had taken over all the territories and put the whole sport under one umbrella, and now wrestling was getting tremendous exposure. I was having a discussion about the validity of wrestling with Randy Ellis, a nice kid who remains a friend of mine to this day, when the question came up again.

"So, Dwayne, is it fake or not?"

"Well, Randy, let me show you. Let me pile-drive you."

I knew all the moves, even then. I was so close to the business that I picked up everything. When you're that deeply involved, you can't help it.

The pile driver can be a dangerous move if you're not careful. But there's a way to do it safely: You just lodge the head tightly between your legs so that it's not protruding at all. I made sure that Randy's head was protruding, which made it extremely dangerous. I could have broken his neck. As it was, he hurt his head real bad when he hit the floor, and he started crying loudly, really wailing. I got a charge out of it at first, because it was exciting to execute a move, but then I got embarrassed because I realized I had hurt my friend. All the other kids were there, and they started yelling at me: "What's wrong with you, man? Why did you make Randy cry?" In a matter of just a few seconds I went from being the biggest babyface to being the biggest heel. I wound up getting suspended from school for a few days, and my mom put a good beating on my ass—didn't even chew me out, just let her belt do the talking. That belt spoke volumes to me, and in this case it was saying, "Get the point, jabroni?!"

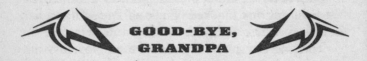

GOOD-BYE, GRANDPA

The man in the hospital bed looked nothing like my grandfather. Peter Maivia was a Paramount High Chief, the highest rank a Samoan can achieve. He had done so much for the wrestling business and for the Samoan community. The man I knew was a bronzed block of a man, very statuesque and proud and full of life. From his chest to his knees, every inch of his body was covered with tattoos. The artwork was reflective of his status as a high chief. Most Samoans who achieve this rank acquire the tattoos over the course of several years; my grandfather, because of his busy schedule, had all of the work done in a period of two weeks. And Samoan tattoo artists do not work with modern tools. They ply their craft the old-fashioned way: with a needle, ink, and a tiny mallet. But there is no denying their talent. My grandfather's massive torso looked to me like a brilliant and vibrant cityscape, with dozens of intersecting lines and angles, each of which told its own little story.

This man in front of me now, in the spring of 1982, was someone else. He was frail and withered. He was tired.

My grandfather had retired from performing a few

years earlier, but he was still actively involved in the business. He had purchased the territory of Hawaii from Ed Francis, another promoter and a man who happens to be the father of Russ Francis, a former All-Pro tight end for the New England Patriots and San Francisco 49ers. While my father was working the territories in the states, my grandfather was busy trying to pump life back into the business in the South Pacific. It had taken some time, but he was beginning to make progress. Unfortunately, he didn't live long enough to see it through. My grandfather was a stubborn guy, so he ignored for years the blood that he sometimes passed in the toilet, the coughing fits that left him exhausted. Don Muraco, *the Magnificent Muraco*, was a good friend of my grandfather's and a contemporary of his on the wrestling circuit. He and some of the other boys would see my grandfather in distress and encourage him to seek help. "Come on, Chief," they'd say. "You have to see a doctor." But my grandfather would simply hold up a hand and shoo them away.

Now there was nothing to be done. The cancer had ravaged his body, and my mother and I had returned to Hawaii to be with him in his final days. My father had remained behind in Portland, Oregon, where he was wrestling several nights a week. This was the hardest time in my mother's life, because she was about as close to her father as a daughter could possibly be.

The hospital room was packed with visitors when we arrived. My mother pushed her way through the crowd and, sobbing like I had never heard, threw herself on top of my grandfather. It was so hard to see her like that. To make matters even worse, two wrestlers who were in the room, a couple of big guys who had never met my mom, and who thought she was just some grieving, desperate fan, decided to act like bouncers. They pulled her off my grandfather and tried to drag her out of the room.

"You'll have to wait outside, ma'am," one of them said. My mother continued to wail uncontrollably. She wasn't even capable of protesting. Fortunately, my grandmother saw what was going on and quickly intervened.

"No, no, no," she said. "This is his daughter."

After my mother stopped hugging him, I walked up and gave him a kiss on the cheek and said, "Hi, Grandpa. I love you." But he couldn't respond. I held his hand and looked down at him, waiting for him to flash that big smile of his, the one that could light up the island. But it didn't come.

Two weeks later High Chief Peter Maivia passed away. There was a massive ceremony in Honolulu, attended by thousands of people. I had always known that my grandfather commanded tremendous respect, but I had never fully understood just how universally well-liked he was. He rests now in Diamond Head, which is a big mountain outside Honolulu. My only regret is that he is not here now to see the fruits of my labor, but I believe he looks down on me and smiles. I believe he is proud of what his grandson has accomplished. I think he's proud of what we've done with sports-entertainment, bringing to the forefront the fact that what we do is showmanship and theater but nonetheless an extraordinary athletic achievement. I think he'd be proud of what we have accomplished. Because he devoted his life to the business.

* * *

My grandfather's final wish was to have my grandmother assume responsibility for his business. And, of course, she honored that wish. She took over the territory and immediately brought in Lars Anderson, who is part of one of the most famous families in wrestling, to act as a booker. She devoted all of her time and spirit to this task, despite the fact that she wasn't a young woman, and soon the business began to flourish. Leah Maivia was no absentee owner, no corporate figurehead, either. She was a hands-on leader and the first woman promoter our business had ever seen. She even wound up being voted vice president of the National Wrestling Alliance, which was more of a political move than anything else, but nonetheless a tremendous honor. She was instrumental in bringing a weekly television wrestling show to Hawaii. She began staging huge monthly shows featuring all of the best wrestlers in the territory. Most important of all, she organized the annual High Chief Peter Maivia Memorial Tribute Show, in which wrestling stars from all over the world would participate. Andre the Giant, a close friend of my grandfather's, always showed up. Ric Flair was a given, too, and of course, you'd have your local guys on the undercard. Every year the Blaisdale Arena would sell out. The tribute show was one of the biggest events on the island.

It was during one of these shows that I got my first taste of the selfishness and politicking that can make wrestling a tough business. I was thirteen years old, and even though my father was in the World Wrestling Federation and we were based in the Northeast, we always went back to Hawaii to help out with the memorial show. At this time Lars

Anderson was not only the booker for the territory but also the Polynesian champion. He was scheduled to wrestle a guy named Bad News Allen on this night; in fact, he was supposed to drop the Polynesian belt to Bad News Allen ("dropping the belt" in our industry means doing a favor . . . *letting the other guy win*). But Lars Anderson balked at the request. About half an hour before the show started I overheard my grandmother and father talking about how Lars was refusing to drop the belt. This happens sometimes in our business. A lot of guys, whether it's because they start to believe their own press or whatever, they sometimes hold up promoters or hold up a show by refusing to do a job.

Lars's refusal was an insult not only to my grandmother but to the memory of my grandfather, and I remember becoming enraged when I heard that this was going on. I could feel my blood boil as I worked myself into a frenzy of anger: *That son of a bitch! This is my grandfather's memorial! This guy is supposed to be here to pay his respects for what my grandfather did for this business, how he helped pave the way for everyone here! And this guy is thinking only of himself?!* The first problem was that Lars was a booker. That was a huge strike against him. Time and again it has proved to be a fatally flawed equation. You can't be a booker for a company and also wrestle for that company. It's a conflict of interest, and it just does not work. Naturally, if you're a booker, you're going to want to schedule yourself on top; you're going to want to appear in the main event. It just makes for a bad recipe.

I wasn't capable of rational analysis at the time: I was thirteen years old, my body was just starting to pump testosterone to my muscles, and my temper often spiked without warning. I wanted everything to go smoothly for my grandfather's sake, for his memory's sake, and for all the other guys. So I made up my mind: *I may be thirteen years old and this guy can kick my ass, but it's an ass-kicking I'm going to have to take!* I stormed into the dressing room and looked around for Lars. At thirteen, I didn't understand why he was doing this, whether it was personal, or simply a matter of business, and I didn't care. All I knew was that he was disrespecting my grandfather's show. I was so angry that I wasn't even aware of anyone else being in the room. I marched right up to him, pointed a finger, and said, "You son of a bitch! You don't want to drop the belt? This is my grandfather's night and you're disrespecting him like that?! What's wrong with you?!"

My dad was off in the corner talking to some of the boys about a few things, and when he heard me yelling, he looked over with stunned disbelief in his eyes. I could see that he was just shocked. Lars was six foot three, 260 pounds—a big, strong, full-grown bear of a man, and here was this kid challenging him, screaming at him, crying, *"I'll kick your ass, you selfish bastard!"*

I thought I was doing the right thing. But everyone was angry with me, including my father and grandmother. They were so busy trying to put on a show that the last thing they needed was me going crazy in front of everyone. My mother took me off to the side and said, "Why did you do that? What happened?"

"This is Grandpa's night," I choked out. "And look what he's doing. He's disrespecting my grandfather. How can he do this?"

Even at thirteen, I remember understanding the situation perfectly and being acutely aware of the implications. "This business is *a work*," I cried. "How can he be so selfish?"

My mother gave me a hug, brushed my hair, and said, "That may be true, but it's not your place to say anything."

With that one sentence I snapped out of it. She was right, as usual. So I apologized to my mother and father and grandmother, and to everyone else who had been exposed to my tirade. I even apologized to Lars Anderson, even though it sickened me to do so. Looking back, I regret losing my temper because it embarrassed my family. But I don't regret speaking my mind. This business is a work, which is another way of saying that the results are predetermined, and we all know it. Winning isn't the point—doing your job and doing it well is all that matters. The people and the business come first. I understood that then, even when I was just a stupid, loudmouthed kid, and I understand it now.

THE PEOPLE'S

chapter 2

PUBERTY

WHEN YOU REACH junior high school, everything begins to change. The world becomes a much more exciting, and sometimes confusing, place. You start getting competitive about sports, and, of course, you begin to see girls in a completely different light.

Actually, for me, the transformation began a bit sooner than it ordinarily does. When it came to fighting and fornicating, I was way ahead of the curve. I don't say this in a boastful manner, or because it's something that fills me with pride. I'm just telling you the way it was.

In my mind, I was God's gift to women . . . the player to end all players . . . the mack of all daddies. I don't recall ever feeling awkward around girls or women the way most boys do. I don't recall stuttering or stammering or breaking out in a sweat just because a girl said hello to me. Then, as now, I could talk the talk, and sometimes that was all that mattered. If you acted confident around girls, they naturally assumed you were mature and experienced. It was all a game, and I excelled at it from a ridiculously early age.

I was living in Hawaii when I met my first girl-friend. I was ten years old; Lisa was thirteen. That's a big difference, of course, and you may wonder how we ever got rolling in the first place. But she was my next-door neighbor, and we got to be good friends before anything carnal took place. We'd hang out together in the morning before school, and then she'd go off to junior high, and I'd go to fifth grade. There was no sex involved in this relationship—not serious, grown-up sex, anyway. But it was a hell of a lot more than hand-holding or spin the bottle. We used to play hide-and-seek with the other kids in the neighbor-hood, and Lisa and I would always run off together, as a team. But we always made sure that we'd never be found. We'd take off deep into the woods and ignore the shouts of the other children as we explored each other's bodies. In retrospect, I realize that I had no business doing what I was doing, but when you're a kid, and an opportunity like that comes along, you tend to go along for the ride. And that's what I did. Sex is a mysterious thing, especially for a ten-year-old boy. Lisa held me tight and provided me with a few clues that would help unravel the mystery. I was grateful for her guidance.

I've always been attracted to older women, and they've often reciprocated. That's one of the benefits of being an early bloomer, I guess. I lost my virginity when I was fourteen, to an eighteen-year-old girl named Maria. Maria was not merely an acquaintance or a conquest. She was, at the time, the love of my life. She was THE ONE!

Maria was a senior in high school. I was a freshman. As any fourteen-year-old boy fidgeting awkwardly on the cusp of adulthood can tell you, that's normally a fatal age difference, especially in the cliquish world of high school. But Maria was a wonderfully sweet and caring girl, a very innocent girl, and I was ... well ... I was THE MAN. Or so I thought.

We were both virgins, but I had convinced Maria that I was not only a really nice, sincere guy (and, for the most part, I was) but also (as the King might put it) ... *a hunka-hunka burnin' love!* After our relationship had progressed to a certain point, and consummation had become something to seriously consider, I took the lead in negotiations. Don't get me wrong. I don't mean to sound like a complete asshole about this. I really cared about Maria. We had a long and terrific relationship. All the same, I was a fourteen-year-old boy who was primarily concerned with getting over for the very first time.

So I put on a big show for Maria. I hinted frequently at my previous sexual encounters, not to be rude or to make her feel bad, but to give her the impression that I was a true swordsman, a teenage Don Juan. By the time we had been going out for a few months, Maria was convinced that I held the Hawaiian record for sexual conquests by a fourteen-year-old. She believed that I had lost my virginity at the age of ten and that women (not just "girls") had been lining up ever since. And I did nothing to dissuade her. Far from it. Whenever the topic came up, whenever it seemed as though Maria might be ready to lay down in the tall grass and let me do my stuff, I willingly, eagerly assumed the role she had assigned to me.

"Listen, baby," I'd say. "Don't worry about a thing. I know what I'm doing. I'll take care of everything. You just put your trust in me. Relax. It'll be okay."

Christ, I sounded like a Barry White song! *"You're my first . . . my last . . . MY EVERY-THANG!"*

We wound up in a public park, on a warm summer night, with a big Hawaiian moon casting a spotlight on our desperate little dance. As we fumbled and groped beneath a blanket, I could feel my heart beating a mile a minute, almost as if it were going to leap out of my chest. Maria was a "good girl," a serious student, and a thoughtful young woman who hadn't given herself to anyone before. Now here she was, entangled with a high school freshman who was trying with all his might not to blow his cover (among other things).

"Just take it easy, baby. . . ."

Thump! Thump! Thump!

"Let me know if you're scared and I'll slow down. . . ."

THUMP! THUMP! THUMP!

"Trust me . . . trust me . . ."

When the sky suddenly lit up, I thought at first that maybe it was just some sort of orgasmic flash, a beautiful and illuminating postcoital rush, like the fireworks you see in cheesy romantic movies. No such luck. The patrol car had sneaked up on us while we were fully engaged, and therefore totally oblivious to our surroundings. That, of course, is one of the dangers of making love in a public place—the possibility that you'll be interrupted, exposed, humiliated. It's also one of the things that makes it exciting, although I'm not sure that played into our thinking at all. The fact is, when you're in high school, especially when you're not even old enough to drive, your options are limited.

The blue spotlight blinded and confused me; Maria was downright terrified. It wasn't until one of the cops said, "Ma'am, please come over here" that we realized what was happening. Maria quickly ducked beneath the blanket and pulled on her dress. She scrambled to the window of the patrol car as the spot light continued to train its eye on me. I didn't move. I just lay there, naked and vulnerable and sticky, having achieved my manhood just in the nick of time.

"Are you OK, miss?" one of the cops asked Maria.

She nodded and forced an awkward little smile. "Yes, officer. That's my boyfriend. I'm sorry. I know we shouldn't even be here."

I squinted through the glare of the spotlight and saw the cops giving me a serious assessment.

"You're *sure* you're all right? You're not being held against your will?"

"No, no, nothing like that. He's my boyfriend."

I guess Maria was believable—either that or I just didn't look like I was capable of any real mayhem—because the cops soon flicked off the light and drove away. But not before telling Maria to fold up the blankets and find another love shack—preferably one not located on public property.

So we went home, our lives having been forever altered. I remember thinking that sex wasn't really all that big a deal, that it was easier than I had imagined, and that I was actually pretty good at it. I'm not sure Maria would have agreed with that assessment, but if she was disappointed, she kept it to herself. For that I can't thank her enough.

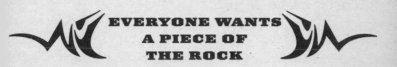

EVERYONE WANTS A PIECE OF THE ROCK

Not only did I attract the attention of older women, I also seemed to get a rise out of men. Older boys, actually. Again, I attribute this to the fact that I appeared to be much older than I was. I don't mean to imply that I was more *mature* than other kids my age—just that I was bigger, stronger, and more confident.

I started working out seriously with weights when I was thirteen. By that time I already weighed about 170 pounds and was more than six feet tall. When you're put together like that, when you're fortunate enough to have a muscular body, and when you happen to have a famous father, you tend to attract attention, some of which you don't necessarily want.

I remember getting challenged frequently when I was in junior high school. The funny thing was, the challenges usually came from older kids. One day the word came down, as it sometimes does in school, that a kid named Billy wanted a piece of me. Now, I had heard about Billy, but I had never met him. He was a high school kid, sixteen years old. I had no history with him whatsoever, but he knew me because I was Rocky Johnson's son, and I suppose that was provocation enough. Back then I wasn't the kind of kid who

started trouble, but I was the kind of kid who didn't mind *ending* trouble. I had a temper, and while I usually held it in check, any legitimate excuse to blow off a little steam was good enough for me. When friends started coming up to me in class and saying things like, "Billy's gonna kick your ass," I felt nothing so much as excitement. I wasn't scared. I wasn't intimidated. I was pretty sure that, in fact, I could kick Billy's ass, and I said as much.

"He wants to meet me after school? Hell, yeah, I'll meet him! Just tell me where."

The deal was this: Billy and I were supposed to tangle in a big park right across from the junior high. A few of my friends asked if I wanted them to stay and help, but I said that wouldn't be necessary.

"Don't worry. I'll kick his sorry butt myself and then walk home," I declared boldly, sounding more than a little like The Rock. The "walk home," incidentally, was about ten miles. At the time, however, I was staying with my friend, José, because my mother was traveling with my father for a few days. José's house was about three miles from school; like me, he typically rode the bus. On this day, though, José was going to walk with me. He was going to be my second, my backup. We had everything sketched out, a whole theatrical number for starting and finishing this brawl. Again, the wrestler in me was bubbling to the surface. This wasn't a work, though. This was real.

"OK, here's the way it's going to go," I said to José. "When Billy shows up, I'll hand you my gold chain. I'll hand you my watch. I'll take them off real slowly, to build up the tension. Then I want you to just go over in the corner, sit back, and enjoy the show."

Now, unbeknownst to me, this kid Billy lived

about a half mile from the school. In fact, as it turned out, all of his buddies lived within a one-mile radius of the school and the park. When José and I showed up after school, no one was there. My first arrogant, cocky thought was, *Well, looks like Billy chickened out.* But that wasn't the case at all. Billy was simply mobilizing the troops. High school dismissal was a couple hours before junior high dismissal, so Billy had decided to go home for a while. When he returned, he wasn't alone.

"What's that?" José asked.

I was looking at my watch, calculating how much longer I'd wait for that punk-ass Billy to show up, thinking, *Hah! He doesn't want a piece of mo!* when I heard the noise, a faint rumbling off in the distance, almost like an approaching storm or the buzzing of a swarm of bees. I couldn't see anything at first, but as the noise grew louder, clearer, they came into view: at least twenty-five kids, all shouting and jabbing at the air, kicking up a lot of dirt with their boots. At the front of the pack, snarling and thumping his chest, acting like a heavyweight champ entering the ring with his entourage, was Billy.

"Oh, shit!" José said.

"What the hell is going on?" I asked. "Who are all those other guys?"

"I don't know, man. His friends, I guess. We'd better get the fuck out of here!"

I watched them coming, a thin gray cloud hanging over their ragged little army, and felt a sick mixture of anger, fear, and adrenaline building in the pit of my stomach.

"I'm not running."

José looked at me as though I was nuts. He shook

his head and sprinted off. I couldn't blame him, really. Two junior high kids against twenty-five high school jabronis? It was suicide. But I didn't care. I was big and tough, and just stupid enough to think that maybe it would be a fair fight—one on one. If that were the case, I was confident I could take care of business.

That wasn't the case.

The fight started almost immediately. There was no debating, no discussion, no attempt at détente. When two teenage boys get together in this type of arena, it's not like one of them is going to extend an olive branch and say, "So, tell me . . . what's the problem? Can we discuss this like gentlemen? Can't we attempt to be civilized?" The situation usually sparks and flames instantly, as it would in the animal kingdom, and that's what happened in this case. The group began to close in around me, like a pack of ugly-ass hyenas, and as it did, Billy stepped forward.

"What's up?" I said.

His reply: "WHAT'S UP WITH YOU?!"

And that was it. *WHAM!* Fists were flying. I got the best of him right away, landed a few solid punches before we locked up and started wrestling around a little. Neither one of us was really acclimated to the rigors of fighting, so we got blown out, completely exhausted, within a matter of just a few minutes. We separated, backed apart a few steps, and tried to catch our breath. As we circled, I saw a flicker of movement out of the corner of my eye, and then felt a stinging pain on the side of my head.

I'd been blindsided by one of Billy's cronies!

I didn't go down right away. Instead, I staggered around, trying to regain my composure. It became clear to me then that this was the plan all along: to "Pearl Harbor" The Rock! From that point on I got my ass kicked . . . big time! They beat the living crap out of me . . . and for absolutely no reason other than my name. When I finally fell to the ground, completely spent and in terrific pain, I thought they'd back off. But that only added to their bloodlust. The scene must have resembled a whole mess of cats terrorizing a mouse, batting him around, slowly tearing him to shreds. I was on all fours, scrambling from one spot to another, trying to cover up and absorb the blows as best I could.

BANG! A shot on the ear.

WHAM! A kick to the stomach.

It went on like that for a while, until finally I broke out of the circle and staggered to my feet. Then I heard someone shouting.

"No, James! Don't be stupid! You'll go back to jail if you stick him!"

Through the tears and the dirt and the blood I could see him coming at me, this kid James, waving a switchblade and squealing like a maniac. He held the knife out and lunged at me halfheartedly, clearly more intent on frightening me and impressing his friends than with actually cutting out one of my organs. James, obviously, had no desire to return to jail.

I stepped aside, and James passed like a drunken bull. I kept backing up, backing up, backing up, until I stumbled into a bush and fell down. Then they were on me again, rat-packin' my butt. In desperation I pulled my jacket up over my head, hoping it would soften some of the shots. There were so many of them . . . and they seemed to be enjoying themselves . . . *God, when would it end?*

"Hey! You boys stop it! Leave that boy alone!"

At the corner, with the window rolled down, was a big black car. Behind the wheel, apparently, was my guardian angel, an elderly woman with a furious look on her face. "Get up off that boy or I'm calling the cops," she said. "Now!"

And just like that it was over. Billy and the boys scattered like cockroaches, and I shuffled on home—to José's house, actually. He and his family treated my cuts and bruises, but they couldn't do much for my pride. Already I wanted revenge. And I would have it . . . soon enough.

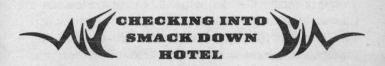 CHECKING INTO SMACK DOWN HOTEL

That night, my mother called José's house to see how I was doing. Whenever she went on the road with my dad, she checked in every day, just to make sure I was all right. When I told her that I had gotten into a fight, we talked for a while, then my father grabbed the phone.

"What happened?"

"They jumped me, Dad. They beat me up. A whole bunch of guys."

I didn't curse them out, like I wanted to, because I was very careful about using bad language around my parents. I was four years old the first time I swore. I said, "You sumbitch!" after hearing my dad say something similar, and my mom instantly dragged me into the bathroom and washed my mouth out with soap. So cursing wasn't an option for me, no matter how pissed off I was.

"OK, just take care of yourself," my father said. His voice was very calm, very controlled. "Stay away from these boys until we get home. Then we'll fix this."

I hung up the phone and smiled at José, because I knew what was coming. My dad had always told me to walk away from fights, and certainly never to start a fight, because fighting is stupid and pointless and usually solves absolutely nothing. At the same time, my father is an extremely proud, tough man who would never back down when threatened. He knows that there are times when a fight is inevitable, when you have to defend yourself, and when the bad guy needs to be taught a lesson. He detested bullies, and Billy, from what he could tell, was obviously a bully. Worse, he was a coward. A sixteen-year-old kid who provokes a fight with a thirteen-year-old and then ambushes him with twenty-five of his friends, some of whom are seventeen and eighteen years old . . . well, in my father's eyes, Billy was lower than whale shit.

My mother deplored fighting; she always told me not to be ignorant in these matters. But my dad could be a bit more complicated. He would tell me to walk away from fights, to use my mind rather than my fists. But in the next breath he would say something like, "It's not whether you get knocked down that counts. It's whether you stay down." He was never into fighting. He was, and is, a very civil person. But he also is an athlete . . . a warrior . . . a man. He will never tolerate abuse of any kind, and he was not about to let his son be abused either.

Naturally, this fight quickly became the talk of the school. When I came in the next morning, there were cuts on my face, welts all over my head and arms. Everyone knew about it—teachers, students, custodians, even the principal. For the most part, everyone was on my side. I was always pretty well-liked by the teachers, because even though I wasn't a straight-A student, I tried to be a genuinely nice kid. I was cordial and polite with my teachers. I treated them with respect. My parents wouldn't have had it any other way.

When my dad got back off the road, he decided to handle this situation in his own manner. He chose not to go to the teachers or the administration. He did not go to the police, even though the beating took place on public property rather than the school grounds. Nah, my dad wanted to resolve this problem in a very personal way.

It didn't happen right away. In fact, I was taunted on a daily basis for the better part of two weeks. Billy and his gang hung out near the junior high after school, so every day when I walked to my bus, I had to pass within sight of him and his buddies. They always made fun of me, laughed, pointed, called me names. I'd answer "Any day, one-on-one!" Then one morning, as I got ready to leave for school, my father said, "I'll be picking you up this afternoon."

When I heard those words I could barely contain my excitement. I remember thinking, *All right, there's nothing better than this! Payback is a bitch, Billy!*

That morning I kept telling my friends, "Be ready after school. My dad's coming. Something big is going to happen."

"Like what?"

"I don't know, but you'll see. They're going to get it today. We're gonna kick some ass!"

His arrival was like something out of a movie, like one of Clint Eastwood's spaghetti westerns, with the wind howling across the desert, tumbleweeds blowing, bad guys pissing themselves at the very sight of the High Plains Drifter.

Of course, my dad didn't ride up on a horse. He came in a big Cadillac with tinted windows. He pulled up in front of the building, and I jumped into the front seat alongside him, my chest thick with pride, my heart racing with excitement.

"Where to?" he asked.

"Around the other side."

We drove slowly around the school, turned a corner . . . and there they were. Hanging out together, probably waiting for me to walk by so they could taunt me some more. Dad wheeled the big Caddy up to the curb, cut the engine, threw open the front door, and got out of the car. The entire group just froze. My father walked—*sauntered,* really—right up to the gang (with me one step behind) and puffed himself up to his full size. Now, remember, my father was not only an impressive physical specimen, he was also a professional wrestler. Which means he was a trained actor. He was a legitimately tough man, but when he wanted to put on the right face, he could be more than just tough: He could be frightening.

"I hear all you kids jumped my son," he said. His voice, as always, was calm, controlled, yet unmistakably hostile . . . and dangerous.

His point was not lost on Billy and his cohorts, one of whom was so scared that he immediately pointed at one of his friends and blurted out, "That guy right there—he's the one who jumped him!"

"Shut your mouth!" my father said, and the kid instantly wilted. "You guys all think you're so tough, huh? All of you, jumping one person. Look how many of you there are here right now. You really ought to be proud of yourselves. You're fifteen, sixteen years old—there's even a few eighteen-year-olds here—and my son is thirteen, and you beat up on him."

My dad was rolling, giving that parent speech that he could give so well, humiliating them all. He walked in and out of the crowd, and at one point he said, "I hear one of you had a switchblade. Which one was it?"

Again, Billy's gang turned out to be lacking in loyalty, not to mention guts. One of the kids pointed at James and, almost crying, yelled, "He did it!"

Dad walked right up to James, got in his face, and snarled. "Big man, eh? Got your knife and all? You know I got a knife, too. Want to see it?"

He reached into his coat and pulled out a little pocketknife. With a single finger he released the blade and held it choot high.

"You want to take your knife out and use it against me like you tried to use it against my son? You think you'd like to try that?"

James stared at the ground and shook his head.

"No, man . . . uh-uh."

I thought that was the end of it, but I should have known better. Dad was a wrestler, and in the wrestling business you never cut a promo without a big ending, a "go-home" line. And Dad was winding up for his.

"As long as you're all here, I'm going to make you an offer. One-on-one, right now, my son will kick the shit out of any of you." I figured something like this was coming, so I was ready. I could feel the blood rushing to my arms and legs; I could feel the adrenaline pumping. I looked through the crowd and didn't see anyone who scared me. Not in a fair fight. Not one-to-one. "Whoever wants to go first, just take a step forward," my father said. "I'll be right over here . . . watching."

There was no movement. Not from Billy, not from any of them. After a while my father let out a sigh of disgust. We walked together to his Caddy, Rocky Johnson and Dwayne Johnson, father and son . . .

Tag-team champions of the world!

chapter 3

O LITTLE TOWN OF
BETHLEHEM

AS IT WAS EVERY day after school, the gymnasium at Freedom High School was hot and cramped and bustling with activity. The musky smell of adolescent energy—a sickly sweet mix of sweat and liniment and Aqua Velva—wafted through the stale November air as a soundtrack of bouncing basketballs and shrill whistles filled the room.

This was my introduction to wrestling. Not professional wrestling, which is more performance art than it is sport, but *real* wrestling. Amateur wrestling. Down-and-dirty, my-head-in-your-armpit, grapple-till-you-puke *wrestling!* We had moved from Hawaii to Bethlehem, Pennsylvania, in the fall of my sopho-

more year in high school. It was too late to join the football team, but it was not too late to be part of another unit, the Navy SEALs of high school sports: the wrestling team.

The wrestling coach, Mr. Llewellyn, was also a physical education teacher, and he had approached me one day during gym class to discuss the possibility of trying out for the wrestling team. Mr. Llewellyn was a nice guy, and he didn't give me a hard sell or anything. He had simply heard about me and my dad, and he had, of course, noticed the fact that I was a pretty big kid (six foot four, 225 pounds by the time I was fifteen)—high school coaches have an eye for this sort of thing—and so he thought I might be worth recruiting.

"Your dad's a professional wrestler, and you're a pretty good athlete," Coach Llewellyn had said. "Why not give it a shot?"

Yeah, why not? I was new in town, eager to make some friends, to be part of a group, and sports, I had learned through years of bouncing around the globe, provided an easy and immediate route to friendship and camaraderie. And, of course, to girls.

In truth, I knew almost nothing about amateur wrestling. I had never attended a practice, never strapped on headgear. To me, wrestling was what my father did. Wrestling was Rocky Johnson laying the smack down in the middle of the ring. It was forearm shivers and suplexes and sleeper holds and backflips off the top rope. It was dropkicks, wrist locks, and pile drivers.

It was a *show.*

I knew amateur wrestling was more subdued. I understood that it wasn't a *work.* Still, I don't think I

realized just how little the two pursuits have in common until I walked into the Freedom High School
gym that afternoon. Everyone stared at me, in part
because I was the new kid and in part because of my
size. It was as though I was being brought in to challenge the king of the ring. And, in a way, I guess I was.

After warming up for a few minutes, Coach
instructed me to work out with the team's number
one heavyweight. As everyone gathered around to
watch, I could feel my blood starting to pump. The
whistle blew and we locked up. Then we started
rolling around the mat, two big kids engaged in some
sort of vaguely defined turf war. I knew right away
that I was stronger than him, and more athletic.
Within a minute or so I had sent him crashing to the
mat with a belly-to-belly suplex. As he hit the floor
with a tremendous *THWACK!* I could hear gasps of
disbelief rising from the throats of his teammates. If
these kids had known who I was, if they had realized
that my father was Rocky Johnson, they might have
applauded . . . or jeered. As it was, they were merely
stunned at the sight of a new kid dusting the gym
floor with their biggest and strongest wrestler . . . their
leader.

Coach Llewellyn smiled at me and I smiled back.
To be honest, though, this little achievement did nothing for me. It seemed too easy, too dry. It lacked
drama. Compared to the shows I had been raised on,
it just wasn't much fun. And after two hours of practice—two hours of calisthenics, one-on-one drilling,
basic fundamentals, all endured without so much as a
smile or a shout—my opinion had only been hard-
ened. Wrestling was, well . . . *boring.*

I left practice knowing that I wouldn't be back the

next day. When I got home, my parents were waiting for me, eager to hear all about my introduction to the *other* kind of wrestling. I think they were hoping that I would love it, though I'm not sure why. But I had to be honest.

"What did you think?" my father asked.

I shrugged uncomfortably. "I didn't really like it, Dad. I didn't like it at all."

He just smiled and said, "Okay." Maybe, in his heart, he understood perfectly. If anyone could understand how amateur wrestling paled in comparison to professional wrestling, it was Rocky Johnson.

The next day I walked into Coach Llewellyn's office and said, "I'm sorry, Coach, but I don't think amateur wrestling is my thing." And that was it, the end of my short, unhappy affair with high school wrestling. I don't mean to take anything away from the sport—amateur wrestlers work extremely hard, and they go through hell in trying to make weight. But I guess I should have known right then that I was more of an entertainer than a wrestler.

SO YOU WANT TO BE A FOOTBALL HERO?

My first year at Freedom High was a little rough. I had started playing football as a freshman in Hawaii and had grown to like the game quite a bit. Because we moved to Bethlehem at an awkward time, I missed football season and thus became something of a man without a country. I worked out a lot to stay in shape and kept mostly to myself. And, on occasion, I got into a little trouble, thanks primarily to my increasingly short fuse.

The first incident stemmed from a rumor that dogged me throughout high school: that I was using steroids and other muscle-building substances. The truth is ... the use of performance-enhancing drugs is not uncommon among world-class athletes and even among big-time college athletes. I can only speak for myself, though. My only experience with steroids was in the summer after my senior year in high school. I had just graduated and was getting ready to play college ball. So I decided that I wanted to get even bigger and stronger. It was stupid. I had no idea what I was doing. From a friend of a friend, I obtained an oral steroid—at least, it was supposed to be a steroid. For all I know, I was taking Advil. I popped this stuff

every day for about three weeks, and after seeing no results at all, and feeling no different, I stopped taking whatever it was. I remember expressing complete and utter dissatisfaction to one of my football buddies, the only guy who knew what I was doing: "This is bullshit, man. It's not working." And that was it. That was my run-in with steroids.

My size, unfortunately, frequently led other people to suspect that I was on . . . *something*. I was fifteen years old and looked like a grown man. And I was constantly in the weight room, jacking iron for two, three hours a day. I'd only been at Freedom High for a few months when the rumors began to intensify, thanks largely to the efforts of this one kid with whom I'd been spending some time. He was telling anyone and everyone that I was using steroids to beef up. And it simply wasn't true. At the time, I wouldn't have known how or where to obtain steroids. I was genetically predisposed to being big and strong. And I worked out—a lot! That's it. There was no magic formula, no special drug.

This kid was big, too, but that didn't stop me from confronting him. Several other people had told me that he was the source of the rumor, so I stopped him one afternoon in the hall and said, "Why are you saying this stuff about me?"

He immediately became hostile and defensive, and it wasn't long before we were throwing punches. I wound up hitting him with a pretty good shot, and unfortunately he fell backward, cracked his head against the lockers, and slumped to the floor unconscious. Obviously, this was not the best way to start my career at a new school. I was suspended for a few days and instantly branded a troublemaker. It would take the better part of a year to alter that perception.

High school football is a very big deal in Pennsylvania. Some of the greatest players in NFL history grew up there, guys like Joe Namath, Johnny Unitas, Dan Marino, and Joe Montana, just to name a few. We didn't have anyone like that at Freedom High—in fact, we basically sucked. We lost as many games as we won during my junior season, and we lost more than we won when I was a senior. But even though we weren't a candidate for a national championship or anything, we enjoyed the game.

My junior year was really my first opportunity to study the game of football. I spent a lot of time watching film and memorizing plays. I played tight end and defensive end—so there was an extreme amount of work involved. I was a team captain and made all-conference in my junior year, but I wasn't really satisfied with the way I played. Looking back, I know I wasn't as focused as I could have been. I would do stupid things, like, as the tight end, I'd seek out the other team's linebacker just to drill him, even if he wasn't involved in the play. Stupid and pointless. But I guess most sixteen-year-old kids are like that once in a while.

I really fell in love with football when I was a senior. At the time, I still thought that one day I'd end up as a professional wrestler. But as my football career began to flourish, and the recruiting letters poured in from colleges all over the United States, I started having aspirations of playing in the NFL. It's amazing what a simple letter can do to a kid's ego. You walk to the mailbox and there's an envelope with *Penn*

State or *Notre Dame* stamped in the upper left-hand corner, and your heart just about does a somersault. Then the phone starts ringing . . . day and night. And then the assistant coaches begin showing up, knocking at your front door after dinner or visiting you at school. It's extraordinarily flattering, and it can really go to your head if you're not careful.

The schools that recruited me with the greatest intensity were Florida State University, Clemson, and the University of Pittsburgh. But Pitt dropped out of the picture shortly after I visited the campus. Not because they lost interest in me but because I lost interest in them. On most recruiting visits you do your mandatory meetings with professors and you get a tour of the campus—dorms, athletic facilities, classrooms, etc. Meanwhile, every high school kid is standing there, thinking to himself, *Okay, great. Now . . . where are the women and the booze?* I'd heard so many bawdy stories that I'd get aroused just stepping into the athletic office. When other athletes are forever saying things like, "Wow, I got to my room and it was a big suite with naked ladies everywhere!" you can't help but have a distorted view of things. There was nothing special about any of my recruiting visits. I had fun but wasn't exposed to anything that could have found its way into *Penthouse Forum*. My most memorable visit was notable mainly because of something that wasn't the least bit inspiring.

I had just finished working out in the weight room at Pitt, and I was invited into the coaches' office. I was sitting with the head strength coach and three or four of his players. The players didn't know me—I was just another recruit. But the coach knew exactly who

I was, and for some reason he started busting my balls big-time.

"You know, Dwayne," he said, "I don't think you could hang with me in the weight room. I'd kick your ass!"

"Is that so?" I was too shocked to come up with anything clever, too surprised that this guy was being such an asshole. I mean, he was supposed to be enticing me to play at his school. And there was an edge to his comments that indicated real meanness. He wasn't just kidding around.

Anyway, we went back and forth for a while. He said something about my dad being a professional wrestler, not an insult, really, but just kind of a smart-ass comment. It was all ribbin' on the square. He'd say something, laugh, and then I'd respond and laugh even harder. But there was an undercurrent of serious anger and dislike, and I don't even know where it came from.

Finally, after a while, I'd had enough.

"It's funny, you know?" I said, and by this time my temples were throbbing I was so pissed. "But not only could you not handle my old man, you damn sure couldn't handle me. And I'll show you right now . . . right here."

He stood there for a moment, kind of clenched his teeth a little, and then started to laugh. The players laughed right along with him. Maybe that was all it was, just a big game, a rite of passage: *piss off the recruit!* Whatever it was, I wasn't buying it. I looked around the room and thought, *Guess I'm not coming here.*

If sex wasn't dangled like a carrot on my recruiting visits, money certainly was. No one offered me cash or cars outright, but I was always told by one of the assistant coaches: "Don't worry, you'll be taken care of. Whatever you need, it won't be a problem." This happened on every one of my recruiting visits . . . with one exception: the University of Miami.

Interestingly enough, Miami was one of the few big-time football programs that did not actively recruit me. By the fall of my senior year, I was being flooded with mail and phone calls from all of the top Division I programs. But Miami was strangely silent. For some reason this piqued my interest. I had given a verbal commitment to Florida State during my senior year, but I hadn't signed anything, and as the weeks went by I became obsessed with Miami's lack of interest. I wanted to attend a school in the South because I missed Hawaii and its warm weather, and I had heard so much about Miami. There was something special about the Hurricanes. Under coach Jimmy Johnson they had won fifty of sixty games in five seasons, including a national championship in 1987. Jimmy was gone now, having accepted the head coaching job with the Dallas Cowboys, but Miami was still considered one of the top programs in football.

It was not considered one of the cleanest. The Hurricanes had a reputation for bending the rules and letting athletes slide through college without so much as breathing the air inside a classroom. So when Jimmy's replacement, Dennis Erickson, came in, he was under tremendous pressure to clean things up. I was part of Dennis's first recruiting class, although I had to take the initiative in the relationship. When it became apparent that somehow I had completely escaped Miami's radar, I decided to find out what had

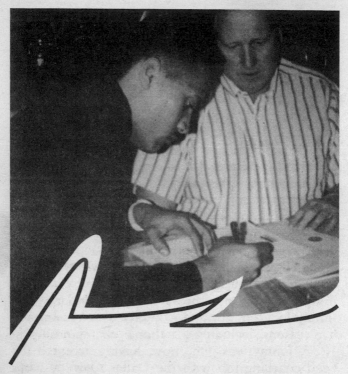

happened. I had a Florida State media guide laying around, so I opened it up to the section that listed all of the Seminoles' opponents. Miami, of course, was there, along with a small box of information about the school. I wrote down the phone number of the athletic department and picked up the phone.

"Good afternoon, University of Miami Athletics."

"Hi, who do I speak to about football recruiting?"

"Who is this, please?"

"My name is Dwayne Johnson and I'm a football player up here in Bethlehem, Pennsylvania."

To my surprise, the secretary immediately connected me to the recruiting coordinator in the football office, a man named David Scott.

"Hi, this is David."

I proceeded to introduce myself and give Coach Scott the condensed version of what had happened. I asked him if I had done something wrong or if Miami had heard something bad about me, something that had squelched their interest.

"Well, Dwayne," he said. "Not that I know of." I heard him shuffling papers. "I have your name right here on our list, as a matter of fact. Why don't I send you some material right away?"

I thanked him for his time and hung up the phone. Within a few days the letter arrived in the mail and I received a phone call from Bob Karmelowics, who at the time was the defensive line coach at Miami. A new round of recruiting had begun.

Coach Karm was a straight shooter. No bullshit. When he came to visit, one of the first things he said was, "Have other schools been offering you money?"

"Yeah, they have."

"Well, I have to be honest with you," he said. "We're not going to do that. I won't offer you anything but a chance to play for a national championship, and a chance to get your degree."

That struck a chord with me. I found it admirable that he was laying it out that way. By this time the novelty of being recruited had worn off. I was sick of dealing with assistant coaches who thought they were so slick. They'd show up with their suits and their rental cars, and they'd pull a piece of paper out of their briefcase and start slinging a line of crap:

"See, here's the deal, Dwayne. We've got you fig-ured in right here for next year. (He points to a spot

*just below the first name on the list, under the head-
ing of* DEFENSIVE TACKLE.*) Jim here is our starter, but
we think you'll be number two on the depth chart."*

"What about this guy here?" (I point to the second
name.)

"Injured."

"And this guy?" (I point to the third name.)

"Transferring."

"And this one?" (I point to the fourth name.)

"Redshirt."

"Uh-huh . . ."

"So, you can see, Dwayne, you're looking at
instant playing time, 50 percent of the snaps from day
one. How's that sound? Pretty good, huh? That's
what I thought. Sign right here!"

At first this little show—and it was repeated by virtually every coach I saw (maybe there's a school
where they teach this stuff?)—made my head spin.
But after a while I got wise to it. I realized that everything he was telling me he was probably telling two
other guys at the same time. So it became a game to
me. Even once I knew I was going to Miami, I would
string these guys along. I'd make them wait all day to
talk to me on their recruiting visits. I'd make them
meet me at a Pizza Hut, along with a dozen of my
friends. Anything to make them uncomfortable. It
wasn't a nice thing for me to do. I know that. But I
really felt like most of these guys were so crooked and
duplicitous that they deserved it.

Not Coach Karm. He said he would offer me nothing, and he didn't. He also said something that made
a lot of sense: "If they cheat to get you to come there,
they'll cheat after you arrive." And I thought, *Wow,
he's right! That's great advice.* Unfortunately, a lot of

kids never figure that out. When you're seventeen, you're basically like Silly Putty. These guys can mold you and shape you any way they want. They can steal your identity and individuality.

Not me, though. Long before the birth of The Rock...I learned the benefit of being hard...of being strong. For me there was no reason to agonize further over the decision. I wanted to be a Hurricane.

RED LETTER DAY

Although we didn't win a lot of games, I had a very good senior season. I had fourteen sacks and more than a hundred tackles and was named high school all-America by *USA Today*, among other publications. Bethlehem is a small city, and the East Penn Conference is not a particularly strong league, so the recognition was nice. I think it might have been a little hard on some of my friends for the spotlight to be so consistently trained on me, but they were always good about it, very true and supportive. I can't say the same thing about some of the other coaches in our league. I was all-America and rated the eighth-best player in the state of Pennsylvania, but somehow I did not make the East Penn All-Conference Team. Why? I don't know. Jealousy, maybe. The coaches voted on these things, and perhaps they simply felt that I had received enough accolades. Maybe they felt their players deserved a shot.

Whatever their thinking, it was misguided and unfair, and I said as much at the press conference to announce my signing with Miami on February 14, 1989. I said, "Gee, it's kind of funny that I'm an all-American, but couldn't make all-conference." Then I paused and looked straight into the camera . . . (Now, at that time I was already doing The People's

Eyebrow, although obviously it wasn't called that. It was just something I started doing with my buddies at school. I'd be walking down the hallway, and if a group of guys was there, and I wanted to get a rise out of them, I'd lift my right eyebrow, as if to say, *You worthless pieces of monkey crap, who do you think you are?* It was just a joke, a way to piss people off and get a reaction.) . . . I looked straight into the camera, cocked my head, and lifted one eyebrow. My buddies all started cracking up. The eyebrow has been around a long time. That's why it's so easy for me to do. To this day, I still get calls from some of my high school friends: "Hey, man, I'm the one who taught you the eyebrow!"

I made a joke out of not being voted all-conference, but the honest truth is that it hurt a little bit. But my mother put it in perspective for me. When she found out, she simply said, "Dwayne . . . small town, small minds." And she was right. I had traveled all over the world before I arrived in Bethlehem. I had lived in thirteen states and in New Zealand. I had a famous father and an unusual ethnic and cultural background. Did this make me a snob? Did it give me an *attitude?* No, I really don't think that it did. But it definitely gave others an attitude about me.

We had a big party at our house after the press conference. Coach Erickson was there, Coach Karm, my whole family—aunts and uncles on my dad's side flew in from Canada; cousins on my mom's side flew in from Hawaii. It was a huge bash. The beer was flowing freely, and over the course of the night, things got a little out of hand. Coach Karm, in particular, indulged a bit too much. At one point my cousin Chad, who is about three or four years younger than me, called to offer his congratulations. When I got off, I handed the phone to Chad's father, my uncle Jay, who had come to the party. Jay eventually hung up the phone, and as he did so, Coach Karm asked, "Who was that?"

"My son, Chad," Uncle Jay said.

Now, by this time Coach Karm was really drunk and obviously no longer capable of determining what was or wasn't funny. There's no other way to explain the next words out of his mouth.

"Really? Well, how big is his penis?"

The whole room went quiet. No one could believe what they had heard. I presume it was meant as a funny reference to Chad maybe being some kind of stud, a hot-shit potential recruit, because he was part of this family of athletes or whatever. I don't know. I only know it was a real miscalculation on Coach Karm's part.

"Excuse me?" my uncle said. And even Coach Karm, drunk as he was, knew that he had said something completely inappropriate. He stammered out an apology, and Uncle Jay said something about it not being very funny before walking angrily out of the room.

Now, I liked Coach Karm, and to this day I still like him. I think he's a terrific coach and a great guy. Sometimes you have too much to drink and you get belligerent and rude and you say stupid things, and that's what happened on this occasion. I'd been drinking, too, so my emotions were getting pretty stirred up. When I heard Coach Karm, and I saw the look on my uncle's face, I started to boil. I followed my uncle into the kitchen and pulled him aside.

"You know, Uncle Jay, I'll be glad to go out there

and kick the living shit out of him if you want," I said. "I'll take him outside and beat his ass for making a crack like that."

Uncle Jay patted me on the back and smiled. "No, that's okay. Let it be."

Good thing he was a gentle man, because if he had given me the green light, drunk as I was, I'd have done it. I'd have dragged Coach Karm right out the door and cleaned the driveway with him. And you know what? I still would have gone to the University of Miami, because that was the type of guy Coach Karm was. He was a defensive line coach, and you needed a certain mentality for that job. He would have appreciated and respected me for standing up and fighting.

Besides, the night was only going to get worse for Coach Karm, regardless of what I did or did not do. Later that evening, about fifteen minutes after he left the party, we got a call from the Bethlehem police. They said, "Mr. Johnson, we have a coach from the University of Miami here who says he was just at your place. Could you come and pick him up. If not, we're going to have to throw him in jail for a while."

What had happened, apparently, is that Coach Karm had stopped off at a 7-Eleven in our neighborhood. He had gone inside to use the bathroom, and when the clerk told him the store didn't have a bathroom, Coach Karm decided to create his own—right there on the floor, directly in front of the guy. Predictably, the clerk called the cops, and pretty soon Coach Karm was in handcuffs, trying to kick out the windows of the patrol car, like some sorry bastard on *Cops* or *Real Stories of the Highway Patrol*.

We showed up a few minutes later, and I remember telling him, "God, man, you're embarrassing. You're

embarrassing to yourself and you're embarrassing to
us. Now get in the damn car!" We took Coach Karm
back to our place and let him sober up for a while.
Eventually he called a limo service and got a ride back
to his hotel. The cool thing was, he left his rental car
behind. So, just to teach him a lesson, I decided to
keep that son of a bitch for a while. I drove all my
friends around for about a week. When Coach Karm
called to apologize for the whole sordid incident, I
couldn't resist making him squirm.

"Geez, Dwayne, I hope this doesn't affect anything."

"No, it doesn't affect anything at all . . ." I said
flatly, ". . . other than the fact that I'm reneging on
my commitment to the University of Miami and I'm
going to Florida State."

There was a long pause on the other end of the line.

"Naaahhh, I'm just kidding," I finally said. "I'll see
you this summer."

JUST A GIGOLO

After we moved to Bethlehem, I maintained a long-distance relationship with Maria, my first love. The parameters of the relationship were vaguely defined, since she had gone off to college in Hawaii and I had moved thousands of miles away. The physical and chronological distance naturally kept us from devoting our hearts to each other, but it would be a lie to say that we simply broke up.

Instead, we remained friends . . . and a bit more. When my family returned to Hawaii on vacations, Maria and I would always get together. In a sense, we were still boyfriend and girlfriend, although neither one of us asked too many questions or expected too much. Or so I thought.

When I was a freshman in high school, I had escorted Maria to her senior prom. That night I promised her that one day she would accompany me to my prom, regardless of where our respective lives had taken us. The fact that I was now leading a totally separate life in Bethlehem, that I had spent the previous three years trying to act like the biggest ladies' man in the Lehigh Valley, did nothing to dissuade me from keeping that vow. Neither did the fact that in the spring of my senior year I was seeing one girl in particular, a girl named Tina, and that she had every right to expect me to invite her to the Freedom High School senior prom.

So I did what any stupid, cocky adolescent boy would do in that situation: I lined up two dates. First, I called Maria and proudly declared my intention to fulfill my promise. She was twenty-one at the time, a junior in college, and you might think that she would have balked at the idea of going back to a high school prom. Uh-uh. She was thrilled.

The next step was to explain the situation to Tina. I could have been honest—just told her the truth about Maria being an old friend to whom I had once made a very important promise. That was one option. I chose another option: I lied. I told Tina that my cousin was flying in from Hawaii and I felt obligated to show her a good time.

"She's going to be my date, and I hope you don't mind," I said. She didn't, of course. Tina, like Maria, had a big heart. She was a good person.

"Ohhhhh . . . your cousin," Tina said. "Isn't that sweet."

Believe it or not, I pulled it off. Maria—my "cousin"—went to the prom as my date, and Tina— my girlfriend—went with a bunch of our friends. The night unfolded like one of those screwball romantic comedies, with me running back and forth between two tables, always trying to stay one step ahead of the two girls. At the end of the night, while sitting with Maria, I excused myself from the table and said that I had to visit the men's room. Instead, I walked over to Tina's table and gave her a little kiss good night and thanked her for her patience and understanding. Then I went home with Maria.

After that, in the eyes of my friends (and in my own

eyes) . . . *I was the man!* Believe me, for a seventeen-year-old guy, it doesn't get any better than that.

Unfortunately, I would later discover that my senior prom had represented a serious withdrawal from the karma bank. And that debt would have to be repaid. I pushed my credit limit to the max by inviting Maria to spend the summer with my family in Bethlehem—after I had learned that Tina would be spending her summer in Cocoa Beach, Florida. After a while, I wasn't sure who I was cheating on anymore. I'd be on the phone with Tina, saying, "Oh, I miss you, too, honey . . . I love you, too . . ." when all of a sudden Maria would walk in the room. I'd quickly lower my voice and change the subject, which bewildered Tina, of course.

It went on like that for a couple months, with me acting like a complete jerk to these two girls, but nonetheless earning huge points with my buddies for being nimble enough to pull it off. Then, on one of Maria's last nights in Bethlehem, my luck ran out. I was out of the house helping a friend move, and Maria was packing her stuff, getting ready to leave, when the phone rang. (The following is a reenactment, courtesy of my mom, who got a huge kick out of seeing her two-timing son get nailed.)

"Hello," Maria said.

"Hi, is Dwayne there?" It was Tina!

"No, I'm sorry, he's out. Who am I speaking to, please?"

"This is his girlfriend, Tina. Who's this?"

"This is his girlfriend, Maria."

"Maria?! I thought you were his cousin!"

"Cousin! I'm not his cousin! We've been going out for the past four years!"

It went downhill from there. By the time I walked in, an hour after the phone had rung, Maria was sitting at the kitchen table, the receiver cradled between her head and shoulder, a cigarette burning in her hand. What made this an especially stunning sight was the fact that Maria did not smoke. I looked at Maria. She barely acknowledged my existence. Then I looked at my mother, who just stood at the sink, shaking her head, as if to say . . . *I told you so.*

I quickly and blindly embraced the impossible task of straightening everything out. I talked with Tina on the phone, and then I talked with Maria. I twisted the truth some more, backpedaled and tap-danced all over the place. I tried to convince them both that I was really still a good guy and that I cared about them deeply (which actually wasn't a lie, although I know it's probably hard to believe). Somehow, I managed to avoid making a mortal enemy out of either Tina or Maria, but things were never the same. During my last few weeks in Bethlehem I was no longer a big shot with two girlfriends. I was flying solo, which was probably just as well. I had graduated from high school. I was leaving town and going off to college. I was starting a new chapter in my life. It was better to start clean.

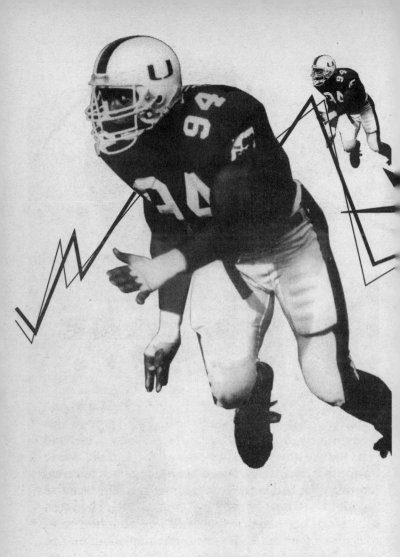

LIKE A HURRICANE
chapter 4

WE WERE JUST a couple weeks into pre-season practice, in the summer of 1990, when I was summoned to Coach Karmelowics's office. He told me to take a seat and then pointed to his desk, where a copy of the *Miami Herald* was folded back to reveal a story that had been written about me. The headline read: FRESHMAN CATCHES EYE OF COACHES. I had seen the story but hadn't really paid any attention to it. Because of my father, I knew something about the ups and downs of celebrity life. Included in both categories was media attention. Sometimes you wanted it, sometimes you didn't. I had learned at a relatively early age that it was best not to take yourself too seriously and to ignore most of what was written about you. This particular story included the usual background information about my father and his wrestling career, as well as a photo and some flattering words about how I had been performing on the practice field for the University of Miami. To me, it meant almost nothing. Miami football was huge when I was there, and there were always several stories in the paper each day. Reporters needed copy, and eventually they got around to writing about almost everyone. They got to me early, but I didn't think anything of it.

Coach Karm had a different take on it.

"Did you read this?" he asked.

"Yeah, I did, Coach."

"Tell me, Dwayne...what about this article excites you the most?"

I could tell he was irritated by my lack of enthusiasm, so I picked up the paper and looked over the copy once again. Nothing registered. "I don't know. What should?"

Coach Karm sighed and went right to a quote from Dennis Erickson: "'Dwayne Johnson will probably not redshirt this season.'" He lowered the paper and stared at me like I was the dullest tool in the shed. "You know what that means?" he said. "You're eighteen years old and you're going to be playing for the University of Miami this season. You're going to get time. You're going to get snaps. Does that not make you excited?"

"Sure it does," I said. "It's great."

In point of fact, it really was one hell of a tribute. A huge percentage of football players at Division I-A schools—especially those that typically are ranked in the top 25—do not make the active roster as freshmen. They are "redshirted," which means they serve an apprenticeship. A redshirt practices every day, endures all that his teammates endure, but does not suit up for games. Instead, he uses the first year of college to grow, physically and emotionally, and, if he chooses, to get a handle on academic life as well.

When I arrived at Miami in July, the word was that all freshmen linemen were going to be redshirted. My position, defensive tackle, was particularly deep. At the top of the depth chart was Russell Maryland, a six-foot-two, 275-pound senior. I had met Russell during my visit to Miami and had found him to be a strong presence—personable, confident, and helpful. (In fact, Russell is one of the most impressive and honorable athletes I have ever known, and we remain friends to this day.) He was also a sensational football player who would go on to win the Outland Trophy as the nation's outstanding collegiate lineman and later help the Dallas Cowboys win two Super Bowls. I had no illusions of unseating Russell Maryland as a freshman, but I did believe that I was capable of making the active roster, of avoiding redshirt status, regardless of what the rumor mill was churning up. That's one of the reasons I wasn't all that worked up about the *Herald* article. It was good news, but it was news that, to me, was not entirely unexpected.

I'm not saying the transition was easy. It wasn't. By the time I got to Miami I was six foot five and weighed nearly 235 pounds. Having grown accustomed to being the biggest dog in the pound, I was at first shocked to see some of my new teammates. A lot of guys were bigger than me, and some of the upperclassmen, twenty-two- and twenty-three-year-old men with sensational, sculpted bodies, were downright intimidating. The intensity of practice was like nothing I had ever encountered. On the very first day we spent a lot of time drilling, running through plays, working on technique. Most of the freshmen were completely lost. I was lucky: Russell Maryland took an immediate interest in my development and helped me along. But I still remember thinking, *So this is what's it's gonna be like: hard, hard work. And we've got another practice this afternoon.*

As a senior in high school my reputation was such that I could do pretty much whatever I wanted. I wasn't a slacker—in fact, I was known as the hardest worker on the team—but if there was a drill I didn't like, I would tell the coach that I was going to work on something else. I'd grab a couple of other linemen, usually good friends of mine, and we'd pretend to keep busy without working up too much of a sweat.

Nothing like that ever happened at Miami. This was a national power, and every minute of every practice was perfectly scripted. No time, no movement was wasted. The staff was so large that on each drill a coach would be standing next to you, shouting in your ear, dressing you down like a fresh recruit in boot camp. And, in addition to field practice, there were daily sessions in the weight room. For all its success and history, Miami has an austere approach to strength training. If you visit Nebraska, Penn State, or any number of traditional football powers, you'll find palatial weight rooms equipped with tons of gleaming metal, rows and rows of Lifecycles and Stairmasters, and viewing rooms where visitors can gawk at the muscles on parade. Not at Miami. The Hurricanes' weight room, even now, is a big, dirty, chalked-up place where serious work is undertaken. There's not much new equipment, just a lot of iron. Mud and grass dragged in from the field cover the floor. There is no air-conditioning, so the place is hot enough to choke the breath out of you, especially when you're straining beneath 350 or 400 pounds, fighting to complete one last set of bench presses. There were days we worked so hard in that room that we'd vomit. But it was a special place, and it was part of the Miami mystique.

The daily routine was incredibly intense, especially once we began working out in full pads. At that point practice became not only exhausting but violent, hostile, territorial. With seven or eight people competing at each position, emotions sometimes boiled over. You chose your friends carefully, and you tried not to screw up too badly. You learned little tricks, like putting your hands on your hips rather than bending over and holding your knees, even though you were so tired that you thought you might pass out. With so much at stake, weakness was not to be revealed casually.

Despite all the pressure and competition, I was confident from the very beginning. I tried to listen to Coach Karm, who gave me a simple piece of advice: "Speed kills." What he meant was this: *If you do everything at full speed, you can never go wrong. You won't get hurt, and you'll impress your teammates and the coaching staff.* Technique will come later. That attitude not only helped me avoid being red-shirted, it catapulted me over almost all of the other defensive linemen. The depth charts for each position were posted daily in the locker room. You'd see some guys walk by the board, smile, pump a fist quietly. You'd see others staring off into space or hanging their heads dejectedly. The day I truly realized I belonged at Miami was the day I looked at the depth chart and, under defensive tackle, saw this:

R. MARYLAND
D. JOHNSON

I didn't look at spots three through eight. I was too pumped up to care. Not only was I going to make the active roster, I was going to get some serious playing time.

Predictably, I sensed some jealousy over my ascension, especially among guys I had surpassed. I was a freshman, and when you're a freshman you're supposed to just kind of sit there and keep your mouth shut, speak only when you're spoken to. It's a lot like being a rookie in the wrestling business. The upperclassmen would be in one corner of the locker room, and the freshmen would be huddled in another, praying that they wouldn't be the targets of any jokes or pranks. When a freshman was plucked out of that station and assigned to a more prominent role, it made everyone a little uncomfortable. Fortunately, I had Russell on my side. Russell commanded tremendous respect. Everyone in the locker room turned to him for leadership and advice. If Russell said you were all right, then you were all right. In Russell's eyes, thank God, I was all right. His philosophy was simple and logical: *If the guy is going to help this team, that's all that matters.*

MIAMI BLUES

As August was about to give way to September, I felt pretty good about myself. I had come down to Miami a few weeks early in order to get acclimated not only to the football schedule but to campus life in general, and now that head start was paying off. At Miami, as is the case at most big-time football schools, you get the idea right away that you are not a student-athlete; you are an *athlete*-student. The football program generates millions of dollars, so it's a priority for the entire school. When a football player arrives on campus, he discovers immediately that he is there to play football. If not for football, he'd have no scholarship. So it's up to each person to balance the rigors of being a Division I football player (which is basically a full-time job) with the rigors of being a college student.

For a while I felt like I had a good handle on everything. I had purchased all my books, I knew what to expect from my classes. And I was second-string behind Russell Maryland, the best lineman in college football. It was almost too good to be true.

In fact, it was too good to be true.

On the last day of double sessions, just ten days before the season opener against Brigham Young University, my world began to unravel. We were in pads, finishing up the afternoon session, working on

what was known as "middle drill." Middle drill was when you let your nuts hang out, so to speak. It was linemen and linebackers on defense, linemen and running backs on offense (and a quarterback to hand the ball off). It was game situation, full contact in the middle of the field. No passing allowed, no break-aways allowed. The quarterback would hand the ball off, and the running back would hit a hole. If the running back broke free, the whistle was blown and you'd do it all over again. Middle drill lasted about fifteen minutes and was almost always conducted near the end of practice, with the whole team and coaching staff gathered around. It was where positions were won and lost, reputations made and dismantled. It was, in short, where you made a man out of yourself. Even now, just thinking about it, I get goose bumps.

I had been doing well in middle drill simply by remembering that speed kills . . . by using my strength and quickness. My technique was improving, too. But on this day I was the victim rather than the assassin. The ball was snapped and I blew past the offensive guard and right into the backfield. I was ready to make a tackle—and it would have been a seriously impressive play—when I was driven into the ground from behind. If it had been an actual game, a whistle would have blown and flags would have flown, and a penalty would have been assessed. Instead, there was merely the grunting and groaning of more than a dozen young men, the crackle of pads hitting pads, and, finally, the sound of a scream rising from my throat.

I knew right away what had happened. My shoulder had absorbed the brunt of the blow and popped out of its socket on impact. That piece-of-shit offensive lineman had been beaten, and he'd tried to cover his mistake by riding me down from behind—an obvious penalty, and one that now had dire consequences. I remember laying on the turf, my face mask stuffed with dirt and grass, unable even to roll over. When the trainer arrived and asked what had happened, all I could say was, "I can't feel my arm." Trainers are used to this kind of thing; they're like battlefield medics. They see a lot of injuries and they hear a lot of anguished cries. It barely fazes them after a while.

"Hold still," the trainer said. I was having trouble staying conscious, but I did as I was told. The next thing I knew he was twisting and rolling my arm, kneading it like an uncooked baguette. Finally, after what seemed an eternity, there was a horrible *pop!* as the shoulder snapped back into place. My arm hung limply at my side as they packed me into an ambulance and whisked me away to Doctors' Hospital in Coral Gables. They shot some X rays and did an MRI. The results were not good: I had a separated shoulder and torn ligaments. The only way to repair the damage was through surgery.

The next day I met with Dr. John Urbie, one of the top orthopedic surgeons in the country. He laid out two options, neither of which was particularly appealing.

"We can let you play," the doctor said. "It'll heal partially and you'll be able to get back on the field relatively soon. But you'll be in a lot of pain and the condition is likely to get worse."

"Or . . . ?" I said.

"Or we perform surgery now and correct the problem, in which case you'll miss the entire season. But you should be as good as new next year."

There really wasn't much of a choice. We had eight other guys who could play defensive tackle, and I was only a freshman. The risks of playing with this type of injury far outweighed the benefits. I would have the surgery.

Two days later, as I emerged from the fog of anesthesia, I realized something: Until that point, I had never really known what it was like to be in pain. I had been injured before, but never seriously. Even the shoulder separation itself couldn't compare to the pain I was now experiencing. The entire left side of my body throbbed. They gave me medication for the pain, but I was reluctant to take it. Within a few hours after I had awakened, I just wanted to get the hell out of the hospital. The confinement . . . the claustrophobia . . . of being in a hospital bed was almost as bad as the surgery. I was an eighteen-year-old athlete and I'd never been hospitalized for anything. It was hard for me. It was hard for the nurses, too, because I was such an enormous pain in the neck. I got up in the middle of the night and tried to walk around, which made everyone kind of nervous. The nurses were yelling at me: "What are you doing? Get back to bed!" I just kept saying, "Please! I want to get out of here!"

The next day I got my wish. I was released from the hospital. But the hardest part was still to come.

THE INVISIBLE MAN

The worst part about being injured is that you quickly become a ghost. When you're healthy, you're in the mix every day. You practice, lift weights, attend meetings, prepare for games. In every way imaginable, you are part of something special. You are part of a team . . . a family. It's really a great feeling.

For me, unfortunately, that feeling was swept away in a matter of just a few short days. I was removed from the active roster and placed in a pile along with the other redshirted freshmen. Unlike the other redshirts, though, I couldn't even practice, so I felt truly ostracized. My perception of the situation was more severe than the reality. It's true that The Show Must Go On. There were ninety players on the University of Miami football team, and the coaching staff had to concentrate on those who were healthy enough to make a contribution. In defense of the program, I have to admit that I was encouraged to come to meetings, watch game film, be part of the defense, at least in a spiritual way. But the combination of physical pain and emotional isolation left me depressed and angry. Being around my teammates, watching them sweat and struggle, only exacerbated the situation. Before long I had removed myself from the atmosphere of the team.

What made this withdrawal especially painful was the fact that I had no one to whom I could turn. Until that summer I had never spent much time away from my family. And now that my days were no longer jammed with a frenzy of activity, the loneliness set in. When you're busy, running around at a hundred miles an hour all the time, you don't even think about whether you're lonely or happy or sad. You just keep moving. Now, all of a sudden, I was sitting in my dorm room, feeling sorry for myself, wishing like hell that my mom and dad were right down the hall. I spent a lot of time on the phone with them. My dad, who's pretty much a stoic, kept saying, "Hang in there, it'll be all right." My mom was more sympathetic. From the time I was in high school I wasn't big on showing my emotions to my parents—I wanted them to think I was an adult. But I remember crying a lot in those first few months, especially with my mom. Every time we'd talk, I'd say the same thing, over and over: "I want to go home. I don't like it here."

When classes started, the situation deteriorated. My entire identity was tied into being a football player—*a Hurricane!*—and now I was just a big kid shuffling around campus in a funk. The frustration I was feeling led me to hate my whole environment. The mature, sensible approach to my predicament would have been to continue to work hard on my rehabilitation and throw some of my excess energy into my classwork. I chose another option: I stayed in bed. By the end of September I had skipped more classes than I'd attended. I was sure that I was going to be leaving school anyway, so I saw no point in putting any effort into my academic life. I've always been a big advocate of making changes when you're

unhappy: *If you don't like your situation, do something about it*. Of course, taken to its irresponsible extreme, that philosophy can have disastrous consequences, which was what happened to me that fall.

In late October I flew to Toronto to attend my uncle's wedding. I had been looking forward to this event for weeks because it was my first opportunity to see my parents and other family members. I was finally out of my sling and starting to feel a little bit better. But it took only a few drinks and a terrible misunderstanding on my part for the entire weekend to be nearly ruined.

The night before the wedding we had a big party at a restaurant. It went on for hours. The alcohol flowed freely and everyone seemed to be having a good time. My father has a very big family, eleven brothers, so there were a lot of people there I barely knew; some people I had never seen before. At one point a couple that I did not recognize began to get loud. The woman was yelling and pointing in the direction of my father. She was smiling, too, but in my drunken stupor I interpreted that as arrogance. After a while I saw my father stand up and point at the woman.

"Hey, keep your voice down!" he shouted.

She waved a hand at him, laughed, and shouted back, over the din of the dining room, "Fuck you!"

Now, it should have registered, even in my ethanol-soaked mind, that no one else seemed even slightly offended by this exchange, including my father. But it didn't. At that moment, when I heard her words, all of the hostility and frustration that I had been experiencing bubbled to the surface. I jumped out of my seat, tossed my chair aside, and stumbled to where the woman was sitting. In my twisted state, I was thinking, *This bitch is talking like that to my father? In front of my mom? And me?*

The next thing I knew my hands were wrapped around her throat, squeezing the oxygen out of her tiny body. As she began to turn blue, I could hear people screaming. I could feel them pawing at me, telling me to stop. But I was enraged.

"Apologize to my father!" I said.

This poor woman weighed about 120 pounds. I was moving her around like a rag doll, clearing glasses and dishes from the table with her body as she choked and gasped and scratched at my wrists.

"Apologize to my mother! NOW!"

There are few incidents in my life that have filled me with more shame and regret than this one. I guess I'm just lucky that my mother reached me in time, and that she was able to cut through what I can only describe as a psychotic break.

"Dwayne!" she said. "It's okay! I know her . . . we're friends!"

I felt my mom's hand on my back, comforting me, calming me. Slowly my grip loosened and the woman slipped free. After that it was like . . . *Party's over! Dwayne fucked up everything!*

Dozens of people were in my ear, screaming at me, telling me I was out of my mind. Everyone, that is, except my parents. I had a temper as a kid, and I had been known to get into a few scrapes. But it was not my nature to terrorize anyone, especially a woman. So they realized then that something was very wrong. After I had finished apologizing profusely to both the woman and her boyfriend (they were surprisingly gracious and understanding about the whole thing), I talked with my mom and dad. I told them how hard the semester had been, and that I was seriously thinking about leaving school. This wasn't an easy thing to admit, because my parents had been talking about moving to Tampa in order to be closer to me.

"When you start playing again, everything will be different," my mother said. "You'll see. Be strong."

I nodded in agreement, mainly because I didn't want my parents to worry about me anymore. I returned to Miami feeling completely lost and alone, certain that whatever my future held, it didn't include playing football for the Hurricanes.

SCHOOL DAZE

In December Coach Karm called me into his office again. I'd spent a fair amount of time there in the preceding months, usually to get some sort of pep talk about staying focused, preparing for the next season, and avoiding the trap of self-pity. I didn't listen to much of it. By now I didn't think anyone could offer me worthwhile advice. I preferred stewing in my own anger. I wasn't sure what the subject of this particular meeting would be, but I presumed it would be some sort of variation on what had become a familiar theme: *Chin up, Dwayne*. During a phone conversation with my father I had let it slip that Coach Karm had scheduled a meeting with me.

"What do you think it's about?" my dad had said.

"Ah, they're probably getting ready for the spring and they can't wait for me to come back," I lied. "Russell Maryland is gone and now it's my turn."

In my heart I knew this wasn't the case. I knew the meeting, which was arranged in a more formal manner than usual, probably involved some sort of bad news. I just wasn't prepared for the depth of it.

"Have a seat, Dwayne." Coach Karm pointed to a chair, just as he had the previous August when he showed me the article in the *Miami Herald*. And, once again, he wanted to discuss something that was lying on his desk. It was a slip of paper, small and flimsy, yet strangely foreboding. I knew what it was, even though I had never received one:

A college report card.

"Would you like to tell me what the fuck this is all about?" he said, waving the paper disgustedly.

I shrugged. I knew my first-semester grades were bad—after all, I had missed a lot of classes and even skipped two final exams. Still, I didn't realize just how poorly I had performed. Or, perhaps, I had deluded myself into believing that my status as a football player—even a phantom, redshirted football player—would somehow carry me through.

It didn't.

"Point-fucking-seven?!" Coach Karm said. He let the report card drop to the surface of the desk. "Do you know how hard it is to get a point-seven? What have you been doing all semester?"

The obvious answer was: *nothing . . . squat . . . jack-shit!*

Coach Karm screamed at me for a while, but most of what he said didn't register. I was too busy staring at my report card. In that moment I felt about as worthless as I had ever felt in my life. I had let my parents down, I had let my teammates and coaches down, and I had let myself down.

After accepting his admonishment and mumbling something about trying harder, I walked out of Coach Karm's office. I don't know why, but for some reason I did not catch the first bus out of town. Instead, I decided to stay.

The next semester was among the hardest and

most degrading periods of my life. I was placed on academic probation, which is sort of like having the word *idiot* stamped on your forehead. It's bad enough that most people think big-time college athletes are morons who have no business taking up space in a classroom; I had proved the stereotype to be correct. Now I had to rectify the situation. I'm a firm believer that perception becomes reality. For three months I had soaked in misery, been frustrated at the world, and generally acted like a complete jerk-off. Three months is a long time for people to perceive something, especially on a college campus. My reputation was in serious need of repair.

So I accepted the terms of my probation, which included additional hours in study hall and weekly sessions with a tutor. I had to leave Christmas vacation early to prepare for class. They were hard on my ass, and I deserved it. I tried to tell myself that each time I walked up to a professor after class and asked him to sign a note saying that I had attended that day's lecture. Humiliating? Absolutely. And way beyond anything the university required. As far as the college was concerned, I was on academic probation and it was up to me to get out of that hole. But there were no special guidelines or restrictions. That was left up to the athletic department. At Miami the administration believed in letting each sport police its own athletes. So, for the next few months, I became a legitimate *student*-athlete. If I missed a single class, I was not allowed to participate in any football-related activity that day. And I needed proof of attendance—thus the note from each professor. If I showed up at the weight room, I had to present a note. If I wanted to attend a meeting, I had to present a note. I felt like

I was eight years old. After every single class I had to walk up to the professor and say, "Sir, I think I'm mature and fairly responsible, although I know that my acts haven't shown it in the last few months. Could you please sign this note saying I was in class so that I can work out this afternoon?" And he'd take the little slip of paper and write, *"Dwayne was here today—Professor so-and-so."*

Making matters worse was the fact that things weren't going great at home for my mom and dad. Their relationship was okay, but they had some financial pressure. My father had made a good living when he was wrestling—in his best year he had earned between $150,000 and $175,000, which was a lot of money in the early 1980s. But like a lot of wrestlers from that era, he had received no exposure to financial planning. Not that we lived a lavish lifestyle or anything, but there was never much thought given to investing for the future. My parents always just assumed that the money would be there. Now, as my father's wrestling career was winding down, money was getting tight. By 1990 he was out of the business and faced with the prospect of having to go find a regular job. The guy was forty-six years old and didn't even have a high school education. He was lost. So he did what a lot of men do in that situation: He turned to the bottle.

I knew all of this was happening, but I had been too busy wallowing in my own gloom to do anything about it. Now, I realized, it was time to put an end to the bullshit. It was time to stop disappointing myself and everyone around me. It was time to go to work.

chapter 5

CUPID,
DRAW BACK YOUR BOW

WHEN YOU'RE A freshman football player at the University of Miami, or any other Division I school for that matter, you hear a lot about fringe benefits ... perks. You hear about easy courses taught by generous professors who happen to be big football fans. You hear about fat-cat boosters stopping by the dorm and opening their checkbooks. You hear about easy access to drugs. And, especially, you hear about sex. Cheap and easy sex. Down-and-dirty style, with hot-and-cold-running groupies.

Most of this is merely fantasy, as I discovered during my first few months in Miami. There were a few restaurants I could count on to give me a free meal, but other than that, boosters were practically invisible. They'd been purged in the wake of Jimmy Johnson's departure, just as Coach Karm had said. A notable exception was the presence in the locker room of Luther Campbell, the lead singer for 2 Live Crew, one of the biggest and nastiest of the hard-core rap groups in the early 1990s. Luther was not a University of Miami graduate, but he had grown up in Miami, and he loved the Hurricanes. He was a big fan. Like the Hurricanes, Luther was brash and cocky. He was arrested once for his "lewd" behavior onstage. By today's standards, he was actually fairly tame, but back then he was considered extremely outspoken and controversial.

So Luther naturally dug the cockiness of the Miami football team, and to show his appreciation, he'd offer prize money for certain accomplishments. For example, when we played Florida State, Luther would let it be known that there was a bounty on the head of Charlie Ward, the Seminoles' Heisman Trophy–winning quarterback. The player who hit Charlie the hardest would get a reward, usually $500. Sometimes there was cash for sacking the quarterback or for making a great catch. It differed each week. But you could always look forward to Luke's Pot until the NCAA cracked down on him and he was tossed out of the locker room.

As for the football-loving professors . . . well, they may have been out there, but they sure as hell weren't teaching any of my courses, as my first-semester transcript demonstrated. Similarly, the Sexual Olympics in which I had expected to be an eager participant had apparently been canceled. There were, of course, girls who were clearly attracted to football players, but the

Roman orgies—the *Animal House* debauchery—
seemed to be missing.

Until now.

"This is the night," one of my teammates said with
a wink. I smiled at him and went about the business
of preparing for a long, hard evening of carousing. I
styled my hair, splashed on some cologne, and sang to
myself. I shared a suite with two of my teammates,
both football players, and right now there were six
girls waiting for us in the living room. *Two girls for
every booooy . . . !* The girls were just regular students, and football fans, of course. We'd heard a lot
about groupies and gang sex, but thus far had been
sadly deprived of any personal involvement in this
sort of glorious depravity. Now, in the middle of the
second semester, we were finally getting close.

"I'm telling you, man, it's gonna happen tonight,"
I said to one of my buddies. "The three of us with
those six girls. Nine of us in one room doing freaky
shit!"

This wasn't wishful thinking. It had actually been
discussed and agreed upon. The girls were like, *Hey,
that's cool, we're down with it.* I remember walking
into the living room and saying, "OK, who's got the
condoms?" The girls just laughed, and one of them
reached into her purse, pulled out a fistful of Trojans,
and said, rather cleverly, I thought, "Don't worry . . .
we're covered."

Our first stop was a place called the Triangle Club
in Coral Gables. To spike interest and entice kids
from the university to come on out, the Triangle Club
had been passing out fliers in recent days promising
"free drinks for football players." In that way the
club was practically guaranteed a full house. Football

players would indeed show up because football players love to drink for free. And other students would show up not only to rub elbows with football players but hopefully to get a little free alcohol themselves. When we arrived on this particular Thursday evening, it looked like every kid on campus was there. I had never seen the Triangle Club so crowded. I wasn't old enough to drink, but that was no serious obstacle. I was a football player, number 94. The fact that I hadn't played a single game the previous fall was irrelevant. No one was going to card me.

In this kind of atmosphere it's easy to be a big shot, and I was milking it for all it was worth. I'd sidle up to three or four girls and say, "Excuse me, ladies, what are you drinking?" Then I'd order a round for everyone. It was in the midst of this performance, while I was acting like Don Juan, that I fell in love. I mean right there, in the middle of the Triangle Club, while I was *working*. I had a drink in each hand and I was leaning over a table, trying like hell to charm a group of drunken girls, when all of a sudden I felt an elbow in my side . . . a real sharp elbow in my short ribs. This was no accident; it was intended to provoke a reaction. And it did.

I glanced down and my heart instantly did a little flip-flop. There, by my side, was a lean, athletic woman with wide eyes and a big, beautiful smile. I recognized her instantly as someone I had seen in the Miami weight room. She was very exotic looking, not at all the kind of woman you forget. I had been impressed not only by her appearance but by the way she moved. She was graceful, confident, strong. I had heard that she was a member of the Miami crew team, but prior to this very moment, I had never spoken to her.

"Hi," she said.

I leaned closer so that I could hear her over the noise of the nightclub. "Hello."

"I see you all the time in the weight room," she said. "I just wanted to come over and introduce myself."

"Well, I'm flattered. I'm Dwayne Johnson."

She extended her hand. "I'm Dany Garcia." I was startled by her handshake. It was more than just firm—it was powerful. I later found out that her major was international finance and marketing, and that in the course of her various business meetings she had come to believe in the value of a sturdy handshake. I was impressed. And as I looked at her smile, and felt her hand in mine, I knew immediately: *This is the one for me!* I know that sounds corny, but it's the absolute truth. I had been hit with a thunderbolt.

After a minute or so, Dany asked me to dance.

"Well, actually, I'm waiting for a particular song." This wasn't true. It was merely a bit of gamesmanship, my opening move in the courtship ritual. It was designed to give me a little more control over the situation. Dany just laughed.

"What song is that?" she said.

"I'll let you know when I hear it."

"Okay, it's been nice talking to you," she said. And she started to walk away. I hadn't counted on that.

"Where are you going?"

"Back to my friends. They're waiting for me." She smiled again. "Don't worry—we'll talk."

I nodded. "Definitely."

And as she strode gracefully away, I thought to myself, *I have to spend the rest of my life with that woman.*

I quickly lost interest in every other girl in the club. All these other chicks? They were obsolete. I gave Dany about five minutes to get back to her table before taking off in hot pursuit. I found her quickly. As "Groove Is in the Heart" pumped through the sound system, I said, "Here's the song," and invited her to dance. Afterward, we walked off the floor together and talked some more.

"So, how old are you anyway?" Dany asked

"That depends. How old do you want me to be?"

I thought I was being pretty smooth, but Dany wasn't falling for it. She just cocked her head. "Come on. How old are you?"

"How old are *you*?" I replied.

She didn't even hesitate. "I'm twenty-two."

Ouch! Not what I wanted to hear. My mind started racing, coming up with all kinds of reasons why a twenty-two-year-old woman—not a girl— would want to avoid an eighteen-year-old boy. But I gave it a shot anyway.

"Well, I'm eighteen."

Dany's eyes grew even wider as she let out a big laugh. Then she smacked me playfully on the chest. "What's wrong?" I said. "It's just a number."

I was trying to act self-assured, but in truth I was filled with anxiety, simply because I'd never been so attracted to anyone in my entire life. I realized that being eighteen was a huge strike against me. Here I was, a freshman in college, and I was trying to convince this grown woman—on the verge of starting her adult life—that I was the man for her. It was crazy! Nevertheless, I pressed on.

"Do you have a phone?" I asked.

She looked at me like I was nuts. Obviously she

had a phone. Everyone had a phone. Everyone except me, that is. I was dead broke and couldn't afford a phone, so I presumed that most other college students were in the same predicament.

"Of course I have a phone," she said. "Why?"

"Because I'd like your number."

And she gave it to me! Without a struggle! I thanked her and said, "Good night, it's been great getting to know you. I'll call." I gave her a little peck on the cheek, which I thought was the appropriate thing to do. But Dany looked straight into my eyes and said, "Would you mind kissing me on the lips?"

Would I mind? You've gotta be kidding!

So we kissed. And as her lips met mine, I knew I was gone. A few minutes later, as my buddies were getting ready to move on to a club in Coconut Grove along with our six girlfriends, I displayed one of the primary symptoms of love sickness: a complete disinterest in cheap, sleazy sex.

"We're outta here, D. J., let's go."

"Nah, I'm not feeling great. You guys go on without me. I'm going back to my room."

Their jaws dropped. I was the ring leader of this whole operation, and now I was backing out on them. I was putting a serious crimp in their plans for a wild, hedonistic night, but I couldn't have cared less. I left the Triangle Club, went back to my room, and immediately picked up my roommate's telephone and dialed Dany's number. I knew she wouldn't be home yet, but I wanted to make my intentions clear. I wanted her to know how much I had enjoyed meeting her. So I left a message. A short time later she called back and we talked for an hour. And we've talked every single day since then. More than nine years have passed and the streak is intact. Wherever the road takes me—Minnesota, Alabama, South Africa, Germany, Kuwait—I always find time to call Dany.

A couple days later we went out on our first "date," an informal lunch. Just hamburgers and fries. The *big* date came the following week. Dany picked me up (she had a car; I didn't) and we drove to a very nice Chinese restaurant. With only forty dollars to my name, I was working without a net on this night. And, of course, I didn't have any credit cards because I couldn't get credit. Nevertheless, I knew I couldn't let Dany pay for the date. So we walked into the restaurant, sat down, and began scanning the menu. Now, if you're in a situation like this, your eyes go right past the description of items and on to the prices. You aren't even thinking about eating. You're just doing math in your head. You're looking for a way out.

God, how am I going to pay for this? I know—I'll sacrifice and have something little. Maybe she'll follow my lead.

I ordered the smallest entrée on the menu and then, in an act of utter desperation, looked at Dany and said, "You want to share?"

"No, thanks—I'm *starving*!"

She pointed to the menu and spoke to the waiter. "I'll have this . . . and I'll have this . . . and I'll have a side of this. Oh . . . and I'd like this as an appetizer, please."

Somehow, I had enough money, although by such a small margin that I wasn't able to leave a tip. I walked out of there with nothing more than a few coins, but I couldn't have been happier. Later that night we sat by a lake and looked up at the stars and fantasized about growing old together. We started talking about ideal mates for life, and I turned to Dany and said, "If I were to date someone, it would be someone just like you."

I meant it, too. As long as I'd been dating girls, I had been in control. The relationship was always about me and my needs and what I wanted to do. With Dany I didn't feel that way. I wanted to be her partner.

GUESS WHO'S
NOT COMING
TO DINNER?

Dany was open-minded about me from the beginning. She thought a lot of football players were jerks and pigs and everything that, for the most part, football players are. But she gave me a chance. I remember telling my parents that they had to meet her, that they would absolutely love her. And I was right. Unfortunately, Dany's parents were a bit less enthusiastic.

Dany wasn't rich, by any means, but she had grown up comfortably middle class in New Jersey. Her parents were Cuban immigrants who were adamant about being *American*. English was always the first language in their home. They wanted their children to assimilate, to adapt and succeed. What they did not want was their daughter dating me, mainly because I was a person of color. So was Dany, of course, but that didn't seem to matter. I was half *black*, and that made me an unsuitable suitor. Moreover, I was a freshman, three years younger than Dany. And I had no money. To them it must have seemed as though Dany had hit the bad-boyfriend trifecta.

"What's he going to do for you?" they had said to Dany on numerous occasions. "He has three years of college left."

"He's going to play in the NFL."

"But what if he doesn't make it?"

"Then he'll do anything he wants. He's a smart guy."

Professional wrestling wasn't really an option for me then. I was still a big fan of the business, and I had been open with Dany about how much I enjoyed it. She liked watching tapes of my dad, and I had made passing reference to perhaps one day following in his footsteps. But I didn't feel a need to share that with Dany's family. I didn't think it was a great idea at that time to say, "Dany, just tell your parents I'm going to be a professional wrestler." Somehow, I got the feeling they might not have found that news to be particularly reassuring.

Whatever I wanted to do, Dany pledged her support, and in return I was committed to not letting her down. I started working harder in class, got all the notes I needed from my professors without complaining, and generally just sucked it up. I went to class every day, met with my tutors, and before long my grades began to improve. By the end of the second semester I was off academic probation. And, in fact, I actually became a very competent and responsible student, so much so that I was elected academic captain in my junior and senior years. My grade point average by the time I graduated was 2.9. It wasn't the highest on the team by a long shot—we had some very smart players, guys with GPAs of 3.5, 3.8, even a couple of 4.0's—but I guess in my case a 2.9 was impressive, in light of where I had started. It showed what a lot of hard work and dedication could produce. I even managed to get a couple of A's, including one in speech communication. Considering that The Rock's popularity today stems largely from his expertise with a microphone, that seems appropriate.

Still, it's funny . . . I can't tell you twenty specific things I learned from all of the classes I took at UM. I don't say that to belittle the quality of the education there. It's just the truth. But I do remember what I learned about sacrifice and having a commitment to being the absolute best. I remember getting up at six in the morning to lift weights and then watch film. I remember summer workouts, running for forty-five minutes in the heat and humidity at 9:00 A.M., and then going into the weight room and vomiting from exhaustion. There were so many things that molded my work ethic. We had a saying at Miami, and it carries over to what I'm doing now: "All it takes is all you've got." I'll never forget that. It's so simple, but so true.

chapter 6

FAMILY MATTERS

WHEN I WAS A CHILD I thought my father was the strongest man alive. Not just physically, but spiritually, emotionally, mentally. He performed what appeared to be superhuman feats each night in the wrestling ring, spectacular athletic maneuvers that made grown men and women, to say nothing of children, stand and scream themselves hoarse. He provided a good home for me and my mom. He was tough, a bit reserved with his emotions, but there never was any doubt that he loved his family intensely and without qualification.

For a long time I never knew that he struggled with the demons of the strange world in which he lived, just like all professional wrestlers. It's a world in which aching joints are anesthetized by the roar of a crowd, and the loneliness of life on the road is soothed by the sweetness of alcohol and drugs and the touch of strange flesh. As with all athletes and entertainers, professional wrestlers struggle mightily against the inevitable: the day when they will not be able to perform, when the back gives out in the middle of a body slam or the knee pops while climbing a turnbuckle. For my father, that day arrived at the end of the 1980s. And, as is often the case, his fall from grace was swift and harsh. Once a world champion, he was reduced to bit-player status. He would take work wherever he could find it—if a small regional promoter needed someone to come in for the night and throw his body around for $100, Rocky Johnson would do it. He had to. He was trained for nothing else.

The serious drinking didn't begin until around 1991. My father had always been a casual drinker, a guy who liked to have a few beers while watching television. Sometimes he went out with the boys after shows. Sometimes he even got drunk. But it had never gotten the best of him. By the summer of '91, when I came home after my first year at Miami, it was clear that he was losing his battle with the bottle. Dad was basically out of the business by then, and he was having a terrible time coping with the tremendous void in his life. He was eating through his meager savings, and he had no job prospects. His pride was battered. For the first time in his life, he was lost. My dad had been kicked out of his house when he was a thirteen-year-old kid. He'd been on his own ever since, and he'd somehow managed to build a pretty good life for himself and his family. Now it was falling apart. His way of coping was to drink.

For a long time, like most alcoholics, my father denied that he had a problem. But as his drinking escalated and he spent more time in bed recovering from hangovers ... as the blackouts became more frequent and the arguments with my mother more volatile ... as the half-empty bottles piled up around the house ... as he descended into a black hole of addiction ... it became increasingly obvious that he needed help. Or he would die.

The irony of his condition—that someone so strong could be so weak—both shocked and disappointed me. I blamed my father for letting it happen, for failing to fight the demons. The truth, of course, was that he had fought ... and lost. The hardest part for me was knowing that my mother was absorbing the brunt of the abuse. I don't mean to imply that my father was physically aggressive or hurtful toward my mom—he wasn't. But he was mentally abusive, and eventually the strain took its toll on their marriage. It never came to the point where my mother simply said, "The hell with it. I don't care anymore." But I wouldn't have blamed her one bit. I remember saying to my father once, after he had promised to quit for at least the tenth time, "God, Dad, why are you doing this? You're destroying yourself and you're destroying our family."

The next year was the hardest, because I was back at school, trying to get my own life in order, trying to be a good student, a good football player, and a good friend to Dany. My parents had moved to Tampa, so they were much closer now, but not so close that I could just jump in a cab and help out whenever my father went on a bender. By the fall of 1992, I had all but given up hope. There comes a point when the friends and family of an addict can do nothing but cut him loose. You can love him, but you let him go because it's too painful to hold on. I had reached that point when my father called me one night at school.

"I've quit drinking," he said.

"Uh-huh." He'd said this before. Many times. I saw no reason to believe him.

"Yesterday," he said. "I quit yesterday."

"Okay, Dad . . . I hope you mean it. I really do."

He'd been attending Alcoholics Anonymous meetings for months, but usually they prompted only indignation on his part. The men he encountered in those meetings—sad, pathetic men with bad skin and yellow teeth and not a penny to their names—only reinforced his belief that he did not have a problem . . . that he was *not like them*. He was, of course, and in his heart he knew it. Acceptance simply took time.

I'm happy to say that my father quit drinking— cold turkey—that day in 1992. He has not touched a drop of alcohol ever since. He cleaned up his act, got a job driving a truck, and went about the hard business of life, just as he had when he was younger. He likes to say that my mother and I got him through this crisis, that if not for us, he never would have made it. I don't know about that. I think he did most of the work himself. Either way, I just want to say, for the record ... *I love you, Dad. And I'm proud of you.*

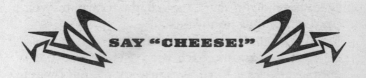

SAY "CHEESE!"

Although things were improving at home and in the classroom, I wasn't terribly pleased with the way my football career was progressing. I had played in nine games as a freshman, including a 22–0 win over Nebraska in the Orange Bowl, a victory that gave us a 12–0 record and Miami's first national championship under Dennis Erickson. Now, in the fall of '92, I was fighting for more playing time. I was getting 30 to 40 percent of the snaps each week, which isn't bad at all for a sophomore, but I wasn't satisfied. I wanted to be a starter, a big shot, and not merely a role player. I became increasingly frustrated, to the point where my emotions boiled over.

The guy who provoked my outburst was Kevin Patrick, a consensus all-American who went on to play for the San Diego Chargers. We were both defensive linemen, so there was a natural tension between us. We were doing a pass drill one afternoon when what should have been a mild disagreement erupted into something out of *Raw Is War*. It started with Kevin and I disagreeing about whose turn it was to participate in the drill. Within seconds we were cursing at each other. Then we were swinging our helmets. The coaches broke up the fight, but I was still steaming two days later when I ran into Kevin in the weight-room office. He said something to me that I interpreted as a smart-ass comment. So I walked slowly to the office entrance and closed the door.

"What did you say?" I asked, the tone in my voice clearly indicating annoyance.

Kevin laughed. It was obvious to everyone else in the room—assistant coach Brad Webber and one of our players—that Kevin was just joking. But I was in a foul mood.

"Look, I didn't mean anything by it," Kevin said. To his credit, he was trying to defuse the situation. The same could not be said for me.

"Sure as hell sounds like you're serious," I said. "So what's the problem."

Well, then Kevin got pissed, too, and pretty soon we were trading "FUCK-YOUs!" and throwing punches at each other. We rolled around the office, onto desks, and finally right through the door and into the weight room. People were screaming, trying to break us up, but I was out of my mind. I wanted to *kill* Kevin. I had him pinned to the floor, and as he struggled to escape, I tried to rip his tongue out of his head. I actually reached into his mouth with my hand, grabbed his tongue, and began pulling with all my strength. There is no way to justify this behavior, no way to make it sound sane. At that moment I was absolutely nuts. My temper had gotten the best of me once again. If I hadn't been pulled off Kevin, I might have permanently scarred him.

The next day I met with Coach Erickson. I apologized for my behavior and tried to express my feelings in a calm, mature manner.

"I just feel like I'm not getting my due," I said. "You've given me some opportunities, and I feel like I've taken advantage of them. I feel like I've outworked everyone out there. So I just want to know— is there something else going on? Is it my temper?"

Coach Erickson shook his head. "No, Dwayne, it's not your temper. We think it's great when you channel your violence in a positive way for us."

I understood what he was saying. Football is all about violence—*controlled* violence. I was not a troubled guy or anything. It's just that I rarely let a disagreement end at the shouting stage. I was still learning the fine art of walking away. Sometimes this attitude led to trouble, as in the final game of my sophomore season, at San Diego State.

The Aztecs didn't have much of a team back then, and we had one of the top programs in the nation. But they were tough. They had a lot of inner-city players, guys with gang affiliations. Like us, they were brash and funky. They talked a lot of trash. But no one talked trash like the Hurricanes. That was our signature. Before every game we'd huddle in the locker room and get a little chant going. Someone, usually a senior or a captain, would say, "Tonight we're going to do three things . . . " And then someone else would respond, "What's that?"

And then the whole team would pick up the chant . . .

"HIT! STICK! AND BUST DICK!"

"And what else?"

"TALK SHIT!"

"What else?"

"TALK SHIT!"

"WHAT ELSE?!"

"TALK SHIT!!"

We always said it three times, just to emphasize the point. If you were playing Miami, whether we were beating the crap out of you or getting our asses whipped, you knew you were going to be subjected to an endless flow of shit-talking. You can see a lot of that now in the character of The Rock, who never stops talking. That's a Miami influence, no question about it.

The incessant trash talking, in both directions, led to a bench-clearing brawl at the end of the game. In fact, it was this incident that prompted the NCAA to create a rule barring players from leaving the bench during an on-field altercation. Any player who broke the rule faced a three-game suspension. I was playing when the fight broke out, so I didn't have to go far to look for trouble. It came in the form of the San Diego State mascot, a grown man dressed as an Aztec warrior. Out of the corner of my eye I could see him charging, arms high, weapon in hand. God only knows what he intended to do. I turned to face him and immediately thought, *I'm going to kill this son of a bitch!* He stopped, turned, and ran. And I went after him!

Now, this was a nationally televised game, so the minute I threw off my helmet and started running, the cameras were on us. Following us. Me, with my hair grown out in an Afro, a wild look on my face, trying to run down the freaking mascot! He sprinted past the sideline and began scaling the stadium wall. I was right behind him, screaming . . .

"I'LL KILL YOU! I'LL KILL YOU!"

With the help of some fans the Aztec made it to safety. But that night my phone would not stop ringing. Apparently, and not unpredictably, my confrontation with the San Diego State mascot had made every sports highlight show in the country.

"What on earth were you thinking?" my mom said.

What could I say? Obviously, if I had been thinking, I wouldn't have done it. In time I would learn to get a better handle on my rage and to use my aggression—as well as my theatrical tendencies—in the pursuit of more practical endeavors.

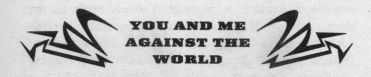

YOU AND ME AGAINST THE WORLD

Dany and I moved in together in the spring of 1993. She was out of school and had recently signed a contract to work for Merrill Lynch. It was a good job with a ton of potential for growth (obviously, since Dany is now a Merrill Lynch vice president), but her starting pay was only $18,000, not much for two people. And I had no money at all. So we got a small apartment and furnished it with a handful of necessities: a bed, a couch, a tiny television set. Our big thing was to go out to the movies on Friday night. We did that almost every week. But there were virtually no other luxuries.

Our decision to share an apartment was the turning point in our lives. It solidified our relationship, and not just because we were living under one roof. When Dany told her parents that we were moving in together, they gave her a choice: *It's him or us*.

She chose me.

I understand that parents want to protect their daughters, that they only want what's best for their children. I can understand Dany's parents being upset by the idea that she was paying my rent. But this wasn't really about money. This was about *me*. It was about who I was and where I had come from. Nothing had ever hurt me more. I believe I can take almost anything. I'm not Superman, but my shoulders are strong . . . my skin is thick. This rejection, however, was painful, because it was an insult to my mom and dad. It was a slap in their faces, as if someone had said, *"What you've created is not good enough for my daughter."* That was hard for my parents to accept, especially my mom.

"My God," she said. "They don't even know you." Which was literally true. Dany and I had been dating for three years, and still I hadn't met her parents. What made it even harder was the fact that my parents had immediately welcomed Dany into our lives and our home. There was no hesitancy whatsoever. I used to rack my brain trying to figure it out. I kept thinking it was an awful dream, and that eventually I'd wake up and Dany's parents would realize that I was a pretty good guy who was madly in love with their daughter. But it wasn't a dream. It was as real as could be.

That was the hardest time for us, especially for Dany. She gave up her family for me, and I will never forget that. When we moved in together, when she made a commitment to me against the wishes of her family, I made a promise to myself: *I'm going to make this work. Somehow, someway. I don't care if I have to eat canned tuna three times a day, every day, I will make this work. Someday I'll pay Dany back, and give her everything she's ever wanted.*

 **GOOD DAYS AND BAD**

In the fall of 1993 I had my most productive season. Warren Sapp, a sophomore who had emerged as a big-time player (he would go on to become one of the most dominant linemen in the NFL), had beaten me out for the starting job at defensive tackle. But I got a lot of playing time. I was healthy and confident, and I finally felt as though I fully understood the Miami system. Our coaches liked to say, "There is no second team here," and it was true in a way. A lot of guys playing backup at Miami would have been starters almost anywhere else. That was part of the Miami mystique.

When I was there, Miami was like no other program in college football. The Orange Bowl was the toughest place for an opponent to play. When we burst through the locker-room doors and into the tunnel, and the music was blaring and the crowd was roaring, we simply knew we were going to win. There was no other option.

I fell in love with football all over again during my junior year. I relished everything about it, right down to the pregame rituals: dressing, taping, listening to my music (always rap on game days to get me geeked, even though I usually prefer country music or R&B),

talking quietly with other defensive linemen, writing "God & Dany" on my left hand, "Mom & Dad" on my right. That was important to me. If I was down in the trenches late in the game, exhausted, not sure if I had anything left to give, I would look down at my hands and see those words—*God & Dany . . . Mom & Dad*—and I'd remember that no sacrifice was too heavy.

We went 9–3 that year and finished fifteenth in the final Associated Press rankings. Not great by Miami standards, but not bad either. There were more than a few memorable games that season, in particular a nationally televised 49–0 thrashing of Syracuse, at a time when the Orangemen had a great quarterback in Marvin Graves and a team ranked in the top ten. They were fighting for the top position in the Big East Conference, and they came down to the Orange Bowl for a night game against the Hurricanes. We hadn't lost at the Orange Bowl in ten years, but Syracuse was supposedly ready to put an end to that streak. By half-time, though, we had a 28–0 lead, and the Orangemen looked like they just wanted to get out town as quickly as possible. They were wilting in the heat and humidity. Some of their guys were throwing up on the sidelines, and you could tell they must have been thinking, *Man, they're kicking the crap out of us, there's no way we're coming back . . . and we've got another thirty minutes of this shit? Oh, God!* ESPN did a nice story on me at halftime during that game. They talked about the success I was having on the football field, and of course they talked about my wrestling background. When the piece ended, the cameras cut to the sideline, where my dad was play-fully applying a sleeper hold to a reporter. I finished that game with six tackles and one and a half sacks.

That was a good night . . . a good year.

I anticipated even better things in my senior year. Having split time with Warren Sapp, I was now recognized as one of the better defensive linemen in college football. I even made a few preseason all-America teams in the summer of 1994. Suddenly the idea of playing in the NFL, which is the goal of virtually every kid who accepts a football scholarship to the University of Miami, didn't seem far-fetched at all; it seemed . . . *appropriate*.

Everything looked great until the first day we practiced in full pads. We were doing what was known as a "bull rush" drill, a purely muscular exercise in which the defensive linemen were supposed to place their helmets directly in the chests of the offensive linemen and attempt to drive them backward. There was little skill or technique involved, but if you were strong, and you got some leverage, you could really do some damage to your opponent. You could also do some damage to yourself, as I discovered.

The ball was snapped and the offensive linemen began backpedaling. I lowered my head and charged, just like a bull. Suddenly I felt a sharp pain in my lower back. It shot down my legs and brought me to a halt. I knew right away that it was a serious injury, just as I had known four years earlier, when I tore up my shoulder. I continued to practice, albeit at half speed, because I didn't want anyone to know the severity of the injury. I knew from personal experience how quickly injured players were tossed on the scrap heap and replaced.

After practice I went to the trainer and explained

what had happened. The trainer blew the whistle, of course, and pretty soon I was meeting with doctors and undergoing a battery of tests. When the results came back, the news was not good.

"Son, you're looking at a career-ending injury," one of the doctors told me. "You might never play football again."

I was stunned . . . and skeptical. You see, I had hurt my back before, when I was a freshman. I had herniated two disks while lifting weights, and after two weeks of rest, I felt as good as new. Wasn't this injury simply a replay?

"No, it's much more serious," the doctor said.

He showed me the results of my MRI. Two disks had virtually exploded, and a third was protruding.

"These disks are completely ruptured," the doctor said, pointing to the two that had suffered the most serious damage. "Do you know what that means?"

I didn't. Not really. But the doctor went on to explain it in graphic terms. A herniated disk merely bulges out between the vertebrae. A ruptured disc is squeezed so severely and traumatically that the softer material within the disk—the nucleus—squirts out. The picture painted for me was that of a jelly doughnut being stomped upon. It was, to say the least, a sobering image.

The prescription was two weeks of rest. No football, no running, no weights. Nothing. I lasted exactly two days.

"What's going on?" Rick Petri, our new defensive line coach, said when I returned. "I thought you were supposed to be taking it easy."

"I'm fine," I said. "Good as new."

That was a lie, of course, provoked by fear and

insecurity. I envisioned my entire season swirling down the toilet, and with it my aspirations of playing professional football. Compounding my fears was the reaction of most of the coaches. Not that they questioned the validity of my injury, but they just seemed generally insensitive. I think that's typical of certain injuries—back injuries, hamstring injuries. They're easy to fake, easy to question, because you can't see them. If you break an ankle, you wind up in a cast. It's obvious. It's real. But when a player says, "Coach, I pulled my hamstring . . . ," the response is often a shrug and, "Ohhhh . . . okay." Same with back injuries. There's always a suspicion that the player might be dogging it.

So I went out and played the entire season with two ruptured disks. And it was a predictably lousy, unproductive season. I endured two to three hours of rehabilitation each day. The pain ebbed and flowed, but never went away entirely. Late in the season, at Pittsburgh, I was in so much pain that two of my teammates, Kenny Holmes and Kennard Lang (both of whom are now in the NFL), had to help me get undressed. I didn't even have to ask them. They were great guys and they knew how much I was suffering. A few minutes later the team doctor gave me a shot to relieve the pressure. In order to insert the needle in the right place, he had me lay down on a bench. Then he lifted my legs in the air. The pain was excruciating, so bad that I started crying for the first time in years. Emotionally and physically, I was spent. The pain had beaten me. That night, on the flight back to Miami, I couldn't even sit in my seat. Instead, I stretched out on the floor near the flight attendants' service area. They had to step over me while trying to do their jobs. It was embarrassing, but I was too exhausted and sore to care.

After the Pitt game I had no choice but to take some time off. I did precisely what the doctor had instructed me to do back in August: nothing. Amazingly enough, after two weeks, I felt tremendous improvement. I couldn't believe it. My back had healed on its own! I wound up getting about forty snaps in the final game of my career. We were playing Nebraska in the Orange Bowl, with the national title on the line. It was tough going out with a loss, especially in a big postseason game played at our own stadium, at the Orange Bowl, where we never lost, but at least I went out on my feet.

Difficult as it was, that final season taught me a few valuable lessons. For one thing, I came to the realization that I needed to have more control over my own life and career, and I began to understand how difficult that would be as a football player. During my two-week rehab, I was expected to attend meetings and meet with the trainers and strength coaches, ride a stationary bike, and do some stretching; but I wasn't supposed to do any weight work. The strength coach at the time was a guy named Dana LeDuc. One day he shouted to me across the weight room: "Hey, bro, can't you do anything for me today?" And I thought, *You motherfucker! I've been busting my ass all season, taking needles in my back, my butt, and everywhere else, just so I can get on a plane. I've outworked everyone this season. Now my body is falling apart and you're giving me this? "What can I do?" You know damn well what I can and can't do.*

I hated that type of mentality, that hard-ass coaching mentality: *He's hurt? Okay . . . move the drill. See ya later. We've gotta get this done.* And when the drill is over, the first question is, "How soon can he come back?" It's an attitude that speaks volumes to each football player: *You're just a piece of meat. And if you can't play, you're a piece of shit.* I don't mean to imply that all coaches are like that, but a lot are. Dana LeDuc knew I wasn't a slacker. Every coach on the Miami staff knew Dwayne Johnson gave 100 percent. I was not a great natural, instinctive football player, not compared to someone like Warren Sapp or Russell Maryland, anyway. That much I recognized right off the bat. But I was always praised for my work ethic. I was a good football player with what the coaches liked to call great upper body violence. No one was going to blow me off the line. I worked too hard to ever let that happen. To have anyone questioning my heart or desire in the final weeks of my college career . . . well, that made me furious. I remember looking at Dana LeDuc and thinking, *One day I'm going to make my mark on this world, and I will remember this.* I didn't mean it in a vindictive way. Rather, it was my way of saying, quite simply, *I recognize that you are an asshole.*

Despite the injuries and frustrations of my senior season, I still wanted to play professional football. I wasn't yet ready to give up on that dream. At the same time, it was becoming increasingly clear to me that my services might not be in great demand. For one thing, I did not receive an invitation to the annual NFL Scouting Combine, which is sort of like an open-air market, beauty contest, and human physiology laboratory all rolled into one. The top college players in the nation all gather in one place for a series of tests and interviews. Scouts from every NFL franchise are on hand, scribbling notes and taking photos as half-naked young studs are timed, measured, poked, and prodded. Like yearlings at a horse sale, the athletes are graded not only on their performance and potential but on their appearance, their musculature.

The Combine may be somewhat degrading, but it's unquestionably a useful tool for the NFL. The cream of the college crop—the ten or fifteen draft picks—often skip the Combine and choose instead to work out privately for individual teams. For everyone else, though, the Combine is a rite of passage. And if you're not even invited to the Combine . . . well, you've suddenly become a long shot.

I knew all of this heading into the draft. That's one reason I had signed with a new Los Angeles-based sports agency rather than with an established agency. To build its client list, this agency had come up with an unusual gimmick.

"We'll offer you a line of credit—up front," my agent said.

"What's the catch?"

"No catch. If you get drafted, you have to pay it back. If you don't get drafted, you don't pay it back. Not a dime."

Needless to say, this attracted a lot of athletes, especially those who were smart enough to realize they were on the fringe. I looked at it like this: I can go with Joel Siegel, an established, reputable agent with great connections who may or may not be able to get me a contract . . . or I can go with this guy, who seems to have his shit together, who seems to be well connected, who seems to know what he's doing,

AND . . . who wants to give me money and doesn't expect to be paid back unless I get drafted.

The agency flew me and Dany out to LA, and we closed the deal over dinner. A few days later I called and asked for what I thought was a reasonable advance: $15,000. The next day I received two checks for $7,500 each. At the time this was an incredible amount of money to me. I had been broke for so long. The first thing Dany and I did was pay off a bunch of our bills. Then I did something for my parents. I invited them both to Miami and gave them a couple presents: a used Hyundai Excel for my mother, so she'd finally have her own set of wheels, and a pickup truck for my father. He was still driving his nasty old red truck, and I knew it wouldn't be easy to get him to part with it. So when he took a nap one afternoon, I drove it to the nearest dealership.

"Here, take this shitbox," I said. "And give me that silver one over there instead." It wound up costing me another $1,500, but when I gave my dad the keys and he responded with a big smile, I realized it was one of the best investments I'd ever made. It was, however, the last gift I would be able to buy for quite some time.

The NFL draft spans two long, tense days. I knew I wasn't likely to be drafted in the early rounds, but each time the phone rang I tensed up because . . . well, because you never know. But it was always a friend or a relative saying something like, "Hey, man, you get drafted yet?"

"No! Now stop calling!"

The first day came and went. No call.

The second day came and went. Still no call.

"Don't worry," my agent said. "We'll get you a free-agent deal."

That didn't happen either. Pretty soon it was July and I was still out of work. It was a very humbling time. I had a national championship ring and a degree in criminology. But I had nowhere to go. I had always presumed that at the very least I would get a free-agent contract, and I was confident I would make the team if I could just get into camp. The NFL minimum at the time was $118,000, which wasn't bad at all. It would allow me to take care of Dany, maybe buy a house, put some money away for the future. Now it was clear that I needed a new plan.

Wrestling was still in the back of my mind, but it was slowly inching its way forward. I was warming to the idea of quitting football and trying something else, anything that would have provided a better life for Dany. At the same time, I was pissed off at the way my football career was ending. I had been training so hard for so many years, trying to outwork everyone, and now it wasn't working anymore. It didn't seem right.

Then, just as I was about to give up, I got a call from my agent.

"You have a job," he said. "Playing football."

"Great!"

"There's just one catch."

"Yeah?"

"It's in Canada."

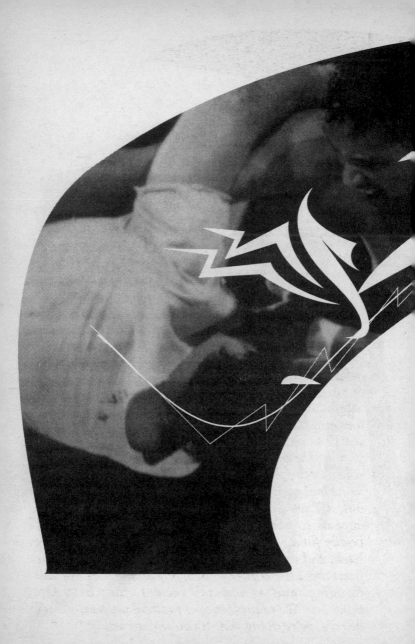

chapter 7

ROCK
BOTTOM

IT'S A HOT SUMMER day in Calgary, Alberta, and we're standing behind a seedy motel, the kind with flashing neon lights and hourly rates. There are four of us, big guys, athletes, and we're stomping around in other people's garbage, trudging through flies and maggots and half-eaten fast-food dinners, in search of a prize. We find it beyond the Dumpsters, a pile of discarded mattresses ten feet high. Most are soiled to the point of revulsion—streaks of semen and urine and menstrual discharge paint a foul mosaic—but still we press on. After a while I find one that appears to have been soaked in the least amount of bodily fluid. I take a deep breath, hoist it onto my back, and walk toward the truck that will deliver us from this little corner of hell. My teammates are still foraging, and as I watch them I can't help but think ... "We're professional football players. I can't believe we're doing this. It's so embarrassing."

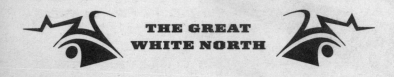

THE GREAT
WHITE NORTH

After recovering from the initial shock and disappointment of being completely ignored by the NFL, I was left with the realization that I still wanted to play football badly enough to accept almost any offer. If the Canadian Football League was my only option, then I'd have to give it serious consideration.

"How do they pay?" I had asked my agent.

"Not great. About $50,000 . . . *Canadian*."

"Okay, how much is that in U.S. dollars?"

He cleared his throat. "Well, it's about thirty grand, maybe thirty-five."

"Any wiggle room there?"

"Practically none," he said. "This is the offer. Take it or leave it."

I thought for a moment. The CFL had served as a path to the NFL for dozens of football players over the years. The quality of play really wasn't bad at all. And the money? Well, thirty grand was better than nothing.

"Let's take it," I said. "I'll go up there and kick some ass."

As always, Dany was supportive, even though it

meant that we'd have to live thousands of miles apart. By now she was getting established in her career, and there was no way I was going to ask her to put that on hold and follow me to Canada. Especially when there was no guarantee that I'd even make a roster or last an entire season.

The Calgary Stampeders' training camp began in June. I did well right from the beginning, although there were certain peculiarities about the Canadian game that hadn't been explained to me, and that caused a few awkward moments. Like the time someone ran back a missed extra point, and I yelled out, "What the hell are you doing?" So the whistle blew and everyone started laughing.

"Uh, Dwayne . . . up here, that's legal."

"Oh, excuse me. I guess I didn't get my CFL rule book. We should probably take care of that as soon as possible."

There were other quirks, too: three downs instead of four on each possession, a stipulation that the defense had to line up at least a yard off the ball (to give the quarterback an advantage, which naturally opens up the offense and leads to more scoring; fans like that). To a fan it might seem like minor stuff, but to a player, born and raised on American football, the differences were dramatic.

Still, I thought I was adapting reasonably well. But there was one particular rule that proved to be my undoing. It was an unbreakable rule, and one that could not be mastered through study or practice. It was a rule regarding Canadian participation. In short, it was a rule that restricted the number of non-Canadians on each team in the CFL. When I first learned of it, I was surprised and disappointed, mainly because there were two other Americans at my position, and it was obvious that there wouldn't be room for all of us on the Stampeders' roster. One of the other Americans was a CFL veteran—in fact, he was an all-league lineman; the other was a guy named Kenny Walker who had played at Nebraska. Coincidentally, Kenny was also the first deaf player in the NFL. He was a nice guy and a good football player. Looking at the three of us, I thought it was fairly obvious that I would be the odd man out. And I was right.

Wally Buono, the Stampeders' head coach, called me into his office and asked me to take a seat. (I knew from experience that it was usually bad when a coach asked you to sit down.) It was not an emotional meeting, like so many I had experienced in college. This was the pros. It was a business, and this meeting was simply part of the business.

"Dwayne, you have two choices," Wally said. "You can either stay with us and work out with the practice squad, or you can go on back home and prepare for next season. We won't hold it against you if you leave, and I really believe, either way, you're a shoo-in to make the team next year."

I thanked Wally for his honesty and for giving me an opportunity, and asked if I could have some time to think about it.

"Sure thing," he said.

So I talked it over with Dany and my agent, and we agreed that it would probably be best if I remained in Calgary. At least I could work out every day and make a few bucks. "Few," as it turned out, was the operative word. Practice-squad players in the NFL at this time earned between $75,000 and $100,000. As a practice player in the CFL, not only would I *not* make that kind of money, I wouldn't even earn the thirty-five grand I had expected. Instead, my salary plummeted to $400 per week . . . *Canadian*. So, now, I was playing professional football for approximately $250 in U.S. currency. Take-home pay? About $175.

Which brings us to the no-tell motel in one of Calgary's less fashionable neighborhoods.

I had thought about quitting because the money was so bad that it barely seemed worth the effort. But I told myself, *Nope . . . I'm not going to quit. I still have goals. I still want to play in the NFL, and I'm committed to making that happen. I'll make the best of this*. To minimize costs, I moved into a shitty apartment across from the stadium with three other practice players—one American and two Canadians. The Canadians were earning even less money, about $300 Canadian. The apartment came with no furniture, so the first thing we did was go off on an adventure to find beds. We could do without a kitchen table, sofas, even chairs and desks. At least for a while. But we had to sleep.

None of us could afford a car, so we had to borrow a teammate's truck. We all piled in and headed off on a glorious quest for bedding. We had no intention of buying anything. We were counting on the kindness of strangers. After a while we found a crappy motel that was in the process of replacing all of its mattresses.

"You can have the old ones," the desk clerk said. "Help yourself."

We began walking down the hall toward the guest rooms. "Where you going?" the clerk said. "They're out back."

We looked at each other and shuddered. *How much worse could this get?* A lot, actually.

The old mattresses had been removed several days earlier. Since then they'd been sitting outside, fermenting in the open air, piled high near the motel's garbage. It had already rained, so the mattresses were soggy and stained and covered with bugs. My stomach started to rise into my throat. I could only hope there was a reason for my being in this abominable situation. Maybe there was something to learn.

We loaded the truck with mattresses—there were no box springs—and went back to our apartment. To keep from crying like babies about the hideousness of the whole situation, we laughed and told bad jokes. Then we went out and bought clean sheets and several cans of Lysol. We sprayed the mattresses until they literally dripped disinfectant; if we couldn't poison the bacteria, maybe we could *drown* it.

And that's the way we lived—four grown men sleeping on piss-stained mattresses in a small, unfurnished apartment. We bought gallon jars of cheap spaghetti sauce and ate pasta almost every night. Most of my meager income was spent on phone calls to Dany. I tried not to burden her with my problems, because she was having enough trouble of her own. She had a demanding job, student loans to repay, and parents who thought she was wasting her life waiting around for me. She was thinking, *Is this the kind of lifestyle I want? Do I want my husband gone for five or six months a year?* And I was thinking basically the same thing.

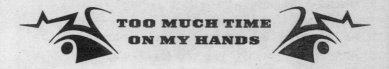

TOO MUCH TIME ON MY HANDS

When you're a practice player in the CFL, you are not the busiest person in the world. You practice only four days a week, and you don't dress for games. When the team has a road game, you don't even make the trip. So it's not exactly the most demanding schedule. Unfortunately, when you don't have any money, there's not a lot you can do to fill the hours.

Most of my time was devoted to figuring out ways to make more money or get a free meal. The latter I often accomplished by attending meetings at which my presence was not required. The Stampeders' schedule was always the same: Thursday was the last day of practice each week. On Friday the players on the travel team practiced lightly, without pads, and went over strategy during an evening meeting. Saturday or Sunday was game day. As a practice player, I was not expected at the training facility after

Thursday. But when I found out that sandwiches were always distributed during the travel-team meeting on Friday night, I made it a point to show up. I would sit down in the back, try to blend in, keep real quiet. The coaches passed out the sandwiches, and invariably one of them would see me and say, "Hell, Dwayne, you don't have to be here. Go on home." I'd try to look surprised and say something like, "Oh, I'm sorry. I thought it was a mandatory meeting. Then I'd get up and leave, but not before I had loaded up with at least one—and usually two—big submarine sandwiches. I never missed one of those meetings. It was one of the most important moments of the week for me, because the sandwiches would last almost the entire weekend. I'd eat half of the first sub that night, the other half for lunch on Saturday. Then I'd eat half of the second sub for dinner on Saturday, and the other half for lunch on Sunday.

I never saw the Stampeders play a game, not in person, anyway. If they were on the road, I'd watch the game on television. Those of us on the practice team received four tickets apiece for home games, but I never used mine. The Stampeders were pretty popular in those days, so I'd usually just walk across the street to McMahon Stadium and scalp my tickets. It was easy. There were always a bunch of people hanging around outside, looking for tickets. I could sell all four for $150. This was an enormous amount of money to me at the time, so I never questioned the morality or legality of it. Nor did I fret about whether it made me a bad teammate. I didn't care. The game wasn't nearly important enough for me to give up the money.

With so much spare time, I found myself daydreaming a lot. And invariably my thoughts would turn to wrestling. I had never stopped following the business, even when its popularity waned in the early 1990s, and I was pleased to discover that many of my teammates in Calgary were wrestling fans. That probably shouldn't have come as a great shock, since Calgary was the home of Bret Hart and Owen Hart, two of the best wrestlers in the business. The Harts were, and are, the most famous family in Calgary.

One day during training camp I walked into the lunchroom and noticed that the World Wrestling Federation's Saturday morning show was on TV. I was pretty excited about that. It was nice to see a bunch of the guys sitting around watching wrestling. The show did not, however, appeal to everyone. At one point Shawn Michaels had come on the screen, and he was doing his patented little song-and-dance act, his little stripper routine, dancing to his theme music, and Doug Flutie walked into the room. Flutie's NFL career hadn't panned out, but he was making a good living now in Calgary. He was a solid little quarterback and he was popular with the fans. But he didn't know shit about wrestling.

"What the hell is this?" he said, gesturing toward the screen.

"That's Shawn Michaels," I said matter-of-factly.

Flutie turned to me and with a look of disbelief on his face said, "Do you watch this shit?"

I didn't lose my temper. Flutie was a star on this team and I was a rookie with a tenuous grip on my job. Besides, I don't think he meant anything by it. I think he was legitimately surprised that all of these grown men were watching professional wrestling. Nevertheless, I felt it was necessary to set the record straight.

"Not only do I watch it," I said, "but it's part of my life. I grew up in this business. My grandfather was a wrestler and so was my dad."

Flutie just shrugged, said, "Oh," and walked away. That was our first and last conversation.

As the season wore on I started toying with the idea of embarking on a wrestling career, although not at the expense of my football career. I hadn't reached that point yet. Instead, I fantasized about becoming the first person to play professional football and work as a professional wrestler simultaneously. I knew it wouldn't be easy, because I was well aware of what it took to succeed as a wrestler. But I wanted to try. So I called Gerry Brisco, a former wrestler who was a friend of my dad's and who was now an agent in the World Wrestling Federation. He also happened to be a huge Miami football fan.

"Hey, Gerry," I said. "It's Dwayne Johnson. Listen, I'm up here in Calgary, and I was wondering if you know of any wrestling schools in the area, someplace where I can roll around in the ring with a few guys."

Gerry was a good man and eager to help. "I know Stu Hart's Dungeon is up there," he said. "But I don't know if the school is open anymore."

Stu Hart was the father of Owen and Bret. The "Dungeon" was actually nothing more than Stu's basement. Years earlier he'd thrown a bunch of mats on the floor and decided to open a wrestling school. A lot of guys got their start in Stu Hart's Dungeon, and the idea of working with him was appealing. Unfortunately, Gerry Brisco's suspicion was correct: The Dungeon was closed.

Now I really felt as though I was merely treading water. My football career was going nowhere, and I had no way to begin my formal wrestling education. A change was needed . . . but how? The answer came in October, in the form of a phone call from my agent. I had just returned to my apartment after practice, and I was sitting down to yet another bowl of spaghetti when the phone rang.

"Dwayne," he said. "They're letting you go."

At first I said nothing. I was too stunned to speak. *Now I'm not even good enough for the practice squad?*

"You're kidding, right?" I finally said.

"I'm afraid not. They want to bring in another guy who just got cut from the NFL. And he's taking your spot."

"Yeah, right. They're going to bring in an NFL player, making NFL money, and they're going to give him $400 a week?! That son of a bitch won't last a week?" I was hurt, angry, embarrassed. I couldn't believe this was happening.

"That may be," my agent said. "But it's not our decision."

At that moment it began to sink in: My football career was over. There was nowhere else to go.

"Make sure I'm on the first flight out of here tomorrow," I said.

Early the next morning I met with Wally Buono. It was a short, cordial meeting. He thanked me for my hard work and said he hoped I'd return the next year, but right now he wanted to sign a lineman who had been playing for the Jacksonville Jaguars. I told him that I understood perfectly and that there were no hard feelings. I extended my hand, told him I appreciated the opportunity, and said I'd talk to him in a few months. In my heart, though, I knew I wouldn't be back.

That meeting was the start of the longest day of my life. I flew from Calgary to Toronto, and then from Toronto down to Miami. Along the way I had a lot of time to think—time to think about what I wanted to do with the rest of my life. I was twenty-three years old, and all I really knew for sure was that I no longer wanted to pursue football. Dany and I sat on the couch at her apartment and talked for hours that evening. We talked about how hard the last few months had been for her, and all the pressure she'd been getting from her family to let me go. As usual, Dany was strong. She told me not to worry about any of that but to focus instead on doing whatever it was that I wanted to do.

"And what do you want to do, Dwayne?" she said. "What do you *really* want to do?"

I looked her square in the eye and said, "I want to start training to be a wrestler."

I didn't know what sort of reaction to expect. Dany had been going through so much bullshit here at home, and I'd been off in Canada, leaving her to deal with everything on her own. She had every right to tell me I was crazy. But she didn't. She just sat there and listened. I told her I wanted to move to Tampa to train with my father. I told her I wanted to give wrestling a real chance, I wanted to do what my heart was telling me to do. And then, suddenly, my words began to sound ridiculous.

Wrestling? You have an obligation right here! Right now! Take care of business!

"Never mind," I said. "Why don't I just stay here in Miami and find a job. I can make some money and help you out. You've been living like this long enough."

Dany shook her head and smiled. "No," she said. "The best thing for you to do is to go to Tampa and start your new life. Start your career. I know this is what you want to do—"

I cut her off. "I absolutely do want to go, but I believe I should stay here and help you."

She put up a hand: *Stop!*

"No . . . you're committed to this and I know you'll be great at it," she said, and then she began to cry. "You take care of your end and I'll straighten out my end . . . my life. Everything will be fine."

I can't begin to explain what that meant to me, what an incredible thing it was for Dany to do. *Go to Tampa!* She said it with such emotion and intent.

We hugged and cried for hours. Finally, around 11:00 P.M., I walked to a nearby drugstore to get a few things. There was a pay phone outside the store, and when I saw it, a thought went through my mind: *I'm not staying here any longer than I have to. I'm going to get my life rolling.* As upset as I was about this chapter of my life ending, my wheels were already spinning. It was time to make the hardest phone call of my life.

"Collect call from Dwayne Johnson. Will you accept the charges?"

"Yes," my mother said. "Dwayne, what's wrong?"

My parents knew I had been released by the Stampeders and that I was flying back to Miami. They had no idea that I was thinking of changing careers.

"Mom, I need to start training." I think she heard something in my voice, something that told her I was serious and that I needed her. It's a mother's love, I guess: unconditional acceptance.

"When do you want to come home?" she said.

"Right away. Tonight. I need Dad to come get me."

She put my father on the phone, and his reaction was predictably fatherlike. "What's wrong?!" he said.

"I need to come home, Dad."

"Why?!"

"So I can start training."

"Training?! For what?!"

"For wrestling."

"Wrestling?! What about football?!"

Right about then I stopped him and said, calmly and slowly, "Dad, I really need you to come and get me." I didn't answer his question. I was twenty-three years old and standing in a phone booth in the dead of night. I had no money, no car, no job prospects. This was not the time for a debate. I needed my dad's help. *Immediately.*

"All right," he said. "I'm on my way."

chapter 8

THE MAKING OF A PROFESSIONAL WRESTLER

THE DRIVE UP TO Tampa seemed to take forever. It's a 280-mile trip, and my father, for all his courage and aggressiveness in the ring, had a tendency to drive like an old woman. He picked me up in the same silver truck I had purchased for him the previous spring, and we drove together through the calm blackness of a south Florida night.

I didn't say much at first, and my father didn't try to force the conversation. Instead, I stared out the window and reflected on my life and how I had arrived at this point. I had exactly seven dollars in my pocket. I was moving back into my parents' home. By this time I had hoped—no, *expected*—to be enjoying the fruits of my labor in the National Football

League. Instead, I was starting all over. In some ways, of course, it was disappointing . . . even demeaning. But it was also exciting.

My father was skeptical. He had spent the better part of his life in the wrestling business, and he knew what a hard world it could be. Like any parent, he wanted a better life for his children. Wrestling had once been good to him, but it also had left him bitter, frustrated, and lost.

"Listen, Dad, I know what you went through. But I just feel like this is what I was born to do."

He clutched the wheel of the truck and stared out at the road. Without turning to face me, he said, "How do you know?"

My dad could be a very black-and-white kind of guy. He saw things one way or the other. With all that I had been through in the past few years, I had come to believe the world was mostly gray. "I really can't tell you," I said. "But I do know what I feel, and I can tell you about that."

My dad nodded. *Go on . . .*

"I've been thinking about this, off and on, since I was ten years old. In my heart I believe this is the right time to give it a try."

"But what about football?" he said. My father loved football, and he loved the fact that his son was a professional football player. He wanted me to continue along this path. He'd wanted that for a long time. I no longer wanted it. I began telling my dad about all of the disappointments I had experienced in Calgary, about what a shitty year it had been . . . the sacrifices, the emotional roller-coaster, not being able to make ends meet . . . realizing, in fact, that the ends weren't even close to meeting. They were miles apart.

"You know, this business, wrestling . . . it won't be any different," he said.

"That may be true," I said. "But I'm prepared to face it. I'm ready to make sacrifices for this business. It's something I'm looking forward to doing. I don't feel that way about football anymore."

He didn't say anything, just took it all in.

"And Dad . . . "

"Yeah?"

"As much as this business was a part of your life . . . it was just as much a part of mine."

The negotiations did not end there. For the better part of a week we talked and argued about what I was going to do. Although my mom was encouraging and supportive, my father was adamant about me not going into wrestling. He wanted me to take some time off and return to football the following spring. When my agent called that week, and then Wally Buono called, both to give me a pep talk about staying in shape and preparing for the next CFL season, my dad became further convinced that I was making a terrible decision.

The situation reached critical mass one night after I got off the phone with Wally. "I'm sorry, Wally," I said. "I appreciate your interest, but I'm never coming back to Calgary." When I hung up the phone my father was sitting at the kitchen table, glaring at me. My mother was next to him. We then proceeded to get into a heated argument, me and my dad, with my mom acting as the mediator.

"You know what?" I said. "I know I have something to offer this business."

"You don't know that," my father said. "You've never even been in a ring."

I remember feeling as though this was the end. There would be no more arguing. "Dad, are you going to train me or not? Or do I have to go to someone else?"

That was all it took. My father did not want me to enter the business, but if I was determined to do it, then he damn sure wasn't going to let anyone else be my teacher.

"Okay . . . ," he said. And then he left the room.

I winked at my mom, and a thin smile began to cross her face. "All right," I said. "Here we go."

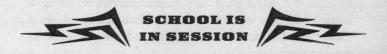

SCHOOL IS IN SESSION

I got a job as a personal trainer at Bally's, which turned out to be a pretty good part-time gig. The money was terrible, but at least I was working in a fitness environment. I'd work out early in the morning, then spend the rest of the day motivating and guiding rich housewives, lawyers, and doctors through their training sessions. One of the benefits of this job was that it helped refine my people skills. I was not the best personal trainer money could buy, but I knew a little bit about the body and fitness, and I knew how to motivate people and make them comfortable with the idea of working out. Before too long, I was one of the busiest personal trainers at Bally's. Unfortunately, the money all went to the club. That was part of the deal. If you had a membership, and you wanted a trainer . . . you got one. I had to be satisfied with my hourly wage. And, for the most part, I was, primarily because my focus was somewhere else.

My very first training session came on a Thursday evening after I had gotten off work, under the direction of a man named Ron Slinker. Ron was a former wrestler, like my father, and a friend of the family. He was a renowned martial artist, as well. One time he appeared on *ABC's Wide World of Sports*. It was a memorable performance. An archer stood about sixty feet from Ron and fired arrows directly at him. As the arrows whistled toward his head, Ron deftly snatched them out of the air with his bare hands! My father liked and trusted Ron, and since Dad knew he'd be busy working a lot of the time, he enlisted Ron's services as an assistant trainer. Together, they would oversee my education.

Ron picked me up at seven and we drove to the air force base in Tampa. I wasn't nervous, but I was excited. I was eager to get started. When we arrived, Ron led me to a hot, dimly lit room filled with mats. "Okay, let's learn the basics," he said. "Walking around, locking up. That's all we're going to do today, just walk around . . . lock up."

In wrestling—amateur or professional—most matches begin with a bit of posturing, circling, sizing each other up. The action begins when the two wrestlers "lock up." Essentially, it means you put one hand behind your opponent's neck, and your other arm becomes intertwined with your opponent's arm. Your faces are pressed against each other, cheek-to-cheek, so as to avoid butting heads. In amateur wrestling, of course, this is the first stage of the battle. In "the business," it's the opening move in a very complicated, heavily choreographed dance; it's a way to ease into the show. Locking up is fundamental, just as dribbling is fundamental to basketball, which is why it was the first thing I had to learn.

So we circled each other for a few minutes. Ron was a big man, about six four, 260 pounds, and even though he was fifty-one years old, he was in good shape. He was strong. After a minute or so we fell into each other and locked up, and as our arms became entangled, I felt a surge of adrenaline. Out of the corner of my eye I could see my reflection in a mirror, and I liked what I saw. Finally, I looked like the man I had envisioned, the man I had always wanted to be. At that very moment, I knew: *This is what I was born to do!*

"Okay, break," Ron said, and we pulled apart. "Again!" We circled some more, locked up again, and broke apart. And that was the way it went for the better part of ninety minutes: *Circle . . . lock up . . . break! Circle . . . lock up . . . break!* By the end of the session I was spent. I was also completely hooked.

When I got home that night my parents were waiting.

"How did it go?" they asked.

"It went great. Really great. We just did some lock-ups, a few headlocks, stuff like that. Very basic. But I liked it."

Typically reticent, my father said, "Good," and left the room, leaving me and my mother alone together in the kitchen. I got a drink from the refrigerator, and as I turned around she said, "It really went well?"

"Mom," I said, "this is it."

She smiled at me then, a smile as big as Florida, and got up to give me a kiss. She knew. So did Dany, who I called that night.

"I've got to be honest with you," I told Dany. "As stupid and corny as this sounds, I know now that wrestling is for me."

"I believe you," she said. "I believe you."

It was crazy, but I knew in my heart that I had found my calling. I could not have been more certain,

just as I knew on the night I met Dany that we'd
spend the rest of our lives together. Some things can't
be explained. Some things don't *need* to be explained.

On Saturday my father got involved. We went to a
different gym, an old sweaty, musty gym popular with
local boxers and martial artists. It was like something
out of *Raging Bull* or *Rocky*, a real traditional hard-
ass kind of gym, with speed bags and heavy bags and
a lot of grunting and groaning. At the center of activity was a boxing ring. When I climbed through the
ropes, I felt my heart racing. Not so much because I
was about to work out with my father, but because I
was getting into a ring with Rocky Johnson. I had no
real wrestling gear at the time. I wore basketball
sneakers, plain shorts, and a T-shirt. My dad was
dressed in sweats. We started circling. Almost immediately my father began to dance like Muhammad Ali,
which was something he used to do quite often when
he wrestled. He was a skilled boxer, and he liked to
use those skills to pump up a crowd. He bounced
around the ring, one foot skipping along neatly
behind the other. *Ha! The old man's still got it!*
    "Come on," he finally said. "Let's get it on." So we
leaned into each other, a very aggressive intergenera-
tional lockup, as if we each had something to prove,
which I guess we did. From there my father put me in
a headlock, and finally a hammerlock (with my arm
up behind my back, in much the way a cop might sub-
due a suspect in the process of an arrest).
    "Now . . . reverse it!" he yelled. Without even hav-
ing gone through this with Ron, I knew exactly what
he meant. I broke his grip (with his help, of course),
spun around, and put my father in a headlock.

"Take me over!" he said.

Again, instinct, combined with all of the subliminal teaching, took over. I dropped to one knee and put him on the mat, with the headlock still intact. From the side of the ring I could hear Ron laughing. "Well, we didn't try *that*," he said. Before we went down my father had called a "spot" (that's wrestle-ese for a specific move or sequence): "One tackle, drop down, get it again." So now he quickly broke my grip and bounced to his feet. He shot me off (tossed me into the ropes), and as I came off he was waiting for me to tackle him. He went down . . . I hit the opposite ropes . . . he rolled over on his stomach . . . I jumped over him. As he rose to his feet, he fed his body neatly into my arms and I got him into another headlock.

One tackle, drop down, get it again.

Incredible! Less than five minutes after stepping into the ring, we not only were doing things I had never done, we were running spots. I'm sure my father was impressed, but it wasn't his style to put me over . . . to put anybody over. (By the way, in wrestling, "putting someone over" is a good thing; if you put your opponent over, for example, you've let him beat you.) When we got home that night my mother said, "How did it go?"

My father's answer? "Not bad. He still has a lot to learn."

He was right. I did have a lot to learn. But I could not have been a more eager and willing student. Whatever it took, I was going to become a professional wrestler.

Another thing working in my favor was that the manager of the gym, Beau Moore, who was a national drug-free powerlifting champ, was also interested in getting into wrestling. Beau was six foot one, 330 pounds, and we began training together. We'd get up at six, have breakfast at the gym, right in the ring, and then start throwing each other around. My days soon became a blur of training, study, weight lifting, and work. It was harder than anything I had ever endured, harder even than my first season at Miami. But I didn't mind. I carried a notebook to Bally's every day, and whenever I was struck with an idea for a spot, I'd write it down. My mind raced constantly. I could think of nothing but wrestling.

Within the course of my training I started to realize that I was pretty athletic and that I should incorporate some of that athleticism into my work. For one thing, I could already do a "nip-up," which is when a wrestler jumps straight to his feet from a prone position, without rolling over and helping himself up. So my father and I agreed that every time I was down, I would get up by nipping up. That's a hundred nip-ups a day, which, by itself, is a pretty demanding workout. The other thing I wanted to do was land on my feet every time someone gave me a hip toss or backdrop (a backdrop is when you launch your opponent into the air and over your back after he comes off the ropes). Typically, after either of these moves, you land flat on your back. I wanted to land on my feet, because I knew it would present a dramatic, athletic image to a crowd. My dad had done it occasionally when he was working, and the fans always ate it up. It took a while for me to execute the move, but one day, while working with Beau, it happened. I took a backdrop and landed square on my feet, turned around, and nailed Beau with a dropkick.

There were always a bunch of boxers and martial artists in the gym, and when I completed this move they all stopped and applauded. It was a great feeling.

At the same time that my training was progressing, I was beginning to think about a "look." Not a character, necessarily, but an appearance. I was sure I didn't want to wear face paint. I wanted to wear simple trunks and boots—no leather, no armor, no capes, no masks. I even starting thinking about a name. It was funny—I had no idea where or when my first match was going to be, but already I was trying to come up with a stage name. The one thing I knew was that I did not want to try to cash in on my family's reputation. I didn't want to be known as Rocky Johnson Jr. or the grandson of Peter Maivia.

"It's important to me that I go out there and make it on my own," I told my parents. They didn't take this news very well. I think they felt my attitude was disrespectful, which wasn't at all what I intended. My mother suggested Rocky Maivia, and I said "Absolutely not! That's what I'm trying to get away from. *Rocky Maivia?!* That's both names. I'll be cursed! I'd rather go out there as plain old Dwayne Johnson."

After a while we dropped the name issue. "The most important thing for me is just to have a match," I said. "I don't care what my name is."

"I agree with you," my father said. "I've kind of been thinking about that all along. You know, so many guys in this business . . . they get their name and they get their gimmick, and they get everything else before they even know how to work. It's too easy for guys to call themselves professional wrestlers. Wrestlers they may be. Professional they're not."

That really hit a chord with me. I wanted to be known as the real deal, not some half-ass cartoon character skating along on his family's name. The next step toward making that happen was to schedule a match. It was time for my audition.

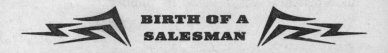

BIRTH OF A SALESMAN

Success is not achieved in a vacuum. I did the necessary work. I put in the time. I busted my butt every day for months. But unless I could find a way to be recognized, my career was going nowhere. That's where Pat Patterson entered the picture.

Pat had been a legendary worker in our business. He had wrestled against my grandfather, and I had known him since I was a kid, although I hadn't spoken to him in many years. Pat was now working as a matchmaker and agent for the World Wrestling Federation. He was an influential figure in the business, and he happened to be living right there in Tampa.

"What I'd like to do," I said to my parents, "is give Pat a call, and see if he's willing to come down and watch me train. Then he could gauge my progress and let us know how far away I am from being ready for a match."

My parents liked the idea. I'm sure they would have made the call for me, since they had been in contact with Pat regularly over the years, but I felt it was important for me to take this step. I wanted to represent myself ... not only as a wrestler but as a man. So, on a Tuesday afternoon in February, I called Pat Patterson.

"Pat, this is Dwayne Johnson."

"Who?"

"Dwayne Johnson . . . Rocky and Ata's son."

There was a brief silence on the other end of the phone as Pat put the pieces of the puzzle together. "Rocky . . . ohhhhh . . . Dwayne, how are you?"

"I'm doing fine, Pat, thanks. I know you probably aren't aware of this, but I've been training to get into the business—"

He cut me off. "You want to get into *this* business?!"

"Yes, Pat, I do. My partner, Beau, and I have been training for the past five months. Now, I know you're busy, but if you wouldn't mind, I'd like you to come down and watch us work out with my dad. Maybe you could give us some insight, some advice."

"When do you train?" he asked.

"We'll be there on Saturday."

"Okay, why don't we plan on that?" Pat said. "I'm off on Saturday. I'll come down and take a look."

"All right, Pat. I really appreciate it."

Suddenly I was preparing for one of the biggest weekends of my life. Already Dany was coming up from Miami for a visit, and now I was going to work out for Pat Patterson.

We arrived at the gym early. It was a complete family affair: me, Mom, Dad, and Dany; my grandmother, Leah, who also lived in Tampa; and Ron and Beau. I warmed up for a while, stretched, tried to control the excitement I was feeling. Pat showed up around ten o'clock, and after a lengthy round of hugs and handshakes, I climbed between the ropes.

Dany had never, ever seen me wrestle. She'd heard me talk about it a lot, and she'd seen videotapes of my father. But since she lived in Miami and I lived in

Tampa, she'd never had the opportunity to watch me in action. Wrestling, like any athletic endeavor, is very different when viewed in person. On television, on tape, the physicality is diluted. The danger seems minimized. In person, at ringside, it's one hell of a show: fast-paced, exciting, and even a little scary. Or, in Dany's case, a lot scary.

Dad was my opponent (my partner, really) on this day. We jumped right into the meat of it—no circling no locking up. *Headlock, tackle, drop down.* Then my dad slammed me to the mat. Whump! The whole ring shook. I jumped to my feet and he slammed me again. *Whump! And again . . . Whump!*

I was on the mat, grimacing as though I was in agony. Like I had completely blown out my back. In reality I was just "selling," which is another term used frequently in the business. It means exactly what it sounds like it means. When you're selling, you're emoting, doing everything in your power to convince the audience that what they're seeing is real. Well, not *real*, but *convincing*, in a hyperbolic sort of way. The more you act, the more you *sell* . . . the better the show. Now, Dany, of course, was completely familiar with my back problems, and when she saw me stretched out on the mat like that, holding my back, writhing in pain, *screaming* . . . for her the violence suddenly became all too real.

"That hurt!" she screamed. "Dwayne's hurt!" She jumped out of her seat (we have this on videotape, in a very special place in the family library) and grabbed my mother. "That's enough! THAT'S ENOUGH!"

I get emotional thinking about it even now, because . . . well, because that's love. *And because I knew it was working. It was one hell of a performance.*

When I heard Dany screaming, and I looked up and saw the tears in her eyes, I stopped the match. I went right over to her and said, "It's okay, I'm not hurt. Really."

For that moment of tenderness . . . weakness . . . I absorbed all kinds of heat from the guys—from my father and Pat and Beau and Ron. "Oh, come on! That's bullshit! You can't stop a match! You think you're going to be able to do that in front of twenty thousand people?"

I turned to them and said, "Hey, relax. This is Dany. It's not twenty thousand people. I'll be right there."

I turned back to Dany and brushed a tear off her cheek. "Are you all right?"

"Am I all right? I'm fine. How are you?"

"I'm fine, too," I said. "Don't worry. I'm just selling."

When I was sure Dany was okay, I climbed into the ring and went back to work. After about twenty minutes Pat interrupted us and said, "Dwayne, can you work heel?" In our business there are two basic characters: heels and baby faces. The former are bad guys, of course, and the latter are good guys. At the time I had been working under the assumption that I would be a baby face, just like my father. I was doing pretty arm drags and hip tosses, showing a lot of fire, smiling . . . charismatic stuff. It had never occurred to me that I might work as a heel. But I kind of liked the idea.

"Well, I guess I could give it a try," I said to Pat. "I mean, what's the difference? Should I just be myself . . . but more aggressive? And be an asshole?"

"Yeah, just do what comes naturally."

I bore in on my father, went right to town on him, kicking him in the gut, pushing him into the corner, nailing him with one punch after another: all traditional weapons in the heel arsenal. My dad seemed stunned by my enthusiasm. We were in the corner, and I was really putting the boots to him, reveling in the viciousness of it all, not even giving him a chance to breathe.

"Jesus Christ!" he said. "You're too stiff!"

That snapped me out of it. My father had always been the kind of guy who, when he was really getting potatoed (in wrestling, when you're getting hit real hard—*too* hard—it's called "getting potatoed"), he would let his opponent know it by shouting, "You're too stiff!" right in the middle of the ring. Not in a whiny way, but in a serious way, just to keep the other person honest, to remind him that it was all an illusion.

"What's wrong with you?" Dad said to me. "You're too damn stiff."

I dropped my arms and started laughing. "What's the matter?"

"Ah, the hell with it," he said. "I've had enough. Beau, you go in."

Although it would be some time before wrestling fans would get to know him, the character of The Rock first came to life that day. With each kick and snarl and grunt, I remember feeling rather intensely ... *This is more fun than being the good guy. This is me—a violent son of a bitch!*

Afterward we were all standing around talking. There were several conversations going on at once. Eventually Pat and I started talking. This was my chance to find out how I had done.

"Pat, I just want you to be honest with me," I said. "I know you've never helped anybody get in the business, nor am I asking you to help me get in the business. That's not what I want."

He gave me a quizzical look, as if to say, *Then why am I here?*

"I just want you to tell me if you think I've got what it takes to make it. That's all. If you think I have what it takes, just say so. If you think I'm the shits, or if you think I need to work on something in particular, then just let me know now."

Pat smiled. "You're going to be okay."

Coming from Pat Patterson, that was high praise indeed. Inside I was euphoric, but I tried to remain calm on the outside. "Okay," I said. "That's great. Thanks."

"You just keep training," Pat said. "Everything will work out."

He went outside to share a smoke with my parents. They talked for a while longer and then we all left the gym. I was thrilled. Pat was not one to bullshit. He was a man of integrity. If he had thought I was terrible, he would have told me. I had passed the first significant test.

In an industry populated by far too many sharks and liars, Pat Patterson was, and is, a man of his word. A week later he called me at my parents' house.

"I spoke with Vince McMahon," he said. My heart skipped a beat. As the owner of the World Wrestling Federation, Vince was the most powerful and influential man in professional wrestling. It was virtually impossible to become a star in the business without Vince's approval.

"You did?" I said. "Really?"

"Yeah, I spoke with Vince, and he'd like to see you work."

"Where? When? I'll do it anytime." My mind was racing again. I was trying to stay calm, listen to what Pat was saying, take it all in.

"We're trying to figure something out," he said. "We might bring you into a TV taping and have a dark match."

"What's that?"

"A dark match is just for the house. Just for the people. No cameras, nothing."

Television meant nothing to me. I would have performed in a barn if they had asked. "Sure, that's fine. Just tell Vince that I appreciate it. Whenever he wants, that's cool with me. I'll be ready."

One of the secretaries in the World Wrestling Federation office called the next day to confirm the details. My tryout would be in Corpus Christi, Texas, the following week. "Do I need to call anyone?" I said. "Do I need to do anything?"

"Nope. Just call Vince's office and give the secretary your address so that they can send your plane tickets."

There were a dozen other things I should have said, questions I should have asked, but I was so excited that I couldn't think straight. All I could do was say, "Thank you."

I called Dany right away and told her the good news. She was ecstatic. Then I celebrated by going to the gym and working out, and having a great lunch. Very quickly, though, the reality began to set in. My first match was only a few days away, and I didn't even have a proper pair of wrestling boots. I didn't have trunks.

Hell, I still didn't even have a name.

chapter 9
FLEX KAVANA

IT ISN'T ALL THAT easy to find a pair of wrestling trunks on short notice, especially when you're my size. I turned for help to a wrestler named Meng, a huge, gentle, Polynesian man who had been a very close friend of my grandfather's. Meng was known affectionately to my family as "Uncle Tonga," and he was the only person I could think of who might have a pair of trunks that would fit me.

Uncle Tonga was a lot like my grandfather, only taller. He had dark, leathery skin, cinder blocks for arms, and a massive torso that dropped in a straight line from chin to waist. He was widely considered the toughest son of a bitch in the business. But, like Peter Maivia, he was also a sweet, kindhearted man, especially where his friends and family were concerned. Uncle Tonga, who also lived in Florida, happily agreed to meet me at the gym one day. He brought along a bag containing a half dozen of his old trunks, all of which were too large for me. I tried them on and chose the pair that were the least baggy—electric purple trunks that looked like something left over from an early 1980s Prince concert. My father gave me a pair of his old white boots (two sizes too small), and I completed the ensemble with a set of white kneepads from Sports Authority.

Strangely enough, when I stood in front of a mirror at my parents' house, fully decked out in this patched-together ensemble, I did not think I looked bad at all. Rather, I thought, quite honestly, *Okay . . . now I'm ready for my tryout.*

When I arrived at the arena in Corpus Christi, I was greeted by two men: Downtown Bruno, who had been involved in wrestling most of his adult life as both a referee and manager; and Steve Lombardi, who was better known as the Brooklyn Brawler. Steve was part of the welcoming committee because he would be sharing the ring with me that evening.

"Hey, Dwayne, nice to meet you," Steve said. "I have your match tonight. I'm looking forward to it."

We shook hands. Steve had been around a long time, and it was reassuring to know I'd be working with a real pro. "Let me take you around and introduce you to some of the guys," he said.

One of the people I met that day was Vince McMahon. Vince, of course, had grown up in the business, just as I had. His father, Vince McMahon, Sr., had been a highly visible figure for many years as a wrestling promoter and owner; his grandfather, Jess McMahon, was also a promoter. Vince Jr. bought the Capitol Wrestling Corporation from his father in 1982 and immediately began taking the business national. Now he stood at the helm of a sports-entertainment empire. When I walked into Vince's office in Corpus Christi, there were several people in the room.

"I'm sorry to interrupt, Vince," I said. "But I'd like to introduce myself. I'm Dwayne Johnson." I had met Vince when I was a boy, but this was much different. This was low-key, but formal. It was important. "I just want you to know I really appreciate this opportunity, and I'm going to do my best."

Vince shook my hand and said, "I'm sure you will do your best. You know, your dad has provided us with many great memories over the years, so thank you, too." And that was it. I left and went off to get something to eat.

The lunchroom was a veritable "who's who" of the business, circa 1996. The Undertaker was there. So was Bret Hart. My head was on a swivel as I tried to take it all in. These were guys I had admired for years. Now, at least for a couple days, I was part of the troupe.

Steve and I discussed our match over lunch. As we began to map out a strategy, Steve was patient, understanding. "What can you do?" he asked.

"Whatever you want to do. Dropkicks, arm drags, basic moves like that. I'm pretty athletic, but I'm not a real high flyer. I don't come off the top rope a lot. Really, Steve, if you wouldn't mind, I'd like you to put this match together. Just tell me what you'd like me to do."

So we constructed a little eight-minute routine.

Steve had done this thousands of times, so the details were instantly placed on file in his mind. I wrote down everything he said and spent the next few hours walking around with a piece of paper, committing each move to memory. Probably 99 percent of all wrestlers have their first match in a rundown gymnasium or bar before twenty or thirty half-conscious spectators. I was making my debut at a World Wrestling Federation event, a television taping, in front of fifteen thousand people! There was no way I was going to allow myself to screw this up. I wasn't going to take a chance on getting all excited and having my memory short-circuit at the last second. If nothing else, as always, at least I would be prepared.

I shared a dressing room with all of the big-name stars, which was a humbling experience. They had their lavish outfits, their expensive boots and trunks ... they looked like a million bucks. Meanwhile, in my purple trunks and white boots left over from the '70s ... with my hair too long on the top, growing straight up and fanning out, kind of like a pineapple, I looked like someone who had slipped through a wrinkle in time. And everyone was smiling at me, sort of chuckling under their breath, saying, "Look at the rook over there." One look at me and you just knew I didn't have ten bucks to my name. I wasn't embarrassed, though. I was excited and motivated: *One day ... I'm going to be here.*

I found a quiet corner, said a brief prayer, just as I had before every football practice and game, and then began walking toward the "gorilla position." The gorilla position is the area directly behind the black curtain that separates the audience from the backstage crew, and through which wrestlers make their dramatic entrances. It's called the gorilla position because, for a long time, it was directed by a famous wrestler named Gorilla Monsoon. The gorilla position was being run by Bruce Prichard. It was Bruce's job to communicate with the television production team, and make sure that guys were ready to roll, ready to hit the curtain as soon as their music was cued. Joining Bruce were several agents, Vince McMahon, and a handful of technicians, who were in constant contact with the production trucks housed deeper in the bowels of the arena.

"Who's coming up?" Bruce said.

I walked over and introduced myself. We shook hands.

"You ready?" Bruce said.

"I'm ready."

He smiled. "What are we calling you, anyway?"

I didn't hesitate. The name game hadn't been important to me in the months leading up to this tryout, and it didn't seem terribly important now. "Dwayne Johnson," I said.

Bruce stared at me like I was nuts. Here he was, surrounded by guys with bold nicknames like *the Undertaker* and *the Hitman*, and along comes ...

"Dwayne Johnson? That's it?"

"That's it."

Bruce shrugged his shoulders. "Okay. Dwayne Johnson it is."

There was one other piece of business. "Bruce?" I said. "Do I have any music?"

"You want music?"

"Sure, if it's not too much trouble."

"No trouble at all," Bruce said, and he picked up his headset and made a call to the truck. The best they could do was to recycle a ten-year-old theme from a tag team of wrestlers known as the Young Stallions. It was loud and cheesy, 1980s, Hulk Hogan-style music—*DAH-DAH-DAH!*—not at all the kind of stuff that I like, and so far from The Rock that it was almost comical. But I didn't care. The music hit and I walked through the curtain. . . .

"Ladies and gentlemen . . . from Miami, Florida, weighing 270 pounds . . . Dwayne Johnson!"

The jeering began with my first step. Wrestling fans are very vocal, very passionate. If they don't know you, then they know you're part of a dark match, and that you're probably there just to do a job. One thing they know for sure is that you are an absolute nobody. And they treat you accordingly.

"You suck!"

"Get the fuck outta here!"

"Go back to Miami, loser!"

I tried not to pay attention to any of it. Instead, I concentrated on the match, kept running spots over and over in my head. Pretty soon the Brooklyn Brawler was introduced, and the crowd went nuts, cheering and roaring like he was the best thing since wholesale carpet. They had no reason to believe the Brooklyn Brawler wouldn't make quick work of this neophyte, but that wasn't the plan. For some reason—whether it was because I had a certain look, or because they thought I had potential, I don't know, and I've never asked—the office had decided that I should win my very first match. So we wrestled for about eight minutes, put on a respectable little show, and then the Brooklyn Brawler put me over. I beat him with a small package, a move in which I took his head and legs and wrapped him up into a little pretzel.

One-two-three ... middle of the ring!

The crowd applauded modestly. I jumped to my feet and thrust my arms into the air. The sound washed over me, the most beautiful sound imaginable. It was euphoric.

"Ladies and gentlemen, the winner ... Dwayne Johnson!"

When I got backstage, everyone was congratulating me, saying things like, "Great first match! Looked like you've been working for months!"

I just nodded, said "thanks" a lot, and tried to keep moving. I was so excited I couldn't even sit down. Steve Lombardi came back a few minutes after me. The Brooklyn Brawler approached with a smile on his face and we shook hands.

"Nice job," he said. "Very nice."

I had him to thank for it, of course. He had put me over in my first match, and he had done it in style, in front of a packed house ... in front of the World Wrestling Federation brass. Believe me, it doesn't always work that way. Even now there are wrestlers whose egos prevent them from doing a job and doing it right. But Steve was an absolute pro.

Gerry Brisco was there, too. Gerry gets a kick out of reminding everyone of just how far we go back. "I knew The Rock when his name was Dewey," Gerry will say. Dewey is what my parents sometimes called me when I was a little kid. "I knew him when he was eating dirt and he had shit in his diapers." That's Gerry's favorite line for me, and he'll use it anywhere, anytime. Doesn't matter if we're at a black-tie dinner.

Now, though, I was seeing the other Gerry, the one who realized when someone deserved an honest pat on the back. "You had a great match, Dwayne," he said. "You look like you've been at this for a long time. Just keep working . . . and get ready for tomorrow night."

He was referring to the second half of my tryout, a match the following evening, again in Corpus Christi. My opponent this time was Chris Candido, a younger, more versatile athlete than Steve Lombardi. Chris could do almost anything. He could be a high flyer or he could work on the mat. That's why the office put me in with him, to see how I'd adapt. Right away I could tell I was in a different league—not that Chris was a better worker than Steve or anything, but he was clearly schooled in a newer, more athletic, cutting-edge type of wrestling, with a lot of contemporary spots that I had never attempted. Early in the conversation, for example, Chris suggested we incorporate a Frankensteiner, which is a big-time athletic move. I would stand upright and Chris would jump on my shoulders from the front, so that my face would be in his gut and his legs would be hanging over my back. Then he'd do a backflip, landing on his head and arms and dragging me over in the process. In other words, he'd use his legs to hook my head. If executed properly, it was a sensational move. And Chris wanted to up the ante by doing a Frankensteiner off the top ropes, which would add another ten feet to the fall, making it an incredibly long, elegant, show-stopper of a move.

And, for someone who had never even tried a regular Frankensteiner, it had the potential to be a disaster. I never told Chris of my inexperience. Any trepidation I might have felt I kept to myself. I knew that we had planned a good match, and that if we could pull it off, I'd be one step closer to achieving my dream. To be candid, I was not lacking in confidence. I believed that even though the Frankensteiner was new to me, I was capable of performing the move smoothly and safely. I was equally confident in Chris's ability. So we went out and put on exactly the show we had discussed. It ended with Chris beating me with a Frankensteiner off the top rope.

One-two-three! Dwayne Johnson's record falls to 1-1.

WEEKLY OIL CHANGES

I spent a few anxious days in Tampa, waiting for my report card to arrive. It came via Federal Express, in the form of a contract with the World Wrestling Federation. The compensation wasn't much—a guarantee of $150 per night—but the opportunity was immeasurable. A door had been opened and I had been invited inside. The rest was up to me.

I signed the contract and sent it back to J. J. Dillon, the Federation's talent relations coordinator. J. J. was candid in his assessment of my ability and potential, and in describing the long road that still lay ahead.

"You had a great tryout, Dwayne," he said. "You showed no signs of that being your very first match. Usually a guy in his first match will be looking all around, fiddling nervously with his trunks, acting skittish. You looked like a complete natural. But . . ."

Uh-oh. Here it comes.

". . . Obviously, you're not ready for the World Wrestling Federation right now at a big-time level."

I'm not?

"So what we'd like to do is send you to Memphis."

Memphis was the home of the United States Wrestling Alliance, which served as a training ground . . . a farm club . . . for the World Wrestling Federation. It was a good place for young guys to refine their techniques and to prove just how badly they wanted to make it. In that sense, it wasn't a lot different from any other minor-league operation. Although I would have loved to have jumped straight to the majors, I realized that Memphis was precisely where I belonged. I was grateful for the opportunity.

"When do I go?"

"I want you to call a guy named Randy Hales," J. J. said. "He's the booker there, and he'll set up a date for you. We'll be keeping an eye on you. We'll receive film on you every week, and we'll be watching your progress."

"That's great, J. J.," I said. "I really appreciate it."

With my modest savings I bought a used Isuzu Rodeo. On May 13, I loaded it up with almost everything I owned, and drove to Memphis, Tennessee. It was a long trip, so I had a lot of time to think. I missed Dany and hated the idea of being separated from her again, but I also felt thoroughly confident that I was doing the right thing, that soon all of the hard work would pay off. It helped that I loved my new job, the craft of wrestling. Compared to the way I had felt when I left for Calgary the previous year, I was the happiest guy on earth.

Somewhere between Gainesville and Tallahassee I started thinking about my name. I had proved that I could wrestle, that I could handle the basic athleticism of a career in the ring. Now I had to face the fact that "Dwayne Johnson" just wasn't going to cut it. It was a fine name, a name to be proud of. It was even a pretty good football name. But it was not the moniker of a World Wrestling Federation Superstar. I needed something better, something flashier. Something memorable. Something at once reflective of my athleticism and unusual heritage.

I've got it: Flex Kavana!

Okay, in retrospect it wasn't a great idea, but it seemed pretty cool at the time. I was still insistent upon not cashing in on the reputations of my father and grandfather; and yet, I wanted something exciting and exotic. "Kavana" was a Hawaiian word, and I liked the sound of it. "Flex" is a bit harder to defend. It was just one of those muscular, heroic nicknames, or so it seemed to me at the time. When I said the name aloud—"Flex Kavana"—it sounded like a name I could live with. It had a nice marketable ring to it. One thing was for sure: Nobody else had ever called themselves Flex Kavana. For better or worse, it was my name.

Flex Kavana made his debut the day after I arrived in Memphis. It was a tag-team match on a Saturday morning, on live television. My partner was "Too Sexy" Brian Christopher, who is now in the World Wrestling Federation. We went up against Jerry "the King" Lawler and a guy named Bill Dundee. It wound up being a big "schmozz," which is what we call a free-for-all, when everybody gets involved in a fight and chairs are thrown and tables are tipped over, and ultimately everyone is disqualified. It was wild, a lot of fun. But it sure wasn't like being in Corpus Christi, wrestling in the World Wrestling Federation. This was the minors.

Being in Memphis was a lot like being a triple-A baseball player. You worked as hard as you could, did your job, and tried to laugh at some of the craziness you saw. And all the while you tried to keep your eye on the prize: the day when you'd be called up to the big leagues. The work was hard, no question about it. On Saturdays I worked a live TV show in Memphis in the morning, then drove to Nashville for a show at the Nashville Fairgrounds that evening. After that show I'd climb in my truck and drive back to Memphis. I almost never stayed overnight because I couldn't afford a hotel. My pay, as it turned out, was $40 a night, not $150. The higher fee applied to wrestlers who had ascended to the World Wrestling Federation and not to those who had been assigned to the USWA. So I took my forty bucks, and whatever else I could earn by hawking my own photos after shows, and I tried to make the best of it. I rented a run-down efficiency apartment in Memphis. I put more than seventeen hundred miles a week on my truck. I worked in crappy arenas in front of hostile, drunken crowds. I worked in barns . . . *real, working barns* . . . the kind of venue where fans sit on bales of hay and the smell of manure takes your breath away. I worked in the parking lot of a car dealership. I worked in rings that sagged and heaved, and I worked in rings with so many nails protruding through the boards that you were afraid to take an honest fall. I worked at fairs and carnivals and almost anyplace else where people would gather.

And, for the most part, I enjoyed it. I was improving with each performance, and I was learning so much about the business and about myself. Unlike my CFL experience, I never doubted that I was in the right place, that I was moving inexorably toward something bigger and better. I set goals for myself, big, bold, long-term goals: *In two years I want to be the intercontinental champion; in four years I want to be the World Wrestling Federation champion; in five years I want to be a millionaire.* Things like that.

Meanwhile, I continued to lobby on behalf of myself. I was calling J. J. Dillon just about every week, bothering the shit out of him, saying, "Hey, listen, J. J., it's me, Dwayne. I just want to let you know I'm doing great. I appreciate everything. And whenever you guys have an open spot for me to come up there and work a dark match, and show you what kind of improvement I've made so far, or if you think I need to improve on something else, just let me know." And J. J. would say, "Okay, Dwayne, I'll let you know. We have your number." It was the same answer every time.

Finally, in August of 1996, after I'd been in Memphis for nearly six months, J. J. made the call. The Federation wanted me to fly up to Columbus, Ohio, for another tryout, this time with Owen Hart. At the time Owen was wearing a fake cast on his arm as a gimmick. Having been in Memphis, though, I wasn't aware that Owen's cast was merely a gimmick. I watched the weekly World Wrestling Federation television show and presumed that Owen, tough guy that he was, had injured his arm and decided to keep performing.

The cast was on his left arm, which is the arm you always work during a match. That's just one of the basics of wrestling: the left arm is the arm you grab. Everyone knows it, and that knowledge allows the dance to progress smoothly, fluidly. Well, when our match started, and I saw the cast on Owen's arm, I thought, *Shit, I don't want to hurt the guy any more than he's already hurt.* So I grabbed his right arm and started working it, twisting it, putting it up behind his back. It felt terribly awkward, like suddenly trying to write with your left hand when you're naturally right-handed. Although most spectators wouldn't have noticed my mistake, to anyone in the business it would have seemed like an obvious, egregious error. If you're a wrestler, and you see this happening, you immediately realize (1) that it's the wrong arm, and (2) that this guy doesn't know what the hell he's doing.

As I worked on Owen, he tried to get my attention. "Hey . . . that's the wrong arm," he said.

"I know. You've got a cast on the other one."

"Yeah . . . take the one with the cast," he said.

"But I thought your arm was broken."

And with that Owen started laughing uncontrollably. He was known for his jokes, for his sense of humor. But to me, at that moment, it was kind of embarrassing. Here I was, trying to be nice to the guy, and I got duped. I imagined that Owen and all the other veterans were looking at me and thinking, *Man, you've got a lot to learn.*

The match actually ended up going quite well after that. I put Owen over and we got a real good pop from the crowd (a "pop" is the roar that goes up when a crowd responds emotionally to a match). A short time later Owen pulled me aside in the hallway outside the dressing room.

"Vince just asked me what I thought of you," he said.

"Great. What did you tell him?"

"I told him you're the shits." I stared at Owen for a moment, unsure of whether he was telling the truth or merely busting my balls again. It was hard to tell with him. Finally he smiled and said, "Nah, I'm only kidding. I told him you're better than half the guys we have on the roster now."

"Really?"

"Yeah."

"You know, Owen, I really appreciate that."

He waved a hand, as if it was nothing. "Well, it's the truth," he said. "Just keep up the great work and you'll be fine."

By this time I was on cloud nine. I had just been paid a compliment by Owen Hart, who was a phenomenal person and a phenomenal worker. And he had shared that compliment with Vince McMahon! How much better could it get?

"Hey, Dwayne!" It was Pat Patterson.

"Hey—did you see the match?"

"Yeah, I saw it."

"What did you think?"

"It was all right," Pat said. "But your punches . . ." He scrunched up his face, as if he had just sucked a lemon. "They were the shits!"

I knew he wasn't kidding. Pat was incapable of being anything but brutally honest.

"You did okay," he added. "But when you get back to Memphis, keep working—especially on those punches, for Christ's sake. You can do better."

I wasn't about to feel sorry for myself. Instead, I did exactly as Pat suggested. In fact, I made a silent promise to throw the best punch in the business. I started watching videotapes of some of the best punchers around. I practiced constantly in front of the mirror, snapping off thousands of punches each day. In time I was able to throw my full force behind a punch and still stop within a hair of the target. There is an art to throwing a punch, of course, especially in professional wrestling, where the object is to make the blow look nothing short of devastating, while inflicting no real damage.

Within two weeks of my match with Owen Hart, I got another call from J. J. Dillon. When J. J. called, it was usually good news. But this set a new standard.

"We want to take you out of Memphis," he explained. "We don't think it's as conducive to your development as we'd like it to be."

The plan, J. J. said, was for me to move to Connecticut, where the World Wrestling Federation had its corporate headquarters as well as its own world-class training facility. He gave me the address and told me to be there in a few days.

"We'll make the necessary calls to the Memphis office and let them know you're leaving," he added.

After calling Dany and my parents to give them the good news, I started bouncing around the apartment. There was no hurry. I didn't have to leave right away ... but I saw no reason to stay. I grabbed a suitcase and began cleaning out my dresser drawers. I threw all of my dirty laundry into an empty pillowcase. In less than an hour all of my possessions were packed up and ready to go. I climbed behind the wheel of my Rodeo, fired up the engine, and drove away, leaving Memphis and the minors in my rearview mirror.

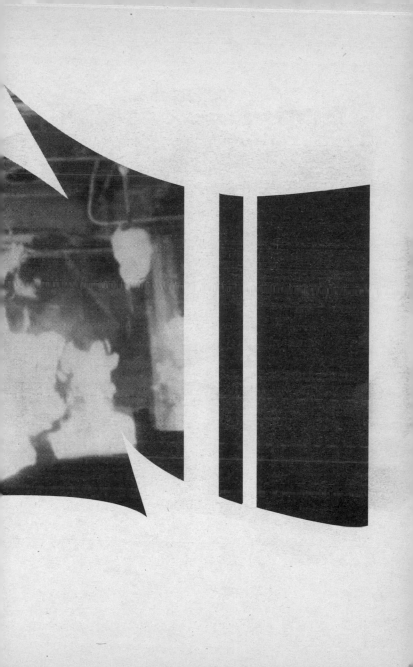

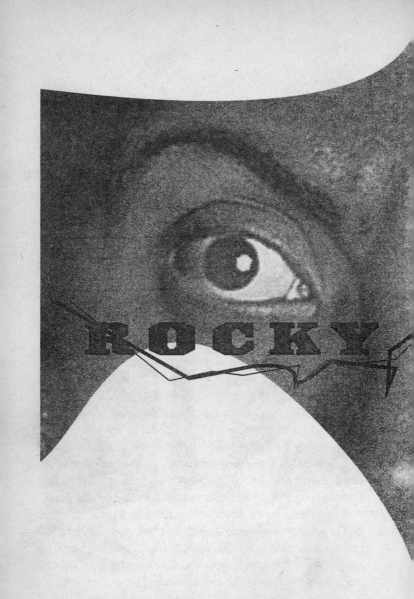

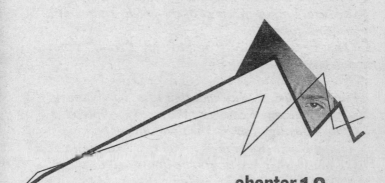

chapter 10
MAIVIA

NOVEMBER 16, 1996 *(New York)—*
Madison Square Garden ... the Mecca of arenas. I'm
backstage in the catering area, eating lunch with some
of the boys. In a few hours I'll make my official debut
in the World Wrestling Federation, in a big Pay-Per-
View event known as the Survivor Series. This is not
a tryout. I'm on the roster now. I'm part of the team.

Gerry Brisco pulls up a chair. He wants to start
going over the evening's matches. No one knows the
outcome at this time. We only know that there will be
eight of us performing, and that at the end of the
night, one man will be the winner ... the survivor.

"How's your wind?" Gerry says to me with a
smile.

"My wind is great."

"Good . . . good. Because tonight you're going to need it. Tonight . . . you're the man."

It takes a moment for this to sink in. I am the rookie here. I'm the greenest of the green. There must be some mistake.

"That's great," I say, trying to play it cool. "What do you guys have in mind?"

"You're going to win the Survivor Series."

I'm so excited, so shocked, that I can barely speak. Down the hallway I can hear the sounds of preparation, the whirring of drills, the pounding of hammers, the popping and cracking of fireworks. And music . . . lots of music. In a few hours the doors will open and 20,000 people will fill the building. Ready or not, it's time for my close-up.

I had been training in Stamford, Connecticut, for more than two months, primarily with Tom Prichard, Bruce Prichard's brother and himself a fifteen-year veteran of the business, and Mark Henry, an Olympic weight-lifting champion. During that time I had gotten to know everybody in the office and the studio, and had begun to feel like part of the World Wrestling Federation family. It was an invaluable learning experience. We trained for several hours each day, working on all kinds of moves and routines. With no spectators, no referees, no television cameras, we were encouraged to push the envelope, to really work on all aspects of the craft.

It had been decided that I would make my debut in the *Survivor Series* in November, and as that day drew near we began discussing my character and ring persona. Flex Kavana was gone. We needed something better than that, and Dwayne Johnson wasn't the answer. Ironically enough, the name suggested by the office was the same name my mother had proposed: Rocky Maivia. It was Tom Prichard who first presented it to me. He had no idea that I had already been down this road with my parents.

"I'm sorry, but there's no way I can do that," I told Tom. "That's my grandfather's name and my dad's name."

The office, however, was sold on the idea, so Tom set up a meeting with Vince McMahon and Jim Ross, a Federation vice president as well as a longtime broadcaster. Together they tried to convince me that there was nothing shameful or insulting about working under the name Rocky Maivia.

"We're not asking you to go in the ring in bare feet like your grandfather did, or to do a Samoan dance or anything like that," they said. "And we're not asking you to do the jabs or the Ali Shuffle like your father did. You are your own man now. This is just a way of showing your respect."

Maybe they were right. My father already liked the name, and if my grandfather had been alive, he probably would have liked it, too. So . . . Rocky Maivia it was.

When I found out that I was going to win the *Survivor Series*, I realized that my life was about to take another sharp turn. It wasn't *winning* that excited me, because I have always understood that this business is a work and that no one actually *beats* anybody. You follow the script—you know your role, as The Rock might say. That's just the way it's done. But I was excited about the prospect of being the winner . . . of what it would mean to be *Rocky Maivia— champion of the* Survivor Series. It was a tremendous opportunity, and it spoke volumes about how Vince and the rest of the front office felt about my potential.

The crowd at Madison Square Garden was, shall we say, a little less enthusiastic. As my music hit (more dumb, generic arena rock) and I walked from the gorilla position to the ring, there wasn't much of a reaction at all. I was a curiosity: *Rocky Maivia, the one we've never heard of.* But thirty minutes later, after I had pinned Goldust to win the *Survivor Series,* they knew who I was. Wrestling fans are not stupid, especially in the 1990s. They're in on the con, and that's part of the reason the business has become so popular. Our fans love the serpentine story lines, the wild soap-opera element, the comic-book violence . . . as well as the extraordinarily high level of athleticism. When Rocky Maivia won the *Survivor Series* in his World Wrestling Federation debut, the fans knew they were looking at a guy who was going to be around for a while.

The character of Rocky Maivia didn't have a lot of depth back then. He was a babyface, a technically proficient wrestler who smiled a lot and communicated almost nothing; he didn't get a lot of time on the microphone. That was fine with me because I was still new to the business and content to merely keep learning. Shortly after the *Survivor Series,* I began working regularly. I went on my first international tour that winter. We spent a few days in Europe and then went on to the Middle East. It was grueling experience, and sort of lonely for me. I was the new kid, only twenty-four years old. I really didn't know anyone, and no one knew much about me, other than the fact that I had been tapped to win a big match in my debut. So I pretty much kept to myself. It was Bret Hart who finally decided to make things easier for me. He went out of his way to sit with me on bus rides, to give me advice whenever he could. This was priceless to me, and I'll never forget it. Here was a guy who was the Federation Champion, one of the biggest stars in the business, and he was willing to take the time to help a neophyte. All too often in this industry—and, I suppose, in any celebrity-driven industry—people forget their roots. They attain a certain level of stardom and they become assholes. It's easy to forget what it was like when you were scratching and climbing. Bret is one guy who has never forgotten.

Owen Hart was basically the same way, except that he had a wicked streak that manifested itself most often in the form of practical jokes. The fake cast incident was my introduction to this side of Owen, but it wasn't my last experience.

Near the end of our international tour, after working the undercard for more than three weeks, I was scheduled to work the main event at a show in Dubai. It was a big, eight-man tag-team match involving some of the Federation's biggest stars, including the Undertaker, Owen Hart, and Bret Hart. And me . . . which I thought was pretty cool. Well, as the match went on Owen became the center of attention, thanks to some serious work being done on his leg, courtesy of the Undertaker and Bret Hart. They took turns twisting and kneading Owen's leg, and as they did so, Owen howled in pain. He threw his arms out, as if begging for mercy. He screamed at the top of his lungs. In short, he was selling like a pro.

Finally, it was my turn. Bret tagged me in and I took my place above Owen's prone frame. I grabbed his leg, the same one that had been causing him so

much apparent pain, and went to town. I kicked it, stomped it, twisted it, and just generally abused it. As I was working the leg with everything I had, Owen propped himself up on one elbow, smiled at the crowd, and with his other hand simulated the motion of smoking a cigarette. *Ahhhhh ... isn't this relaxing?*

This, of course, was Owen's way of welcoming me to the company. Here I was, jumping up and down on his leg, trying to do the best job possible in my first big international match, and Owen was clowning around, acting as if it didn't hurt a bit. I wasn't one to joke in the ring, so I looked at Bret, and then at the Undertaker, as if to say, *"What the hell?"* They just lowered their heads and snickered. After a while Owen jumped to his feet and said, "Shoot me off ... I'll reverse you ... give me a big tackle." Exactly those words. I went along, even though, at this point, I wasn't sure I could trust Owen.

Now, normally when you give a guy a big tackle, he goes down with authority. *Wham!* If it's solid enough and makes a big noise, it becomes real for the audience, which is good, because then you get a nice reaction. So I shot Owen off, he reversed me, and as I came off the ropes I gave him a big, hard tackle. But instead of going down with authority, Owen did a long, dramatic, slow-motion fall: *TIM-BERRRRRR!* And everybody started to laugh: the other guys at ringside, the audience, the referee ... even me. Owen was gifted that way. Not only was he a great wrestler, but he knew how to make people laugh. He knew how to make them feel good.

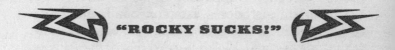

"ROCKY SUCKS!"

One of the low points for the World Wrestling Federation came in early 1997, when Shawn Michaels decided to relinquish the Federation Championship. This was not planned. Shawn went on *Raw Is War*, the Federation television show, and announced that he would not be defending his title at *WrestleMania*. This kind of thing happens in our business sometimes. Guys will refuse to do a job or balk at following a story line. What Shawn's reasons were ... I don't know. And I don't care. I only know that it led to yet another opportunity for me.

After Shawn relinquished the Federation title, the office felt that something was needed to spike the fans' interest. So, on a special Thursday edition of *Raw*, in Lowell, Massachusetts, I became the heir to the throne.

Hunter Hearst Helmsley was the World Wrestling Federation Intercontinental Champion at the time. The Intercontinental Championship is the second most important title in the business, one rung below the World Wrestling Federation Championship. Both, of course, are orchestrated by the Federation. The Intercontinental Champion naturally gets a lot of exposure and publicity. If he's talented and charismatic enough, and the fans seem to embrace him strongly enough, he could become the World Wrestling Federation Champion. But there are no guarantees. A lot of Intercontinental Champions do not become Federation Champions. Still, the Intercontinental title is considered one of the biggest prizes in the industry, and when I learned that Triple H was going to drop the title to me on *Raw*, I was shocked.

So were a significant number of our fans, who, perhaps not unjustly, felt that Rocky Maivia was being forced down their throats. At the same time that this was happening, the World Wrestling Federation was experiencing a dramatic attitudinal shift, at the core of which was Stone Cold Steve Austin. Steve was just starting to become the popular antihero then. He was giving the finger, saying "ass" on television, and generally exhibiting behavior that in the past would have made him a complete heel. But the fans loved it!

Meanwhile, over here, we had Rocky Maivia, who was supposed to be an all-around good guy. I was always told back then, "Rocky, you can't smile enough when you get in the ring. Remember ... you're just happy to be there. You're happy to be in the World Wrestling Federation. You want to win, of course, but if you lose, you know, you just kind of go 'Damn! I'll be back next time!'" It was the typical, nauseating, babyface bullshit. The character of Rocky Maivia was very traditional, very typical of a babyface in the 1970s and 1980s: American as apple pie and all that. He was the type of guy who helped old ladies cross the street and kissed babies. It's funny, I always like to say now that The Rock is the kind of guy who won't kiss a baby and he'll *throw* an old lady across the street! But not Rocky Maivia. He was sweet. The fans would look at Rocky, in his nice, pretty blue outfit, and then they'd look at Stone Cold Steve Austin, cursing and giving the finger and popping open cans of Budweiser, and they'd say . . . "Rocky Maivia? Forget it!"

If there was any doubt that the business had undergone a sea change, it was laid to rest on March 23, 1997, in Chicago, site of *WrestleMania XIII*. I had brought my parents and Dany to the match, thinking it would be a wonderful night for all of us. But it wound up being one of the strangest. I was defending my Intercontinental title against the Sultan, a notorious heel from the Middle East who was managed by another notorious heel from the Middle East, the Iron Sheik. So I made my entrance in typical Rocky Maivia babyface fashion. And within five minutes the majority of the crowd at the Rosemont Horizon had inexplicably turned against me. Cries of "ROCKY SUCKS! ROCKY SUCKS!" echoed off the walls.

Wait a minute . . . I'm the good guy! That was the first thought that went through my mind. Somewhere along the line, something had gone terribly wrong. I had put in so much work, and I had done exactly what I was told to do. I had embraced a character who was supposed to be a classic babyface, and for some reason that character was now reviled. It made no sense. And regardless of whether the business is a work, it was unappealing, to say the least. As the jeers continued, I thought, *When this match is over, I'm going to fix all this.*

That proved to be easier said than done. I beat the Sultan—*one-two-three . . . in the middle of the ring!*—and got a decent pop from the audience. But even as I was leaving, the chanting continued. The fans didn't boo me out of the building or anything, but they let me know that I was no champion in their eyes.

"ROCKY SUCKS!"

It's funny how things work out, how the crowd's hatred of Rocky Maivia, something that bothered me in the beginning, turned out to be the best thing for my career. The saying caught on after that, and I'd hear it every night, in every building.

"ROCKY SUCKS!"

Some places it was only 20 or 25 percent of the people chanting, other times it was 40 or 50 percent. But it was always there. After a while the signs started to pop up: *"ROCKY SUCKS!"* and *"DIE, ROCKY, DIE!"* At first I smiled right through it all, until it became ridiculous to keep up the facade. If you're a human being, it's virtually impossible to ignore that kind of abuse, especially when your character has been designed to elicit exactly the opposite response. Eventually the smile disappeared. I wasn't cursing at the crowd or anything, but I damn sure wasn't going to pretend I was happy. Not anymore.

That spring I dropped the Intercontinental title to Owen Hart. I also tore the posterior cruciate ligament in my knee during a match against Mankind. Those two incidents, taken together, gave me a chance to step out of the spotlight for a while. I called the office after my injury was diagnosed and spoke with Jim Ross. I told him the doctor was confident that surgery wouldn't be necessary, that my knee would heal with rest and rehabilitation. Jim was very understanding and told me to take eight weeks off. It was in that period of time that Rocky Maivia took to heart the advice of wrestling fans everywhere . . . and began to whither away.

GOING TO
THE CHAPEL

By this time Dany and I were engaged to be married, although we hadn't told her parents, primarily because our relationship with them had continued to deteriorate. I still hadn't even met them, even though they now owned a condominium in Miami, just a few minutes from the apartment that Dany and I had rented. For six years I had been dating their daughter, and still not one word had passed between us. It was hard for me, but it was awful for Dany. Her strength through the entire mess was tremendous. I've never seen anything like it. She nearly lost her family because she refused to compromise not only how she felt about me but also her own beliefs. Dany would not attend any family functions knowing that I wasn't welcome. She recognized that behavior for what it was: complete bullshit.

Finally, as our wedding day approached, we decided to make one final effort. We would drive to their condominium together and confront Dany's parents. After that, whatever happened . . . happened. Dany was prepared for the possibility that it might be the last time she would ever speak to her mother and father.

We made our way over to their condo and walked

in unannounced. It was a complete surprise. After a few minutes of awkward conversation involving the four of us, I walked outside with Dany's father so that we could speak privately, man to man. I was extremely angry, but I kept my emotions in check. I wasn't loud or belligerent or anything like that. More than anything else, I wanted to convey a feeling of pride—pride in my relationship with Dany, pride in who I was and what I was doing with my life. At some point in the conversation Dany's father said. "I could never approve of you guys living together . . . at least not until you're married."

That was my opening.

"Well, now that you've said that, I've come here to tell you this: I'm going to marry Dany." It wasn't a question. I wasn't asking for his daughter's hand in marriage. I made my statement and that was that. It was an important moment and what would prove to be the turning point in my relationship with Dany's parents.

The ice thawed a bit after that. Dany's mother started to get heavily involved in the planning of the wedding. Her grandparents even got involved. But we paid for the wedding ourselves. The scars hadn't healed so quickly or completely that I was willing to accept any money from Dany's parents.

We were married on May 3, 1997. It was a very unique and beautiful Samoan/Cuban wedding, with a Polynesian band and Polynesian dancers. Kind of like a luau. My mother danced a lovely Samoan dance for us, and our wedding hymn, "The Hawaiian Wedding Song," was beautiful. After dinner, in addition to the traditional wedding cake, we brought out dozens and dozens of chocolate chip cookies (at my request,

because I'm a big fan of cookies), along with gallons of fresh milk. Everyone had a great time.

Many of my relatives from Hawaii came to the wedding, including my Aunt Sharon (who did a wonderful job coordinating the whole affair) and my Uncle Tonga. Pat Patterson was there, too. In addition, a lot of Samoans and Polynesians we barely knew simply showed up. That's another wonderfully quirky Samoan custom: if an "important" Samoan (I had achieved a degree of notoriety by this time, and, of course, my last name, Maivia, was well known throughout the Samoan community) is getting married, other Samoans in the region will drop in, even if they haven't been invited. It's not considered rude; in fact, it's a sign of respect. Many Samoan dignitaries came, including my Uncle Neff Maivia, who flew all the way from Hawaii to surprise Dany and me.

Our wedding day also was the first time that my parents met Dany's parents. It was a surprisingly stress-free introduction, in part because my parents are such unselfish people. Their attitude, basically, was this: *Now that they're going to get a chance to know you and see what type of person you are, everything will be fine. And we're proud of that. We're also proud that you're getting married today. This is your day and there's no room for bickering about all those years when they didn't like our son.*

I couldn't thank my parents enough for their generosity and kindness. On the most important day of my life, they really came through like the stars that they are.

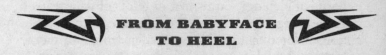

FROM BABYFACE
TO HEEL

No one in the World Wrestling Federation works in a vacuum. Rocky Maivia's fall from grace may have been felt most acutely by me, but others certainly noticed what was happening. Frequently in this business the fans dictate character development and story arcs. When the fans' allegiance shifts, you have to be ready to move with them. So it was that in early August of 1997, Jim Ross presented me with a wonderful option.

"How would you feel about turning heel?" he said.

This was my first day back with the company, after more than two months of rehabilitation. I knew that some sort of change was in order, and I was hoping our writers and front-office personnel would agree, but I didn't expect anything to happen quite so quickly.

"Jim, I would love to turn heel," I said.

"Really?" He seemed somewhat surprised by my enthusiasm.

"Absolutely. What did you have in mind?"

"We're thinking about having you join the Nation," Jim said.

Hmmmm. This was an interesting development. The Nation of Domination—or "the Nation," for

short—was a highly militant faction run by a character named Faarooq, who was in reality a wrestler
named Ron Simmons. At the time, the Nation was
perceived by fans to be almost like the Black Panthers
in terms of ideology, or at least in terms of its apparent dislike of white America. Initially, the Nation was
an organization that included wrestlers from a variety
of ethnic backgrounds, including Puerto Rican,
African American, and Caucasian. Nevertheless, at
the time that I was invited to join, the Nation was
clearly drawn as a hard-core, militant, black group.
Bad Guys!

I didn't have to think long about the offer. "Jim, I
would like nothing better than to do that," I said.

"Great, I'll talk to Vince and let him know you dig
the idea."

It didn't take long for the new plan to be put into
effect. That very night, at a show in Jackson,
Mississippi, Rocky Maivia stopped smiling. I didn't
wrestle. Instead, I did what's known as a "run-in."
Faarooq was wrestling a guy named Chainz, and at
one point in the match Chainz seemed to have
Faarooq beat. He was hammering the crap out of
Faarooq, and the referee was down, having been
knocked senseless during the course of the match.

Suddenly, there was Rocky Maivia, sprinting down
the aisle and leaping into the ring. The crowd, under-
standably, thought Rocky was there to help Chainz,
the good guy. They hadn't seen Rocky in more than
two months, and they had no idea what was about to
happen. In one of those great 180-degree shifts that
make wrestling so much fun, Rocky grabbed Chainz
and set him up for The Rock Bottom, which would
later become the signature move of The Rock. Of

course, it wasn't called The Rock Bottom at the time. It was usually just called "an unbelievable maneuver!" While standing side by side—me facing one way, him the other—I hooked Chainz's head and neck with my right arm and lifted him up in the air. Then I swept his legs out from beneath him and drove his upper body and the back of his head into the mat. He landed with a terrific *CRASH!* and lay dazed on the ring floor. As the crowd watched in stunned silence, Rocky Maivia dragged Faarooq over and placed him on top of Chainz. Then he shook the referee from his slumber, and the referee counted Chainz out. *One! Two! Three!*

As Jim Ross and Jerry Lawler, who were broadcasting that night's show, feigned shock for the television audience—"I can't believe Rocky did that!"—I sauntered around the ring with Faarooq. Together we raised our right arms into the air and clenched our fists: *The Nation Salute!* Boos cascaded down upon us, and for the first time in my career, I felt right at home. I felt as though the hate had been earned. I was now, officially, a heel.

There was just one problem. I was concerned about the Nation's image and the possibility that my character might be perceived as racist. I wanted to be a heel in the worst way, but after all I had been through in my personal life, I wasn't comfortable with the notion of perpetuating stereotypes. So I went to Vince Russo, our head writer, and told him how I felt.

"I think I need an opportunity to tell people why I turned heel, and why I joined the Nation," I explained. "It's extremely important to me that people don't think I joined because of the color of my skin." To me, a conversion based on that simple premise was not only revolting but limiting as well. You know . . . that lame bullshit: *I'm black and I'm pissed!* Well, who gives a flying fuck, really? I just felt like there was a lot more depth and personality to me than that.

At my request, the Nation was then given interview time on television, an opportunity for the new Rocky Maivia to cut a killer promo and explain himself . . . all in one shot. As soon as we walked out, the crowd started chanting "ROCKY SUCKS! ROCKY SUCKS!" Right away I thought, *Man, we've got something here. This is great.*

Faarooq spoke first, then handed the microphone to me. As the baton was passed, the jeering intensified. Clearly, I was perceived as the baddest of the bad guys. I had taken a lot of care in writing this promo. I wanted to entertain the fans, but I wanted to make my feelings clear. The line between Dwayne Johnson and Rocky Maivia was about to be blurred, so it was important that I kept the promo as close to my heart as possible. I lifted the microphone to my mouth and said, slowly and loudly, with great conviction . . . "Die, Rocky, Die!" That caught their attention. Suddenly the arena was quiet. They had no doubt expected a typical, old-school wrestling promo— "LET ME TELL YOU PEOPLE ONE THING . . . GO TO HELL!"—and instead they got this. Now, at the very least, they would hear me out.

"That's the response I get from you people? After giving my blood, my sweat, and my tears? For months and months? Signs that say 'Die, Rocky, Die'? And hearing 'Rocky sucks!' at every arena across the country?"

Those words—"Rocky sucks"—were the ignition the crowd needed. Now they had been engaged. Now it was time to have some fun.

"*ROCKY SUCKS! ROCKY SUCKS! ROCKY SUCKS!*"

I let it go on for a moment. I soaked it up, enjoyed it, let them have their fun, because, after all, a great live promo is a collaborative effort, a verbal joust between fans and star. Finally I held up a hand and the noise diminished. *That's cool. I'm in control. They want to hear what I have to say.* "I just want to make one thing perfectly clear right here, right now. Rocky Maivia is a lot of things, but 'sucks' isn't one of them. Joining the Nation wasn't a black thing. It wasn't a white thing. It was a respect thing. And one way or another, from now on, Rocky Maivia is going to get respect . . . by any means necessary."

We walked off to a chorus of boos, but I felt confident that I had made my point, and made it well. From now on Rocky Maivia would be much more like Dwayne Johnson: confident, emotional, volatile. I wanted to go out there and be myself. Sometimes I would smile, sometimes I wouldn't. If someone said, "You suck!" I would no longer pretend not to hear it. In the ring, I would be more aggressive, violent. I had the freedom to be a heel, and it was . . . *liberating!*

Over the course of the next few months Rocky Maivia became the hottest heel in the company. The DIE, ROCKY, DIE! signs multiplied. "ROCKY SUCKS!" became almost an anthem to World Wrestling Federation fans everywhere. And I loved it! At last I had found my calling. I went out every night and happily absorbed the venom that was spewed in my direction. I still wasn't getting a lot of interview time, but I was confident that would change. I was just waiting for my opportunity.

The pivotal moment came in December of 1997. Stone Cold Steve Austin, who had taken the Intercontinental title from Owen Hart at the *Survivor Series* in November, had just come back from a neck injury. Now he was in the ring, cutting a promo. And as he was talking . . . in strutted Rocky Maivia. The greatest rivalry in World Wrestling Federation history was about to begin.

"I hate to rain on your little victory parade," I said. "But I just want to come out here and make a special note. And that note is this: Everybody knows that when I was World Wrestling Federation Intercontinental Champion, I was the best damn Intercontinental Champion there ever was!"

"BOOOOOOOO!"

"Stone Cold Steve Austin, I'm challenging you for the Intercontinental championship, and if you have any manhood at all, you'll accept my challenge!"

"BOOOOOOOO!"

One of Steve's trademark lines was "That's the bottom line, 'cause Stone Cold said so." So, as the go-home line to my promo, I said, "And if you do accept my challenge, then your bottom line will say: 'Stone Cold—has-been. Compliments of . . . The Rock!'"

And that was it. With that single promo, and that go-home line, Rocky Maivia became "The Rock," an outrageously arrogant, self-centered, but undeniably talented wrestler who couldn't care less what other people thought, and who always—ALWAYS—spoke in the third person. No one had ever attempted that before, but I was eager to give it a try. I saw The Rock

The Rock—The People's Champion.

Me at six months with my mom.

Me at four with my mom and dad
in traditional Samoan clothing.

Me at four with my dad's Georgia Tag-Team and Heavyweight title belts.

A ten-year-old Rock with his fashion mentor, "Classy" Freddy Blassie (notice The Rock's silk shirt).

Me with the Eighth Wonder of the World, Andre the Giant.

Winning the World Wrestling Federation Championship for the second time over a bloodied, beaten Mankind in the memorable "I Quit" match, *Royal Rumble*, 1999.

The Rock layin' the smack down on Bret "the Hitman" Hart.

The Rock becomes the World Wrestling Federation Champion for the first time at *Survivor Series*, 1998.

Dany's and my
wedding day,
May 3, 1997.

Mom and me
in Hawaii.

The Rock—the Most Electrifying Man in Sports-Entertainment.

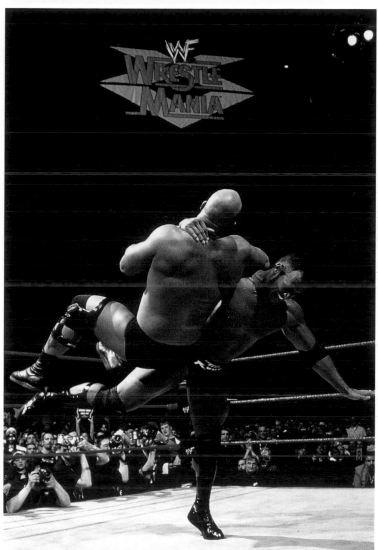

WrestleMania XV, Stone Cold Steve Austin getting The Rock's Rock Bottom in the greatest World Wrestling Federation Championship match in *WrestleMania* history.

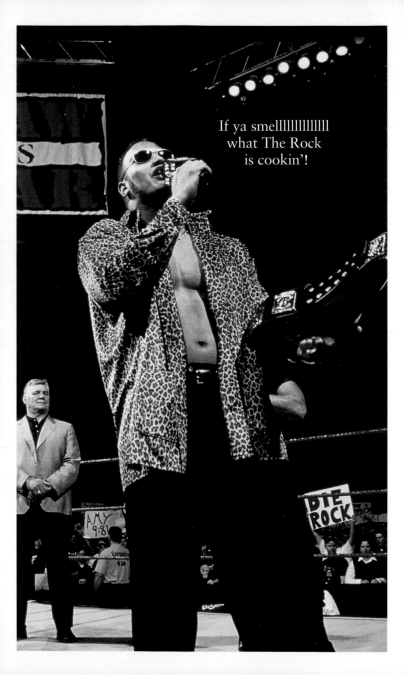

The Rock versus Triple H in one of our classic matches—a ladder match at *SummerSlam*, 1998, for the Intercontinental Championship.

The Great One electrifying a *Raw Is War* crowd.

The Brahma Bull waiting for the Rattlesnake, *Backlash*, 1999.

The Rock filming his Chef Boyardee commercial on South Beach, Miami, Florida.

as an extension of my own personality. He was bombastic, funny, cocky . . . but, at his core, he was an athlete with sound technical skills. He loved wrestling. He loved sports-entertainment.

The Rock was Dwayne Johnson . . . with the volume . . . turned . . . WAY . . . UP!

chapter 11

THE PEOPLE'S CHAMPION

So it's after The Rock cuts his famous promo that the fun really begins. Stone Cold Steve Austin, fool that he is, decides that he has a set of nuts big enough to accept the challenge of The Rock, and that is the start of what The Rock would call "magic." Why? Because The Rock detests Stone Cold Steve Austin. The Rock realizes that Stone Cold Steve Austin is without a doubt the biggest piece of Texas trailer-park trash walking God's Green Earth. Why does The Rock feel this way? Because the guy personifies what trash would be to The Rock. He's the exact opposite of The Rock. The Rock is The Great One, The Chosen One, The Most Electrifying Man in Sports-Entertainment—period! And Stone Cold Steve Austin ... well, it's just genetically impossible for The Rock to like Stone Cold Steve

Austin, because to The Rock it looks like some woman made love to a big piece of crap, and nine months later out popped Stone Cold Steve Austin. And you know what? Stone Cold hates The Rock right back, which is fine with The Rock, because that's what makes their rivalry so special, so mesmerizing, so unforgettable. There is a magical synergy between The Rock and Stone Cold Steve Austin that is very hard to explain. But you feel it whenever they step into the ring together.

Sometimes you feel it when they're outside the ring, as is the case in the weeks leading up to the World Wrestling Federation Pay-Per-View show in December of 1997. For the better part of three weeks The Rock and Stone Cold Steve Austin are personally responsible for some of the best damn sports-entertainment in the history of television. Nose-to-nose, trashing each other on a nightly basis. Of course, Stone Cold is no match for The Rock when it comes to cutting promos, but he damn sure is willing to try. The Rock has to give him that much.

The highlight of this ongoing feud is the infamous "pager incident." One night on *Raw Is War,* our weekly television show, Stone Cold Steve Austin decides he's going to try to be a big shot, just like The Rock. He wants to run his mouth on national television, and he tries to cut The Rock's promo in half by making sure his big, ugly mug is staring out from the Titantron, which is the big-screen TV we use on *Raw.* Well, this doesn't sit well with The Rock, so it isn't long before he and Stone Cold are squaring off, screaming in each other's faces. Their little repartee is starting to get pretty heated when all of a sudden Stone Cold says, "When you're walking through the airport, Rock, and your pager goes off, and you look down and see 3:16 (Just in case you've been living in a cave for the past few years, The Rock will now explain to your monkey-asses exactly what this means. In 1996, just as Stone Cold was becoming one of the top draws in the World Wrestling Federation, he had a big-time brawl with Jake "the

Snake" Roberts. Jake was always quoting the Bible, preaching to anyone who was willing to listen—and to anyone who wouldn't listen, for that matter. So one day Stone Cold threw the Bible-thumping back in Jake's face. "Talk about your John 3:16," he said. "Austin 3:16 says, 'I just whooped your ass!'" And now trailer-trash jabronis all over the planet are guzzling Budweiser, flipping the bird, shaving their heads, and walking around wearing T-shirts that scream "Austin 3:16." Christ, The Rock is sick of it!), you're going to have to ask yourself: Is it live ... or is it Memorex?!'"

Well, The Rock is standing there staring at Stone Cold Steve Austin like he's got three heads, thinking *What kind of funny cigarettes have you been smoking? What kind of Texas Moonshine have you been pouring down your esophagus?* A few minutes later, though, after Stone Cold has apparently left the building, The Rock is in the middle of the ring, holding the World Wrestling Federation Intercontinental belt, the belt that The Rock made famous, when he hears his beeper go off. The Rock thinks this is a little strange, of course, and when he pushes the button on his pager and the son of a bitch says *3:16* ... well, The Rock's eyes about pop out of his head. He's so pissed he's ready to kill someone. Who the hell does Stone Cold Steve Austin think he is, trying to embarrass The Rock on national television, in front of the millions and the millions of The Rock's fans? What The Rock doesn't know is that Stone Cold is about to go postal on his ass. The Rock spins around and sees that big piece of garbage getting ready to jump him. And it's too late for The Rock to protect himself. Stone Cold proceeds to go to town on The Great One!

But that's okay. The Rock is telling you about one of the most famous scenes in sports-entertainment history—he's telling you about getting his butt kicked—so you'll understand something: Any time you've got The Rock involved on TV, cutting promos, kicking ass, laying the smack down, it doesn't really matter who wins or loses. See, The Rock wins either way, because ratings go through the roof and you've got one hell of an entertaining segment.

KNOW YOUR ROLE
AND
SHUT YOUR MOUTH!

WHOSE TITLE IS IT, ANYWAY?

December 7, 1997 (Springfield, MA)—So we go into the Pay-Per-View, and the best match of the night, as if it could be any other way, is Stone Cold Steve Austin vs. The Rock for The Rock's Intercontinental title. And once again Stone Cold decides he wants to be like The Rock, he wants to be a big shot, he's doing everything he can to command as much attention and respect and admiration as The Great One. How does he do this? By driving his Stone Cold Pickup Truck directly into the arena! This beast is all decked out with trailer-park trash, it's got the skull on the side, it's got *3:16* on the back, and it says *Stone Cold* on it. Man, if The Rock were a Stone Cold fan, this would be something The Rock could truly cherish. But obviously he's not a Stone Cold fan, so it's just a big piece of shit to The Rock!

Well, it doesn't take long for Stone Cold and The Rock to lock up and start going at it. For the next fifteen to twenty minutes The Rock beats the living piss out of Stone Cold Steve Austin. You want highlights? The Rock will give you highlights. How about The Rock dropping The People's Elbow on Stone Cold? How about The Rock going for a second People's Elbow and missing? (What, you thought The Rock was perfect? The Rock has never claimed to be perfect. Things like that happen.) In true Rock form, though, The Rock does exactly what he does best, and that's try to win at any cost. He decides he's going to take a pair of brass knuckles and nail Stone Cold Steve Austin! But Steve is one step ahead of The Rock on this night. When The Rock throws what could be the most devastating punch of his life, Stone Cold ducks. Then he gives The Rock a Stone Cold Stunner and covers him—*one-two-three!*—right there in the middle of the ring.

Is The Rock embarrassed? Hell, no! The Rock is a man and a half. He calls a spade a spade. Stone Cold Steve Austin beat The Rock—clean. Can't deny that. But it's only the first volley in a long battle.

The next night on *Raw Is War,* the crowd is really getting on The Rock's case. The fans pretty much revile The Rock at this point. But The Rock doesn't care. The Rock has said from Day One that whether the fans chant "ROCKY SUCKS!" or "DIE, ROCKY, DIE!" or "ROCKY! ROCKY!", that's entirely up to them The Rock will continue to go out there every night and do his thing and prove that The Rock has the ability to make you chant *something*. You cannot ignore The Rock.

Stone Cold Steve Austin knows this better than anyone else, because that evening, on national television, Vince McMahon orders Stone Cold to give The Rock a rematch. Vince is no fool. He doesn't want Steve Austin as the Intercontinental Champion— he wants a real champion, a people's champion! He wants The Rock as his champion! And Vince has enough confidence in The Rock to know that The Rock is going to go out there and whip Stone Cold's sorry ass like there's no tomorrow. Stone Cold knows it, too. When he comes out and sees Vince McMahon and The Rock waiting for him, he proceeds, in that backwoods dialect of his, in that trailer park–trash language that only he can understand . . . he proceeds to admit to the world that he's tired of the beating that The Rock has been putting on him, and that he hasn't physically, let alone psychologically, recovered from the stomping that The Rock gave him the previous night in Springfield. Rather than risk humiliation, rather than risk another beat-down on national television, Stone Cold Steve Austin hands the Intercontinental belt over to the rightful champion: The Rock.

Now, The Rock doesn't blame Stone Cold for one single, solitary second, because if you think about it, who wants an ass-kicking from The Rock? And two nights in a row! *Pleeeeease!* The average man needs at least a week to recover from a date with The Rock (the average woman, too, *if you smell what The Rock is cooking!*). Stone Cold is content to sit back and eat his little hot dogs and drink his beer. He doesn't want any part of a rematch with The Rock. It's a good thing, too, because The Rock wouldn't have served up a can of 100 percent whoop-ass to Steve Austin—The Rock would have served him a big double-Rock Burger . . . with extra Rock Sauce on the side. And instead of shoving it down Stone Cold Steve Austin's throat, The Rock would have shoved it up his candy ass!

The fans, obviously, are shocked by this development. Stone Cold is their hero. He's Mr. "antiauthority . . . say anything . . . gutter mouth . . . flip the middle finger whenever I feel like it." And now here he is, just *giving* the title to The Rock? Who would have guessed? Well, The Rock would have guessed, because he knows what would have happened if Stone Cold hadn't exercised a little common sense for a change.

THE ROYAL RUMBLE

January 18, 1998 (San Jose, CA)—It's a brand new year and The Rock is still the Intercontinental Champion, and he's taking on Ken Shamrock at *The Royal Rumble*. Of course, it should be called *The Rock Rumble*, because The Rock, as always, makes this show special. (Again, for any jabroni who's been living on another planet, The Rock will provide illumination: *The Royal Rumble* is one of the biggest Pay-Per-View events of the year, and one of the most challenging events on the World Wrestling Federation calendar. The reason it's called The Royal Rumble is because it's a battle royal, with thirty participants from the World Wrestling Federation, all in the ring, trying to knock each other out. Unlike a typical battle royal, though, in *The Royal Rumble* the wrestlers don't all jump in the ring at once; instead, two guys start out in the ring, and every couple minutes, another fighter enters.)

The Rock is so big, so magnetic, so charismatic . . . he can't help but steal the spotlight from *The Royal Rumble* itself. And that's exactly what happens when he takes on Ken Shamrock on the undercard. Ken Shamrock knows this, too. That's why he wants to go one-on-one with The Rock. You challenge The Rock . . . hell, of course you're going to get famous. You're going to get your head shoved up your ass sideways, too, but you're definitely going to make a name for yourself. And that's what

Ken Shamrock wants. He's supposed to be this killer, this deadly fighting machine, a multitime Ultimate Fighting Championship winner. Well ... whoopee! Let the party begin! The Rock says, "So what?" to that. Ken Shamrock is from California, so he's fighting in his backyard, but The Rock doesn't care. The Rock goes out and beats the living crap out of Ken Shamrock, from pillar to post, exactly as he promised he would. Before the match Ken Shamrock is crying and whining about how The Rock is going to enlist the help of the Nation to win this match. Well, The Rock has already made it clear that the Nation will remain in the background——The Rock doesn't need any help. And that's precisely the way it happens. The Rock is by himself, just the way Ken Shamrock wanted it, and just the way The Rock likes it. And The Rock simply beats the pants off Ken Shamrock for more than twenty minutes and retains the Intercontinental title.

But that's not all. As soon as he's through punishing Ken Shamrock for his insolence, The Rock throws his hat in the ring for *The Royal Rumble*. He gets no rest, either. The Rock is the fourth man in the ring, which means there are twenty-six other jabronis coming down, gunning for The Rock. He's got the bull's-eye on his chest, he's got the Brahma Bull tattooed on his right arm. (The Rock has been digging bulls from Day One. He's a Taurus, you see, so it's part of his makeup. He especially likes Brahma Bulls. If you go inside The Rock's office, you'll see a big Brahma Bull skull, complete with teeth and all. One day The Rock said, "Let's go ahead and put a Brahma Bull on The Rock's arm, complete with The People's Eyebrow. Complete with red eyes. See, the Brahma Bull is synonymous with The Rock, because he does exactly what a Brahma Bull does, and that's stomp the living piss out of everything that walks. The Brahma Bull spits on people, he snots on people ... the Brahma Bull *shits* on people, and that's exactly what The Rock does ... without giving a damn.) The Rock is facing a monumental challenge, but he's more than up to the task. He stays in that ring for damn near an hour, but hey, that's okay. The Rock could stay in there for ten hours, because when you're an athlete like The Rock, a gem like The Rock, a diamond like The Rock, exhaustion doesn't concern you. The Rock is a finely tuned machine, and he's more than capable of laying the smack down on every single roody-poo stupid enough to enter the ring against him. And that's what he does in *The Royal Rumble*. He kicks ass for an hour, wiping the mat with one loser after another, until, finally, at the very end, who's left in the ring?

Just two men: The Rock and Stone Cold Steve Austin. Again!

This, obviously, is an electrifying moment—it's always an electrifying moment when The Rock is standing in the spotlight. Having Stone Cold Steve Austin there beside him only makes it better. The Rock then proceeds not only to start pounding his dusty, trailer-park ass but to talk shit while he's doing it. That's something no one else can do. It's been scientifically proven: no one can talk shit and whoop ass like The Rock. It's genetically impossible. In the end, though, Stone Cold Steve Austin ends up cheating (the details escape The Rock's memory—that happens when you've administered so many beatings to so many jabronis) and tosses The Rock over the top rope and wins *The Royal Rumble*.

The thing about *The Royal Rumble* is . . . it's not like there's a $50,000 prize waiting for the winner. The reward for winning *The Royal Rumble* is that you automatically become the number one contender for the World Wrestling Federation title, and you are guaranteed an opportunity to face the champion, whoever that may be, at *WrestleMania*. So now Stone Cold Steve Austin is going to *WrestleMania* instead of The Rock. That doesn't make The Rock happy—he was planning to go to *WrestleMania* and take his size-13 foot, turn it sideways, and stick it straight up Shawn Michaels's candy ass. The Rock was eager to teach the paper champion a lesson. But that's cool. That's okay. As always, The Rock is a man and a half. He puts *The Royal Rumble* behind him. Like the pile of dirt that he is, Stone Cold Steve Austin is swept under The Rock's rug.

WRESTLEMANIA XIV

March 29, 1998 (Boston, MA)—Everybody loves *WrestleMania*, right? It's the biggest show of the year, and it draws people from all walks of life, from the brightest of stars to the dimmest of bulbs. And this year they're all here to see The Rock. Before his Intercontinental Championship match against Ken Shamrock, The Rock receives an interview request from none other than Gennifer Flowers, one-time side dish of The People's President, William Jefferson Clinton. Essentially, Gennifer wants a piece of The Rock . . . she wants a BIG piece of The Rock—i*f you smell what The Rock is cooking*. And you can't blame her one bit, because, after all, The Rock is the one who told Bill: "Hey, listen, man . . . you can't be silly—you gotta cover your Willie!" Now, whether ol' Bill listened to The Rock, well, that's another story. The point is this: Gennifer and The Rock go back a bit, so The Rock feels something of an obligation to grant her request and conduct The People's Interview in front of the millions and the millions of The Rock's fans.

   GF: I'm here with the Intercontinental Champion—
   The Rock: Whoa, actually, Genny, it's *The People's* Intercontinental Champion.
   GF: Excuse me . . . The People's Intercontinental Champion, The Rock. Now, Rock, the people want to know—if you were the leader of this country, how would you run things?

The Rock: Well, actually, Genny, The Rock feels like this. First and foremost, the term "leader" is really beneath The Rock. The Rock feels like a more appropriate term would be . . . "ruler."

GF: Okay, if you were the ruler, how would you handle the homeless situation?

The Rock: I'll tell you what, Genny, that's a touchy subject for The Rock, the homeless situation in America. The Rock feels like this: as long as The Rock still has his palatial palace down on South Beach in Miami, Florida, he really couldn't give a damn whether they live in a Frigidaire box or a Kenmore box. As long as those homeless pieces of trash keep their cardboard boxes off The Rock's freshly mowed grass, everything will be copacetic.

GF: Well, how about the judicial system?

The Rock: Well, first and foremost, as long as all The Rock's fans across the country realize that The Rock is the judge and the jury, everything should be fine. Actually, after The Rock has contemplated that for a second, if The Rock *were* the jury, nine times out of ten he'd be a *hung* jury . . . *if you smell what The Rock is cooking.*

GF: How would you run the White House?

The Rock: Tough job, tough question. But The Rock of course is up to answering it. The Rock feels like this: As long as all the interns in the White House, beneath The Rock, knew their damn role, and they didn't get out of hand, step out of line, and they didn't do anything orally wrong—excuse me, Genny—*morally* wrong, then The Rock wouldn't have to do what he does best, and that's lay the smack down in a major way. Thank you very much, Genny.

Later on that evening, The Rock peels off his $500 Versace shirt and his $200 shades and, once again, lays the smack down on Ken Shamrock. The Rock beats that pile of monkey crap to within an inch of his sorry, pathetic life, proving, once and for all, that The Rock is not only the greatest Intercontinental Champion in the history of wrestling but the coolest thing since the other side of the pillow!

HUMILIATION OF THE NATION

April–May, 1998—By this time The Rock is a true Superstar, touring all over the country, wanted in every city and every town for personal appearances and demonstrations of athletic and theatrical prowess. There aren't enough hours in the day for The Rock to fulfill all of his commitments. And not only is The Rock followed by the legions, by the millions . . . and the millions of his fans, not only is he the most compelling champion in the World Wrestling Federation, but all of a sudden The Rock is having to carry these jabronis in the Nation on his shoulders. Now, The Rock has big shoulders, so The Rock doesn't usually mind a little extra work, but any time you've got a group of guys, and in the middle of that group—check that—at the *front* of that group is a gem, a diamond, a jewel like The Rock, you're bound to have some jealousy. You're bound to have some animosity. And that's exactly what has happened within the Nation. These guys are getting jealous of The Rock. They see The Rock's success—by this time The Rock is making millions of dollars and receiving the adoration and respect of fans all over the planet—and they don't like it. Especially their leader, a guy by the name of Faarooq.

Now, The Rock really couldn't give three quarts of rhinoceros piss about Faarooq, but sometimes it's important to let everyone know who's boss. So The Rock sets Faarooq straight, once and for all, on national television. The Rock presents $15,000 gold

Rolex watches to each member of the Nation, ostensibly to show his gratitude and respect. But for Faarooq, The Rock has something else in mind, something special. He gives Faarooq a big color portrait of The Rock. Why? To show his appreciation for everything Faarooq has done for the Nation. Of course, Faarooq has never done anything for The Rock. But that's okay. The Rock doesn't need help from anyone, especially from a guy like Faarooq. So instead of a Rolex (and by the way, what the hell is a Rolex watch to The Rock? Fifteen thousand dollars? Come on! That's one night's pay for The Rock—and that's a bad night!), The Rock decides to blow up a big picture of himself holding the Intercontinental title belt, a belt The Rock made pretty famous, and he presents it to Faarooq in a gesture of camaraderie and sportsmanship.

You would think that son of a bitch would appreciate The Rock's gift. But no! Not for one second! Faarooq just snarls at The Rock's stunning visage and punches a hole in it with his fist. Well, that's when The Rock realizes that Faarooq is just sick with jealousy . . . he's bleeding envy, and that's not conducive to a healthy relationship. So The Rock has to cancel Faarooq's contract, so to speak. He raises his big right hand and says, "Faarooq, you've got about three seconds—*and The Rock . . . means . . . three . . . seconds*—before The Rock lays the smack down on your candy ass."

And The Rock begins to count:

"One . . . two . . ."

By now it's obvious that Faarooq is too stubborn for his own good. He's holding his ground. The Rock balls his hand into a mighty fist and . . .

" . . . Three!"

WHAM!

The Rock smacks Faarooq across his ugly forehead, sending him crashing to the mat. Damn near knocks him out. The other members of the Nation intercede and prevent The Rock from

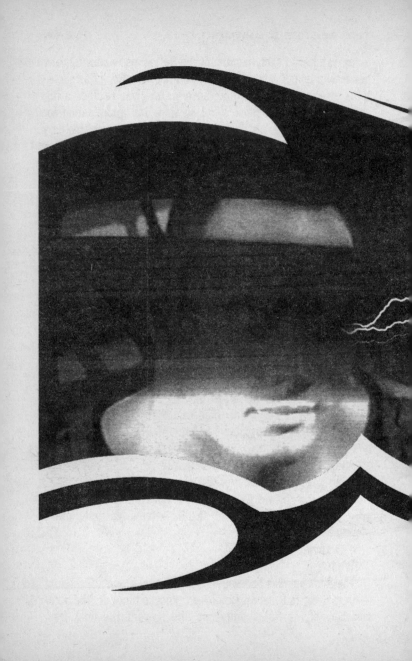

annihilating Faarooq on the spot. Now, in our industry, in the fabulous world of sports-entertainment, after something like that happens you're bound to have a Pay-Per-View match, and that's exactly what happened. The Rock goes out, and like the true champion he is, he disposes of Faarooq to retain his Intercontinental title and take his rightful place as leader of the Nation.

LAYETH THE SMACKETH DOWN!

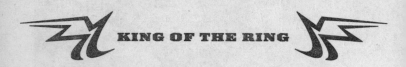 KING OF THE RING

June 28, 1998 (Pittsburgh, PA)—*King of the Ring* is a true test of The Rock's strength and spirit and greatness, not only because he has to beat three men in one night on Pay-Per-View, but because just two weeks earlier he underwent surgery to repair a torn knee ligament. There is not a man in this industry who will sacrifice his body like that. But The Rock will, because The Rock is The People's Champion, the true champion. And now he's in *King of the Ring*, whipping the living crap out of this jabroni and that jabroni. The Rock's semifinal victim is Dan "The Beast" Severn, who goes down, *one-two-three*, right in the middle of the ring. It's a meaningful loss for Severn because it's the first loss of his career, but that doesn't make it anything special to The Rock—hell, The Rock doesn't care who he beats.

So it's on to the finals, and here comes Ken Shamrock one more time. Here's a guy who's doing all he possibly can to bask in the glow of The Rock. It's not enough that The Rock has beaten Ken Shamrock senseless two or three times already. And not just on Pay-Per-View, but on *Raw Is War*. In front of the millions ... and the millions of The Rock's fans, The Rock took a steel chair and planted it dead smack in Ken Shamrock's face, knocked him unconscious, knocked him into tomorrow. The Rock played a Hank Aaron on Ken Shamrock, tried to knock his head over the centerfield bleachers. Some people said The Rock went too far that night. Well, you know what The Rock says? The Rock says ... anytime you get into the ring with The Rock, and you're on your knees, and you do a motion with your hand that says, "Bring it on, baby!" Well, you're asking for trouble, because no one can bring it like The Rock. And that night, on national television, The Rock brung it all right ... he brung it right into Ken Shamrock's brain.

And now he's ready to do it again, if need be. For thirty-five minutes in the *King of the Ring* final, The Rock and Ken Shamrock try to tear each other apart. Finally, the impossible happens: The Rock makes a mistake, and Ken Shamrock puts an ankle-lock submission on The Rock, and The Rock taps out in the middle of the ring. Ken Shamrock is the new King of the Ring, 1998. Well, that's just damn wonderful for Ken Shamrock, who starts running around the ring like a little baboon, jumping up and down like it's Christmas morning and he just got his favorite choo-choo train. He's bouncing all over the place like being King of the Ring really means a flying fuck to The Rock. *Ken Shamrock is* King of the Ring—*well, whoop-de-doo, let the celebration begin! Pop some champagne for Ken Shamrock!* Meanwhile, they're playing Ken Shamrock's crappy music over the PA system, some hideous cross between the *Sesame Street* theme and a Doris Day song. Fine, let him jump around all night, because over in the corner, leaving the ring, is The Rock. And in his left hand he's holding something. What is it? Could it be? We can't really get a good glimpse of it, and then it's in focus, and ... yes! It's the Intercontinental title belt! Ken Shamrock can have King of the Ring. The Rock is still the Intercontinental Champ!

 **"SUMMERSLAM"**

August 30, 1998 (New York, NY)—It's August. It's hot (just like The Rock). It's time for the *SummerSlam* ladder match. And, of course, it should be called *The Rock Slam* because this is another Pay-Per-View made famous by The Great One. (Incidentally, The Rock is the only true Great One. Let's not talk about that other guy, the hockey player, because The Rock asks you: who the hell did he ever beat?!) The Rock is taking on a long-haired candy ass named Hunter Hearst Helmsley, "Triple H" for short. And short is what his career is going to be if he keeps trying to pull stunts like this. You see, Triple H shows up at Madison Square Garden, The Rock's home away from home, dressed up like The Rock. He has felt sideburns taped to the side of his head. He's wearing an ugly hairpiece. All in all, he looks like a pumped-up lounge lizard doing an Elvis impersonation at a third-rate Las Vegas hotel.

They say imitation is the most sincere form of flattery. But then again, when you're a goof, a candy ass, a nobody, a nothing like Triple H, and you're trying to imitate The Rock, that's far from flattering. And anyway, as Triple H is about to find out, there ain't nobody—and The Rock means nobody!—who could ever be like The Rock. But Triple H keeps running his mouth. He obviously wants his monkey ass to be famous. He's obviously seen how The Rock has taken each and every one of these jabronis and raised them up to The Rock's level—for a while, anyway—each time he's whipped their asses. From Stone Cold Steve Austin to Ken Shamrock to Dan Severn . . . the list goes on and on.

Now it's Triple H's turn. The Rock beats him like the punk that he is for thirty-five, forty minutes. The Rock is doing precisely what he said he was going to do, and that's climb The People's Ladder, rung by damn rung, and grab the title belt. He's near the top, about to snatch the title, with twenty thousand fans screaming "ROCKY! ROCKY!" when guess what happens? All of a sudden, out of nowhere, comes Chyna, Triple H's little sidekick. She climbs up the ladder, sneaks right up behind The Rock, who is justifiably exhausted, and hauls off and nails The Rock right between the legs, smacks him square in the nuts. Well, then The Rock does the only thing he can do, and that's grab The People's Jewels and fall off the ladder in pain. Which, of course, allows Triple H to scurry up the ladder like a rat and steal the title.

That's fine. Once again The Rock is a man and a half. He calls a spade a spade and Triple H the winner. But did Triple H beat The Rock clean? In the middle of the ring? *One-two-three?* Absolutely not! Did Chyna smack The Rock right in The People's

Jewels, helping Triple H to snatch the belt? Yeah, that's the way it happened. Essentially, Triple H cheated his way into a title. But the fact of the matter is this: Triple H leaves with a belt, but The Rock walks out proudly with something even more important, something bigger and better than any title on God's Green Earth.

The Rock walks out of Madison Square Garden, *SummerSlam*, 1998...as The People's Champion!

The 4J Annual Psychodrama Frames Awards

"THE ROCK"

THE GOOD, THE BAD...

chapter 12

THE UGLY

FAME IS A FUNNY thing, especially when it comes on you like a thunderstorm. Three years ago I was nearly broke. I could walk down the street without anyone recognizing me. Now that's all changed. Dany and I have accepted the fact that we can no longer go to the movies anytime we want, or go shopping anytime we want. It's always a calculated decision to go out in public. If we go to the mall, it's within the first thirty minutes after it's opened, or the last thirty minutes before it closes, when we know the fewest people will be there. Every trip has to be carefully planned.

My needs are not extravagant. I spend a lot of my

time in shorts, basketball shoes, and T-shirts. But The Rock likes his clothes; The Rock *needs* his $500 Versace shirts, his $300 shoes, his Rolex watch. It's part of the image. I buy all of my "Rock" gear at a store called Lucky's in Miami. It's a very small shop that deals only in the finest apparel. When I walk in, I'm often besieged by fans who want autographs, handshakes, just a moment of The Rock's time. The owner is more than willing to close the shop for me, and in fact we even tried that once, but it only made the situation worse. When people realize that a store is closed, especially during normal working hours, they know that something unusual is going on. They start gathering around the window, staring, pointing, speculating. Pretty soon there's a mob outside.

The kids in my neighborhood have figured out where I live, so now we have a steady stream of wide-eyed young fans banging on the door, typically five or six a day. When I answer they usually look at me, smile mischievously, and then say something like, "Ummmmm . . . is Jimmy home?"

"No Jimmy here, man."

"Okay . . . see ya!"

I've thought about going into character—*"The Rock says . . . 'Keep bangin' on that door and The Rock's gonna lay the smack down on your candy ass!'"*—but that would probably just increase the flow of traffic. And, sometimes, the visits are genuinely moving. One kid, for example, likes to draw pictures for me. He stops by approximately once a week to drop them off. If I have a big match coming up, he'll write a few words of encouragement, like "Lay the smack down on Austin."

It's a balancing act, this business of handling fame. Dany and I have the resources now to buy a nice house, and that's what we're doing. We'll be moving soon to a gated community, which will afford us a measure of privacy and a respite from the madness once in a while. Don't get me wrong, though. I am immensely grateful for my success. There are a lot of guys in the NFL—even All-Pros—who don't make as much money as the top tier of performers in the World Wrestling Federation. When you've slept on soiled mattresses and subsisted largely on a diet of spaghetti and free submarine sandwiches, you tend to appreciate a good paycheck. And I love interacting with fans. I know they are the backbone of our industry and that without them I would not have a job. I

still find it flattering when someone comes up to me and asks for my autograph, just sticks out a scrap of paper and asks me to sign it. I mean, what could you possibly do with that? Knowing that someone might take it home and frame it or put it in a special box on top of their dresser . . . to me that's just a very humbling experience. And I feel the same way when I see Rock action figures and dolls . . . when I see my likeness on video games and lunch boxes and almost anything else you can imagine.

Does the good outweigh the bad? Absolutely. It's not even close. That's why I'll never understand anyone in this industry, or in any aspect of the entertainment or sports industry, who refuses to sign autographs. I see it all too often in our business, guys who don't take the time to sign autographs and talk with the fans. I try to accommodate as many people as I possibly can. It's becoming increasingly difficult, because the character of The Rock has become so popular in the past year, but I try to remember that the fans are not an annoyance. They're the only reason we're here. All I ask is that when I'm in a restaurant, eating dinner, please wait until I've finished eating. Then I'll be happy to sign. It's my nature to be courteous. Anyone who knows me will tell you that I'm very accommodating when it comes to signing autographs, especially for little kids. I love seeing the looks on their faces, the smiles. Why anyone would want to avoid that response, or ignore it, I don't know. How anyone could insult the people who admire them the most is a mystery to me. And quite frankly I find it sickening.

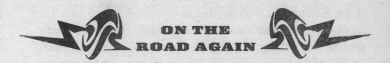

ON THE ROAD AGAIN

I don't mean to imply that being a professional wrestler is easy. It's not. There is an extraordinary amount of hard work involved, and the life can and does exact a toll. I'm amazed at the number of people I meet who think I only work on the days and nights they see me on television. And they are equally amazed when I tell them that every other day that they don't see me, I'm working. At some arena, in some city ... I'm working. I spend approximately 225 days a year on the road. That can put a strain on any relationship. Fortunately, my wife has been wonderfully understanding and supportive. She knew when she married me that we would have to make tremendous sacrifices in our relationship. But that doesn't make it any less difficult.

One of my favorite singers is Willie Nelson, the ageless living legend. One of his best lyrics is "The night life ain't no good life, but it's my life." I often find myself singing that, especially when I'm sitting alone in a hotel room at 3:00 A.M., trying to wind down after a show. There's a huge misconception about life on the road. People think, "God, this guy is a millionaire and he travels all over the world and he has a great, glamorous life." Well, I am *not* complaining about my life, believe me. I love being an entertainer and I love making the fans happy, and I love earning a good living. I've been blessed and I'm very fortunate. But at the same time I feel like I'm earning every dollar. I don't believe there are many people who can fathom the rigors of life on the road.

Want to know what it's like? Okay . . . here is my itinerary from a typical first day on the road:

12:00 noon—Drive to Miami International Airport. I've already packed, worked out for two hours, and had a farewell lunch with Dany.

1:30 P.M.—Flight leaves for Dallas. When you reach a certain level with the World Wrestling Federation, you get to fly first-class, which is a nice perk.

4:00 P.M.—Arrive in Dallas. I head straight to the rental counter, pick up my car, and drive to the hotel. I check in, find a place to eat, and then drive to the arena.

6:30 P.M.—Arrive at Arena. I drop off my bags, chat with one of the wrestlers' agents about the night's activities, and then go to work. At almost every show there is some sort of meet-and-greet with a group of fans. It's usually sponsored by a local radio or television station, and the winners receive a chance to shake hands with The Rock. Typically, the meet-

and-greet is the first item on the agenda after I arrive.

7:30 P.M.—**More fuel.** Everyone who knows me well knows that I have to eat every few hours. My metabolism is like a furnace. So, I always order a second meal—to go—when I'm having dinner; I'll eat it later at the arena.

8:00 P.M.—**Match preparation.** Time to discuss strategy with my opponent. If it's someone with whom I've never worked, we have a lot to discuss. If it's someone with whom I have a long history, like Mankind or Steve Austin, the preparation isn't quite as intense. We know each other's moves and tendencies. Since the story line has been set and the outcome determined, it's usually just a matter of sitting down and discussing tweaks and changes that need to be made. And making sure that when the music hits, I'm ready to go out there and give the best performance I possibly can, to send those people home happy.

8:30 P.M.—**Suiting up.** Oddly enough, I usually take a shower before I work. One of the guys, Kane, likes to tease me about that. "God, Rock, you haven't learned the system yet," he'll say. "You're supposed to shower *after* your match." And then I'll jokingly reply, "Well, you know why I do this?"

"Why?"

"Because I'm *The Rock!*"

Then, of course, it's a matter of putting on the boots and putting on the trunks and the elbow pads. And a little bit of baby oil to give the body a nice sheen under the lights.

9:00 P.M.—**Getting pumped.** The exact time of my match varies from night to night, from show to show. In the minutes leading up to my entrance, however, the routine is always the same. One of the last items on the checklist is a series of push-ups, just to get the blood pumping and the adrenaline flowing—and to give the muscles a bit of a rip before going out onstage. Then I say a little prayer, thanking the Good Lord for all the blessings he's given me in my life.

9:15 P.M.—Showtime! Every night, regardless of whether there are three hundred people, three thousand people, or thirty thousand people in the building, the rush is always there. My heart is racing, my skin is tingling. And then my music hits! *"Do you smell what The Rock is cooking? The Rock says . . . The Rock says . . ."* I'm still a football player at heart in a lot of ways; I got goose bumps whenever I took the field at the Orange Bowl. But I'll tell you . . . there is absolutely nothing that compares to hearing my music, hearing an audience erupt, hearing everyone singing along, chanting The Rock's name. And it's just The Rock—I'm not sharing the spotlight with ten other guys, the way you do on a football field, and I don't have a helmet on. It's The Rock and The People's Eyebrow and the sideburns. It's electric!

9:45 P.M.—Analysis. After the match my adrenaline is still pumping. I'm sweating profusely and I'm completely geeked. When I start to calm down, the first thing I do is get together with Jack Lanza, one of our agents, and talk about the match. Jack has helped me tremendously in my career. As I was coming up through the ranks, regardless of whether I was the main event or not, Jack was always there for me, every night, after every match, eager to sit down and go over everything in detail. I have complete faith in Jack's opinion and judgment. He's a no-bullshit kind of guy, always tells it like it is, and that's a quality I greatly respect and appreciate.

10:30 P.M.—Departure. After chatting with Jack, I shower, dress, and leave. I'm almost always the last guy out of the arena at night. Now that it's getting quiet, I like to take my time, think about the night and the match. A lot of fans hang around outside, so Jim Dotson, head of World Wrestling Federation security, always waits for me to make sure I'm taken care of and have a police escort.

11:00 P.M.—Still more fuel. I have to eat again after the show. If I'm in a city where I know I can get some steak or chicken breast at this hour, I'll go out for a meal. If not I'll just go back to the hotel and order room service.

12:30 A.M.—Still more fuel (different kind). After my late-night dinner I'll go to the nearest gas station and gas up the car, because I'll be leaving early the next morning. I'll have a 7:00 A.M. flight, or I'll be driving a couple hundred miles to the next city on the tour.

1:00 A.M.—Tube and talk. When I get back to my hotel room, I give Dany a call and we chat about the day. Then I turn on the television, kick back, and relax. I'll usually go through about a gallon of bottled water before I sleep, just to make sure I don't get dehydrated. Around 3:00 A.M., I doze off.

6:00 A.M.—Wake-up call! The alarm sounds. Time for another day.

The schedule varies from day to day, city to city. There may be more promotional obligations, for example. Radio and TV spots. Any number of contractual responsibilities, including personal appearances. Basically, though, that's a typical day. Once in a while I'll go out and have a drink after a match, just kind of chill out and relax. But I don't do it often. I'm not saying I'm an angel. God knows when I was in college I used to do my fair share of partying. I went out damn near every night. I drank and got drunk, just like a lot of other college kids. When you reach a certain level in this industry, though, a couple of things happen. You have to make decisions and you have to make sacrifices and you have to make commitments. Each individual performer has to set his own parameters. For me it means making sure that I'm doing all I can to be the best. Period.

There are a lot of demons in this business. I saw them firsthand when I was growing up, and I see them now. If you're a successful, famous professional wrestler, the forbidden fruit is within easy reach. The groupies are there. The women are *always* there. And the availability is high. It's easy to go out and get laid. It's easy to go out and get drugs. It's easy to go out and drink. I don't condemn other guys for doing that. I will never, ever pass judgment. You live your life how you deem appropriate. I'll do the same. But I think I know the demons and pitfalls better than most people because of the world in which I was raised. I know that forbidden fruit can be sweet, and that if you're not careful, you'll eat way too much of it. I saw what alcohol did to my father. I saw what cocaine did to other people. One of the things I'm proud of is that I have never tried cocaine. I've never even tried marijuana. That doesn't make me better than anyone else—it's just how I choose to live my life.

At this point in my career, going out to a busy club or a bar is usually more trouble than it's worth. If The Rock is hanging out in a bar at 2:00 A.M., he's practically asking to be hassled. Anyway, I have a hard enough time getting up early in the morning after four or five hours of sleep without battling the effects of a hangover. It takes all of my energy to stay focused every day, to concentrate on working out, eating right, and being the best performer I can be. But I don't want to sound like some kind of martyr. It's not like I have to work really hard at *not* going out. That's just not me. Not anymore. Nor am I suggesting that to be a top guy in this industry you have to live the way I do. That's not true either. There are top guys in this business who go out almost every night. That's their way of relaxing and having fun. *God bless you and more power to you.* But Dwayne Johnson's idea of having fun, especially on the road, consists of having a good meal and watching a movie, and just trying to relax.

I listen to a lot of music when I'm traveling, too, and my tastes are pretty eclectic. I really enjoy R&B, blues, and gospel. On Sunday mornings, wherever I am, I have to find a gospel station. And the greatest gospel singer of all time, in my opinion, is Sam Cooke. To me, there is just none better. If you check out my CD collection, you'll also find a lot of Al Green, Marvin Gaye, and Luther Vandross.

On long car trips, though, there's nothing like country music, especially the lonesome sound of the steel guitar. Man, you hear that in the middle of the night, when you're driving along some soulless interstate, and it'll just about break your heart. In addition to Willie Nelson, I like George Jones, Merle Haggard, and George Strait. These guys know all about life on the road. They know how lonely and exhausting it can be. I'm a lucky man. Without the Good Lord above and the love of my wife and family, I'd probably be living proof of the music I enjoy so much.

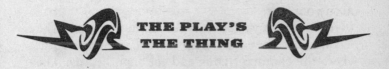

THE PLAY'S THE THING

Surviving and thriving in this business requires more than talent and ambition. This is a strange and wonderful world in which we live, and it takes time to figure out how to deal with the quirks and peculiarities. One of the things that never ceases to amaze me is the consistent hypocrisy exhibited by some wrestlers. There are some guys who reach a level of success and then claim to have it all figured out. They like to boast of their knowledge of the business. And yet, they'll turn around and refuse to help someone else, either by refusing to drop the belt, or refusing to put someone over . . . refusing to do a job! And I want to make something clear here: This sort of behavior happens a lot. You might think that because professional wrestling has become a bigger and more professionally run business, with much more at stake, there would be fewer opportunities for this sort of thing to happen. But that's not the case.

I'm not suggesting that a guy will refuse to lose and therefore turn a work into a real fight. It's not as simple as that. I mean these are all grown men who earn a very good living. But there are many ways you can lose. You can go out there and bust your ass and make the people go fucking bananas, and then put

someone over—*one-two-three!*—in the middle of the
ring . . . or you can lay on your ass and let everyone
know how unhappy you are. Or you can lose through
a disqualification, in which case you will get to hang
on to your belt.

Too many guys get wrapped up in the hype. They
become consumed by their own ego. They forget
where the character ends and the man begins. They
become the character. I'll be the first to admit this is
an occupational hazard, because a key ingredient in
any successful character is making sure the acorn
doesn't fall far from the tree. In other words, I believe
the character has to hit close to home. You see that
with Dwayne Johnson and The Rock. The Rock is
me . . . taken to an outrageous level. But I do know
where the line is and I don't cross it. I would never say
to the kid bagging my groceries at Publix, *"Hurry up,
you load of monkey crap!"* But some guys blur that
line. Their egos get completely out of control, to the
point where they actually start to believe they're legitimate stars. Well, what constitutes being a star?
Because twenty thousand people have paid to see you,
along with twenty other people, on a wrestling card?
Please . . . This business that we are in is the business
of theater, and it is a collaborative effort like any
other theatrical endeavor. You are no bigger than the
business decides to make you, and you look only as
good as your opponent allows you to look.

I'm proud to say that I heard that message, and
accepted it, very early in my career. As a heel, I knew
that Steve Austin's comeback would only be as good
as I could make it. So I told myself, *I will fly, and I
will have him kick the living shit out of me, for as
long as I can keep these people up.* To me, there is no

better feeling than that. Growing up in this business I learned an important lesson: You work for one thing—a reaction. And I will get a reaction from the crowd in any way I can. It doesn't matter whether I'm winning or losing. That's not the point. I was surprised by the number of people who didn't seem to realize this when I was coming up in the business, guys who didn't necessarily refuse to help me but who certainly laid on their asses while helping me—while *saying* they were helping me. I got the sense that they were thinking, *Jesus, this guy has only been in the company for a year, and now I've got to put him over?!* I got a lot of jealousy, some professional, some personal. The professional jealousy I sort of understood, because you get that in any venture in life. But the personal jealousy baffled me because, even to this day, I am very selective about who I get close to. A lot of the guys who were personally jealous of me never even really knew me. And they still don't.

In part because of some of the animosity I encountered, I have made it a point to help any new guy coming in, as long as he wants my help. And not simply because I want to be a nice guy. If I can help someone one day reach my level of success, I'm a firm believer that it will only benefit me in the long run. If the new guy can generate $50 million in revenue for a Pay-Per-View, that's going to be good for the World Wrestling Federation, and that means it's good for me. I'm secure in the position I have within the company, and in my talent. You can never keep talent down, so the more talented a group we have, the better. To me, that's just sound business.

I'm not the only one who feels this way, of course. There are other top performers in the business who

IT DOESN'T MAT

R WHAT YOUR NAME IS!

are equally secure and confident. Not coincidentally, they're also the ones who were most generous toward me while I was coming up through the ranks.

Bret Hart, for example. Bret, as I've said, went out of his way to help me, to take me under his wing. This was a guy who was at the pinnacle of his career. He was the World Wrestling Federation champion. And yet he was thoughtful enough to help me in and out of the ring, even though I hadn't even been in the business for a year.

Steve Austin has been equally generous. Here's a guy who is, at this moment, the biggest box office draw in the history of professional wrestling. And yet, he has gone out of his way, time and again, to help me out. His professionalism and strength of character have made it possible for The Rock to become one of the biggest stars the World Wrestling Federation has ever known. The incredible ascension of The Rock can be attributed directly to his intense rivalry with Stone Cold Steve Austin and the excitement of their matches. That hasn't happened by accident. If Steve Austin doesn't want The Rock to look good, then The Rock doesn't look good. Period.

It's interesting that three of the men who have shown me the most professional respect and personal kindness are also three of the biggest names in the business. You never see the petty jealousy from these guys that you see from performers at a lower level. And that's no coincidence. These are guys who are secure in their talent, in the knowledge that they have accomplished great things in the business, and that they will continue to accomplish great things. It's a testament to their understanding of the business and to them as people that they were able to look at me

and say, "This guy has some talent and a decent attitude. I'll help this son of a bitch because some day,
down the line, he's going to help me." It's encouraging to me that there are people like Bret Hart, Steve
Austin, and the Undertaker in our industry.

There was a very specific incident that demonstrated to me exactly what kind of a man the
Undertaker is. It was while I was teetering at the
upper edge of the second tier, getting ready to leap to
the top tier. The Rock was on the border of super-
stardom, within a breath of reaching a level of success
that only a handful of wrestlers attain. The
Undertaker, of course, was already there, and he was
my opponent on this particular edition of *Raw*. We
were in Detroit, at Cobo Arena, and the decision had
been made that I was going to win the match. So, in
essence, my fate was in the hands of the Undertaker.
He had the opportunity, all by himself, to propel me
to the next level . . . to reach down and pull me up
alongside him. He also had the power to make me
look mediocre. The Undertaker would never deliber-
ately go out there and make someone look like complete shit, because he's a consummate professional.
He's too smart a businessman to do something like
that, which is one reason he's been so successful. But
he did have other options. He could easily have said,
"Well, let's have The Rock beat me via disqualification." He could have said, "Have The Rock hit me
with a chair, knock me out cold." That way everyone
would have said, "The Rock had to use a chair to
beat the Undertaker." It was entirely up to him. All
that had been determined was the outcome: The Rock
would win, the Undertaker would lose. How we
would arrive at that point was up to the Undertaker.

His decision was to put me over clean—*one-two-three!*—in the middle of the ring. Not only that, but he decided it would be best if the Undertaker was beaten by The Rock's signature move, The Rock Bottom. That would ensure maximum exposure for The Rock and maximum entertainment for the crowd. It made me realize what a true professional this guy is. I will never forget meeting the Undertaker before the match and saying, "Man, I just heard it's going to be a clean finish. Are you comfortable with that? Are you sure you want to do that?"

He looked at me and said, without hesitation, "Absolutely. It's your turn and it's your time."

Having grown up in the business, and having seen business conducted that way . . . and not conducted that way . . . I couldn't help but be moved by such an impressive gesture. It really wasn't possible for me to thank him enough, but I tried anyway.

"Somewhere down the road I'll have the opportunity to do the same for you," I said. "And I want you to know . . . I'll do it in a heartbeat."

chapter 13

KNOW YOUR ROLE!

It's interesting the way things begin to take a turn for The People's Champ after *SummerSlam*, 1998. The fans actually begin cheering for The Rock (not that he cares). They admire The Rock. They treasure The Rock. You can't blame them, of course. The Rock's talent is so obvious, so awesome, that even if you don't like The Rock, you can't help but find him mesmerizing. Hell, you can't hold talent down. That's a proven fact. There's no stopping what can't be stopped. Like the cream that The Rock is, he's rising straight to the top of the World Wrestling Federation! The fans aren't stupid. They look at The Rock, with his washboard stomach, his perfect mocha complexion, his penetrating gaze, and his magnificent athletic ability, and they realize: *Hey, This isn't just some loser standing on the corner of Jabroni Drive and Know Your Role Boulevard. This guy has what it takes. This is a guy who will spill his blood for us. This is a guy who will risk everything. This guy is more than just the most recognizable face in North America. He's more than just the most electrifying man in sports-entertainment. This guy is bigger than our dreams. He's bigger than our ambitions. This guy is ... The Rock!*

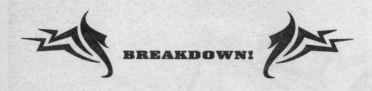

BREAKDOWN!

September 27, 1998—You think you can scare The Rock by throwing a match at him with just twenty minutes' notice? Come on! The Rock can wake from a dead slumber and still smack the yellow off the teeth of any jabroni in the business. The Rock is *always* ready. So when Mankind and Ken Shamrock get a little hair across their asses and decide they want to go two-on-one with The Rock . . . well, The Rock says, *"Show me what you've got, baby!"* These two jabronis figure they'll team up on The Rock— you know, *two minds are better than one.* But not when one of the minds belongs to Ken Shamrock and the other belongs to Mankind. Together, they're a half-wit, at best. So The Rock, fearless guy that he is, accepts the challenge and tells Mankind and Ken Shamrock that he's going to pull their eyelids over their heads and kick their candy asses all over the ring. And that's exactly what he does. The Rock goes thirty-five, forty minutes in a steel cage. He even survives a gash to The People's Eyebrow! These jabronis cut The Rock, and The People's Blood is flowing from The People's Champ, and he's tasting The People's Blood! But like the heroic figure he is, The Rock endures it all and walks out of the ring the same way he walked in: as the one true champion.

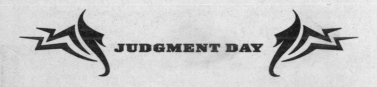

JUDGMENT DAY

October 18, 1998 (Chicago, IL)—Now it's time for The Rock to lay a little smack down on another fat-ass jabroni, a guy by the name of Mark Henry. A big Olympian, Mr. all-America. Well, whoop-de-fucking-doo! Raise the flag and fire the cannons. Let's have a big parade for Mark Henry. The Rock couldn't care less, which is why he promises to take those Olympic medals and shove them straight up Mark Henry's cottage-cheese ass! And when the bell rings, The Rock does what he does best: *Hit, stick, and bust dick!* And what else? *Talk shit!* What else!? *Talk shit!* Can you hear what The Rock is saying? Mark Henry sure as hell hears it, because The Rock, the master of elocution, is delivering a Shakespearean soliloquy even as he's ripping Mark Henry apart. The Rock, a man and a half, is talking trash to this half a man. And in the middle of the ring, as he's stomping the Wheaties out of Mr. Olympic champion, The Rock says, "Hey, listen. It's obvious you're going to get your butt kicked, so it's entirely up to you. You can prove to everyone here that you know your role by leaving the ring now, *without* The Rock's foot up your ass, or you can hang around a little longer and leave *with* The Rock's foot up your ass. So Mark Henry decides to stay, and The

THE ROCK IS COOKIN'?

Rock proceeds to make him regret the day his mama crapped out his slimy little body.

Much to The Rock's chagrin, however, a jabroni named D'Lo Brown, one of Mark Henry's teammates in the Nation, decides to interfere with the match. From ringside he pins The Rock's legs to the mat and helps Mark Henry win the match. But that's all right with The Rock, because once again he proves that he's too much for any single man, to say nothing of a eunuch like Mark Henry.

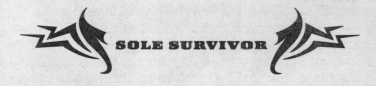

SOLE SURVIVOR

November 15, 1998 (St. Louis, MO)—With November comes Thanksgiving, a time for the millions . . . and the millions of The Rock's fans to give thanks to the hardest working man in sports-entertainment. This year The Rock's fans are especially appreciative, for The Rock is taking part in the *Survivor Series*, with the World Wrestling Federation title on the line. It's one of the biggest Pay-Per-View events of the year because everyone is anticipating a showdown between The Rock and Vince McMahon, the owner of the World Wrestling Federation. The Rock has been

feuding with McMahon for months now. McMahon hates The Rock because The Rock is The People's Champion . . . and everyone knows that Vince McMahon loathes the people. The Rock's popularity, his following, his fan club, has been swelling with each successive performance, and that makes Vince McMahon ill. Tonight, McMahon has promised, The Rock will hit rock bottom.

Winning the *Survivor Series* requires strength, stamina, speed, and showmanship, traits The Rock has in abundance. Still, it's a daunting task. He'll have to go through four jabronis in one night to win his first World Wrestling Federation title. But do you think The Rock is intimidated? Hell, no! Not for one single solitary second. With The Rock's fans chanting his name, The Rock first disposes of the Big Boss Man in a record-setting four seconds. How does he do this? Well, when the Big Boss Man runs into The People's Ring, The Rock hooks him with a small package—only when you're dealing with The Rock, there's no such thing as a small package. Every package is big . . . and lethal. The Big Boss Man hits the mat, The Rock covers—*one-two-three!*—and it's on to the second round.

Up next is that renowned tough guy, Ken Shamrock, whose ass The Rock has kicked all over the world. The Rock is getting tired of laying the smack down on poor old Ken Shamrock, to tell you the truth, but what can The Rock do? The guy keeps coming back for more. So The Rock humiliates Ken Shamrock one more time, punishes him for fifteen minutes before putting him out of his misery and eliminating him from the *Survivor Series*.

So now The Rock comes to the Undertaker, the so-called "phenom" of the World Wrestling Federation. But the Undertaker is nothing special in The Rock's eyes. Here's this guy, he's six foot ten, 320 pounds, with skin the color of bad meat and tattoos all over his body. To The Rock this guy is just a giant waste of flesh! The Undertaker thinks that he impresses The Rock by speaking in tongues and claiming that he can steal the souls of jabronis.

He likes to come out on TV, on The Rock's show, *Rock Is War*, and he likes to take a little dagger and "sacrifice" his opponents. Well, The Rock has said this to the Undertaker before and he'll say it again: *When you live by the dirt, you die by The Rock's shovel.* And that's what happens in Round Three of the *Survivor Series*. The Rock goes through the Undertaker like Ex-Lax goes through his big fat mama!

You want details? The Rock will graciously provide you with details. First, the Undertaker enters the ring in his usual dopey manner: through a cloud of smoke, with crappy organ music blasting through the PA system, and that fat-ass Paul Bearer right by his side. When the Undertaker gets close enough, The Rock tries to whisper something in his ear. Understand that there's a substantial amount of talking in the ring, especially when The Rock is involved. And what The Rock is telling the Undertaker, quite simply, is this: "You don't have enough hair on your dead ass to take a step forward and face The Rock one-on-one." The Undertaker, surprisingly enough, accepts the challenge. He takes a step forward and The Rock gives him The Rock Bottom Special: a fist in the mouth and a foot in the ass! End of story.

Now the final match is set, the match to determine the World Wrestling Federation Champion, the most coveted title in all of sports-entertainment, far bigger than any title professional wrestling has ever seen. And make no mistake—The Rock doesn't call himself a professional wrestler. He calls himself a sports-entertainer, because that's exactly what this is: sports-entertainment. And The Rock is the best damn sports-entertainer the world has ever known. The Rock is the *king* of sports-entertainment!

Only one person stands between The Rock and the World Wrestling Federation title: Mankind. Actually, it's not really accurate to call Mankind a "person." If you stare at Mankind for more than a few seconds, you realize it looks as though a big gorilla

ran down the ramp, jumped into the middle of the ring, squat-
ted, took a shit, and out plopped Mankind. That's exactly what
you see in Mankind. The Rock has to be candid and cruel about
this one: When you look at this guy, he is just so *not* The Rock.
The Rock is the quintessential athlete. The Rock has a body that
appears to have been chiseled from granite, as befits his name.
His hair is perfect, his clothes selected from the finest designers.
The Rock is the crown jewel . . . The Chosen One . . . the man des-
tined to lead sports-entertainment into the next millennium.

Mankind? Well . . . here's a guy—a *creature*—who shaves half
his head and wears tattered clothes and a little leather mask. He
makes all these goofy noises and says he lives in a basement or
a boiler room or some other dark, musty place. No one can figure
out what the deal is with Mankind—not even The Rock, with his
superior intellect. The Rock once asked Mankind, "God, Mankind,
what kind of unholy inbreeding did it take to create a mutated
freak like yourself?" And you know what Mankind's answer was?
He looked at his watch and squealed . . . "It's 3:22!" I mean . . .
what in the living hell is that supposed to mean? What does that
tell you about Mankind?

In fairness, it should be pointed out that Mankind suffers
from a certain handicap that makes it difficult for him to com-
pete effectively against a specimen like The Rock. That handicap
is "lack-of-testicle-itis." Not too many people know that about
Mankind, but The Rock knows it, and sometimes this knowledge
brings out the humanitarian in The Rock. The Rock can be a sen-
timental man, so he tries not to layeth the smacketh down too
hard on Mankind. After all, this is a man with a wife and children.

But Mankind has a knack for provoking The Rock, and so the
final match of the *Survivor Series* becomes a classic confrontation, a visceral stew for the millions . . . and the millions of The
Rock's fans. It's a match that includes a lot of thrown chairs,
steel railings, suplexes, and pile-drivers on the concrete floor.

You have a whole range of breathtaking entertainment . . . courtesy of The Great One. In the end, The Rock wraps up Mankind in the famous Sharpshooter, a move first made famous by Bret "the Hitman" Hart. With Mankind flat on his back, the Rock lifts Mankind's legs into the air so that they form a "V." The Rock then steps between Mankind's legs with his right leg, so that his foot is near Mankind's chest. The Rock then proceeds to twist Mankind into a pretzel. He crosses Mankind's legs, hooks the upper leg with his arm, and then rolls Mankind over onto his stomach. The Rock now has both of Mankind's legs hooked and hideously twisted. He rocks backward, in a dazzling display of power and ingenuity. And now The Rock, along with the first ten rows of the arena, can hear Mankind begin to cry. From deep in Mankind's throat comes a pathetic, shrill whine, and finally the sound of submission, as Mankind says: "OW-EE! OW-EE! OWWWEEEEEEEEEE! I QUIT! I GIVE UP!"

The bell rings and now you're looking at the new World Wrestling Federation Champion! But The Rock is still disturbed by what he has heard from Mankind. Here's this huge man, in his thirties, been all around the world, supposed to be some kind of a big shot . . . and he's yelling "OW-EE?" He's screaming like a woman? Good Christ, if you're going to get beat, at least go ahead and get beat with some pride and dignity. Say "AAAAAAAHHHH! That hurts, dammit!" Say anything. But not "OW-EE!"

When the match is over, the real fun begins. Into the ring walk Vince McMahon and Shane McMahon, father and son, hated corporate clowns. The crowd holds its collective breath, anticipating that The Rock will lay the smack down on these duplicitous assholes, that they will be taught a lesson by The People's Champ. But wait just a minute! What's going on? The Rock is hugging the McMahons. He's shaking their hands. He's holding the World Wrestling Federation belt aloft, and they're helping him do it! Moments ago twenty thousand fans were on their feet, screaming The Rock's name, but now they have fallen silent. They can't believe their eyes. How could The People's Champion be aligned with the man who hates the people? How could The People's Champion become The Corporate Champion? It makes no sense.

Suddenly, just before the *Survivor Series* comes to an end, just before the picture fades to black, The Rock's archrival enters the ring. It's Stone Cold Steve Austin, crashing the party, sticking his bald head where it doesn't belong one more time. He's challenging The Rock. He wants a piece of The Corporate Champion. *Soon enough, Stone Cold . . . soon enough.*

 ## MAN WITH A PLAN

A record-setting audience tunes in *Raw Is War* the following night. This is no great surprise to The Rock. After all, there are six billion people in the world, and The Rock would dare say that half of them are big fans of The Rock. So a good three to four billion people are sitting at home wondering . . . *Why, Rock, why? Why are you hugging Vince McMahon? Why did you sell out to the Corporation?*

Well, The Rock has answers, of course. The Rock always has answers. It's just that The Rock knows the value of keeping some things to himself. And that's just what's happening right here. See, it's really quite simple. The Rock didn't sell out. The Rock just got ahead. The Rock is a highly intelligent man, and he did what he had to do in order to become the World Wrestling Federation Champion. You don't think The Rock knows what he's doing? You don't think The Rock has a strategy? Come on! Give The Rock some credit. The Rock began mapping out his strategy years ago. This alliance with Team Corporate means nothing to The Rock. It's just a tool, a weapon in The Rock's growing arsenal. By hooking up with Shane and Vince McMahon, The Rock has set his master plan in motion. But he can't just go on national television, on this night, less than twenty-four hours after winning the belt, and tell his legions of fans all about it. No, The Rock knows his role, and his role is to be the champion—at any cost! So The Rock is using the Corporation for all it's worth. Now the Rock is back in the spotlight, right where he belongs, right where the fans want him.

People's Champion? Corporate Champion? It's all the same to The Rock. Just so long as he's champion. He struts and preens around the ring as only The Rock can—confidently, arrogantly, with his muscles straining against his $800 leopard-skin shirt. And then, out of nowhere, intent on spoiling The Rock's big moment, comes Stone Cold Steve Austin. That piece of trailer-park trash wants a shot at the title. But does he have the *cajones* to ask The Rock for a match? Hell, no! If Stone Cold had simply approached The Rock with the respect and humility befitting an underling—if he had come out and said, "Rock, please give me a shot at your title, a title that you are going to make famous"—then The Rock would have graciously said, "You're damn right you'll get your shot, and tonight The Rock is going to kick your monkey ass!" But no . . . Stone Cold Steve Austin had to go out and get a little bald jabroni by the name of Mills Lane, the boxing referee—the judge, all of a sudden! (And what kind of crock is that anyway? The guy goes from being a referee to being a judge? What did The Rock miss?) So now here's Mills Lane examining Stone Cold Steve Austin's contract, and he declares that there's a clause stipulating that Stone Cold has a legal right to fight for the World Wrestling Federation title that night on *Raw Is War*! An hour and forty-five minutes later, it's The Rock and Stone Cold going at it once again, making sparks fly, making fireworks go off, making magic happen, with the title on the line . . . The Rock's title, in the middle of The People's Ring, The Rock and Stone Cold Steve Austin going nose-to-nose.

It's a hell of a fight, but The Rock begins to take control. He hits Stone Cold Steve Austin with so many lefts that Stone Cold is *begging* for the right! The Rock gives Stone Cold The Rock Bottom. Then he removes his elbow pad and winds up for The People's Elbow. The noise in the arena is deafening! The end is near! But wait . . . what's happening? The Rock is distracted by one of Stone Cold's jabronis, and this momentary lapse allows Stone Cold to escape. Stone Cold catches The Rock with the infamous Stone Cold Stunner. He leaps on The Rock, covers, and referee Earl Hebner begins to count: "One ... Two ..."

Suddenly there's Ken Shamrock, dragging the referee out of the ring. Ken Shamrock, rocket scientist that he is, thinks he's doing The Rock a favor. He's trying to get famous by helping The Rock! As if The Rock needs any help. As if The Rock wasn't about to kick out of the Stunner. So now The Rock is thinking ... *What the hell is going on? How many people want to ride The Rock's wave?* A few more, as it turns out. The Undertaker has been back near the USA Network production truck, and he knows that right now the ratings are going through the roof because The Rock is in the middle of the ring. So the Undertaker decides he wants a piece of the glory. He climbs into the ring with his shovel and hits Stone Cold Steve Austin square in the jaw. Now you have one bald jabroni laid out colder than a block of ice, and you've got one big dead jabroni with gray skin and tattoos, standing there holding a shovel like he's really impressive. And the crowd is going completely nuts!

Meanwhile, walking up the ramp is a bronze Adonis. He's holding the World Wrestling Federation Championship belt. He's smiling. Who could it be? Why ... that must be The Rock!

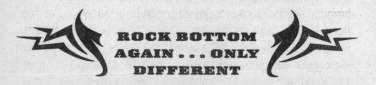

ROCK BOTTOM AGAIN . . . ONLY DIFFERENT

December 13, 1998 (Vancouver, BC)—When The Rock arrives at GM Place, after a luxury-class flight in the corporate jet, he comes to the conclusion that this is going to be a very special night indeed. There are twenty thousand screaming fans in the house, and they're all here to see The Rock. They're here to be part of *The Rock Bottom*, the first Pay-Per-View special ever named after a World Wrestling Federation Superstar. Only The Rock is worthy of such an honor. No one else. When he makes his grand entrance, The Rock is thrilled to see a pair of hundred-foot color posters of himself hanging from the arena ceiling. The Rock has to admit: *This is pretty cool . . . and, damn, that guy is good looking!*

The Rock's opponent is Mankind. With the World Wrestling Federation title on the line, The Rock goes to work. Thirty minutes of kicking ass and taking names, at the end of which he decides to give Mankind his Christmas gift early: The Rock Bottom Special! But Mankind is fighting well, and suddenly he catches The Rock with his signature move, the ridiculous Mandible Claw. The Mandible Claw consists of Mankind putting a filthy sock over his hand, reaching into the mouth of his opponent, and pressing two fingers against the back of his opponent's tongue. When executed properly, this move leaves Mankind's foe temporarily paralyzed. Well, no shit! You should smell "Mr. Socko." He's foul enough to make anybody faint. And that's the only reason the Mandible Claw is effective. The *only* reason!

Anyway, Mankind catches The Rock with the Mandible Claw and now The Rock is motionless on the mat, and Mankind is howling like a sick coyote. But let the truth be known ... let The Rock be frank with the millions ... and the millions of his fans (and the millions of his soon-to-be fans reading this book): The Rock never quit. The Rock never gave up. Mankind did not beat The Rock *one-two-three* in the middle of the ring, which was required in order for the belt to change hands. So that's it. Did The Rock *technically* lose the match? Yes, The Rock *technically* lost the match. Did The Rock *technically* walk out the World Wrestling Federation Champ? Yes, The Rock *technically* walked out the World Wrestling Federation Champ. Is Mankind *technically* 280 pounds of monkey crap? Yes, *technically* he is. And is The Rock *technically* The People's Champ? Absolutely!

HALFTIME HEAT

January 23, 1999 (Tucson, AZ)—What better time and place to utilize The Rock's skills as the consummate entertainer than at halftime of the Super Bowl? World Wrestling Federation and USA Network officials have discussed this matter with The Rock. They've said, *"Come on, Rock. The millions and the millions of The Rock's fans don't give a rat's ass about that cheesy halftime show. They don't want to see Stevie Wonder. They don't want to see Gloria Estefan. They want to see The Rock doing what he does best, and that's laying the smack down!"*

So The Rock agreed. And now he's walking into an empty arena in the Arizona desert, preparing for another battle with that inhuman piece of garbage, Mankind. This is the perfect setting for The Rock, the perfect forum, because The Rock can do what he does best: take his time, take the entire halftime of the Super Bowl, to beat Mankind's ass and entertain the people like only he can. So The Rock doesn't just beat Mankind on Super Bowl Sunday—he *humiliates* Mankind! He kicks and chases Mankind all over the arena. And he provides a running commentary while he's doing it. At one point the Rock stops by a concession stand, dips a tortilla chip into some salsa, tastes it, and then spits it out in disgust. "It's mild!" The Rock shouts. "The Rock likes it hot!" And with that he throws the salsa in Mankind's face. The Rock pummels Mankind. He drags Mankind into the kitchen and damn near sticks Mankind's bulbous, bushy head into a 400-degree oven.

On and on it goes, more entertainment than the Denver Broncos and Atlanta Falcons have provided in the first half of the Super Bowl, that's for damn sure! The Rock snatches up a bottle of whiskey, takes a sip, and begins to sing like only The Rock can: "Jack Daniel's if you please...knock this jabroni to his knees!" *WHAM!* Mankind takes another shot. Eventually The Rock drags Mankind into the management offices and continues to administer a savage beating. He's interrupted by the ringing of a telephone. The Rock answers: "Hello, Smack Down Hotel, Rock speaking . . . No, I'm afraid Mankind's not available right now—he's a little busy . . . WITH THE ROCK'S FOOT IN HIS MOUTH!" A few moments later the phone rings again: "Yeah, Candy Ass Cafe. How can The Rock help you? No, I'm sorry, Mankind's not available right now—HE'S A LITTLE TIED UP!" And The Rock wraps the telephone cord around Mankind's fat neck.

Mankind is no match for The Rock. He has only one chance, and that is to cheat. So Mankind resorts to using heavy equipment—*really* heavy equipment—in a desperate attempt to avoid further pain and degradation. What does Mankind do? He commandeers a damn forklift! While The Rock is on the ground, Mankind jumps behind the wheel of the forklift and drops about a dozen fully loaded beer kegs on The People's Champion. This would have crushed the chest of a normal man, of course, but The Rock is far from normal. He loses the match and his World Wrestling Federation title because he's temporarily stunned and incapacitated by Mankind's treachery, but The Rock will be back. Count on that! And The Rock still comes away feeling pretty good about himself. You know why? Well, let me put it this way,

Mankind: You never beat The Rock *one-two-three* in the middle of the ring. You never have and you never will. And on top of that, how many calls did you get from network presidents after that match, congratulating you on a flawlessly entertaining performance? The Rock got calls from every network there is on TV . . . and a few that aren't even on yet. *Halftime Heat* did record numbers, and it sure as hell wasn't because of your big, ugly puss. It was because everyone wanted to see The Rock!

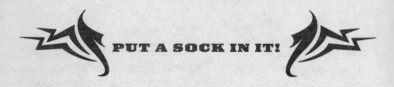

PUT A SOCK IN IT!

January 24, 1999 (Anaheim, CA)—The Rock meets Mankind again, this time in a special "I Quit" match at *The Royal Rumble*. And, once again, Mankind winds up crying like a baby. The Rock nails Mankind in his face, in his head, in his fat ass! The Rock lays him out like there's no tomorrow. Scrambles Mankind like an egg-white omelet. And at the end, with Mankind crawling across the floor, The Rock sticks the microphone in Mankind's mouth, damn near chokes him to death, and orders him to submit. Well, Mankind may be a freak, but he's no fool. He shouts to the world, "I QUIT! I QUIT!" And The Rock withdraws the mike, hands it to the referee, and says, "Jabroni, you get back in that ring and you award The Rock the World Wrestling Federation title."

The second reign of The Rock has begun.

BACK AND FORTH

Sadly, for the millions...and the millions of The Rock's fans, the Great One saw a setback thanks to the combined cheating of Mankind and his buddy, Stone Cold Steve Austin. One night on *Raw Is War*, just as The Rock is getting ready to pin Mankind's back to the mat and defend his title, in walks the party crasher, the biggest piece of Texas trailer-park trash on God's Green Earth. Stone Cold Steve Austin grabs a steel chair and levels The Rock, allowing Mankind to escape. The Rock is laid out cold. Mankind flops on The Rock and covers—*one-two-three!* The title changes hands again. But the beauty of this whole scenario is this: It proves beyond a shadow of a doubt that The Rock is too much for any one man to handle. Did Mankind pin The Rock on his own? Hell, no! And Stone Cold Steve Austin, don't you think for one single, solitary moment that The Rock will ever forget what you did on this night. Come hell or high water, The Rock will exact his revenge!

February 14, 1999 (Memphis, TN)—The Rock is primed. The Rock is ready. On the night of the St. Valentine's Day Massacre, The Rock is in Memphis, Tennessee, home of The King, Elvis Presley, The Rock's all-time favorite entertainer. Now The Rock has an opportunity to bash in Mankind's brains and have it be legal, because this is a "Last-Man-Standing" match. Just as the name implies, anything goes. There will be no disqualifications, no penalties of any kind. The winner of this match is the man who is capable of walking out the door with the World Wrestling Federation Championship belt in his possession: *the last man standing!*

So The Rock does what he does best. He throttles Mankind from one side of the building to the other. He smacks Mankind with a chair. He tosses Mankind onto a ringside table. But that's not all The Rock does. See, The Rock understands the importance of putting on a show. The People's Champ understands the value of giving The People something to remember. So he picks his spot, and when the time is right, The Rock grabs the microphone and says to the crowd, "Here's a little gift from The People's Champ." And then The Rock begins to sing his own version of a song made famous by The King: "Heartbreak Hotel."

"Well, since Rock's baby left him ... he's found a new place to dwell. It's down at the end of Jabroni Drive at . . . Smack Down Hotel!"

The crowd erupts! They love The Rock! In Memphis, especially, they know that any man who appreciates Elvis can't be all bad. And any man who is capable of performing a tribute to The King at the same time that he's whipping Mankind's ass ... well, that man deserves to be The People's Champion. This memorable match ends with Mankind and The Rock smacking each other in the face with chairs and knocking each other out—

simultaneously! It's a thrilling conclusion to another thrilling night of sports-entertainment, courtesy of The Rock.

Despite the fact that Mankind still holds the World Wrestling Federation title, it's now clear that The Rock is the number one personality in sports-entertainment. He's receiving truckloads of mail each day, hundreds of thousands of tear-stained letters from his legions of fans, all wanting to know: *When are you going to be champ again? When will Mankind get rid of the sugar in his testicles and give you a fair shot at the World Wrestling Federation title?* So, finally, Mankind relents. It's late February, and we're in Birmingham, Alabama, for a *Raw* telecast. Tonight it really is *Rock Is War*, because The Rock is out there on camera, cutting the type of promo that only he can cut, challenging Mankind, daring him to step into the ring with The Rock. Mankind isn't eager to accept this challenge, but Vince McMahon intercedes and *orders* him into the ring against The Rock. *Now!* Mankind is shivering with fear. He looks out through that ridiculous mask of his and says, "But I need seven days." The Rock grabs the mike: "Seven days?! Mankind, you don't even have seven minutes!"

Well, pretty soon The Rock and Mankind are joined by a five-foot-ten, 195-pound piece of monkey crap by the name of Shawn Michaels, the Heartbreak Kid, the commissioner of the World Wrestling Federation. Like everyone else, the "commish" wants to ride The Rock's wave of greatness, so he makes the match. The commish orders Mankind to square off against The Great One that evening on *Rock Is War*, with the stipulation that it be a ladder match. Now, this benefits Mankind, who is one of the craziest guys in the World Wrestling Federation, a real whack-job when it comes to risking life and limb. Mankind *loves* ladder matches! But The Rock isn't fazed. He's thinking, *Shawn Michaels . . . HBK . . . making the ladder match*. Well, the initials should be HST—horseshit tonight—because that's what this looks like to The Rock! So The Rock grabs the microphone and says, "You think you're going to impress The Rock by making a ladder match and putting him against Mankind? Well, Shawn Michaels, you don't understand something. This is The Rock, and he emits electricity twenty-four hours a day, seven days a week, 365 days a year—including leap year!"

And with that, The Rock goes to work. He beats Mankind to within an inch of his useless life. He climbs The People's Ladder—rung by damn rung—and snatches the World Wrestling Federation title! The Rock is going to *WrestleMania*, where he will face his old bald-headed nemesis, that piece of trailer-park trash, Stone Cold Steve Austin. We are now just four weeks away from *WrestleMania XV*, the biggest wrestling event of all time, because it's The Rock's *WrestleMania*, a show that The Rock promises to make famous. The Rock stands high above Mankind and every other jabroni in that arena, the World Wrestling Federation Champion for the third time . . . *if you smell what The Rock is cooking!*

THE ROCK SAYS . . .

chapter 14

I LOVED FRIDAY nights when I was a kid. My dad would usually be out working a show, and my mother would be doing some paperwork, catching up on laundry, and cleaning around the house. To keep me occupied, she'd set up a big Panasonic video camera in the corner of our living room. The little red light would come on, and that room would be transformed into an arena or studio, with me playing multiple roles.

"Ladies and gentlemen, this is Vince McMahon, and I'm about to be joined by Jimmy 'Superfly' Snuka."

Jimmy Snuka was one of my favorite wrestlers; he was such a close friend of the family that I called him

Uncle Jimmy. His promos weren't great in a traditional sense, but they were undeniably spellbinding. His interviews were famous for being wildly entertaining...and virtually incomprehensible:

"Brother, when the sun sets and the waves crash down, and you wake up tomorrow thinking it was yesterday, then you must drink the drink of life, my friend. ..."

And after all this whacked-out shit, he'd finish with some big line about an upcoming show:

"And tomorrow, brother, at the Garden, mentally and physically, you will know what the Superfly is saying!"

Jimmy was incredible. You'd sit in front of the television, listening to him, and when he was through you'd think, *What in the hell did he just say?* Then, very quickly, you'd come up with the answer: *I don't know what he just said, but it sure sounds like he's going to kick the crap out of someone this weekend, so let's go down to the Garden!*

In some ways, the character of The Rock came to life on those Friday nights in my living room. I was never Dwayne Johnson in front of that camera. I was always someone else. I imitated my dad, Jimmy Snuka, Roddy Piper, Magnificent Muraco, and of course Ric Flair. Piper, Muraco, and Flair were my favorites because they were the top three heels, and they represented everything a heel should be. I realized even then that heels always seemed to have fun in front of the camera. They cut the best promos, said the most outrageous things. They were rude, arrogant, and almost hypnotically entertaining. Ric Flair was particularly enthralling. I thought he had tremendous charisma. He had the ability to captivate people the minute he started talking, and he held them in the palm of his hand, right up until the end of his promo.

I spent a lot of time learning how to be a fundamentally sound wrestler. While I'm not exactly a gymnast, I have a fair amount of athletic ability, and I work as hard as anyone in the business. That said, I know that The Rock's popularity stems largely from his relationship with the camera, and especially the microphone. To deny that would be a lie. The Rock is charismatic, funny, smart ... and completely over the top in terms of ego and arrogance.

Amazing as it sounds, almost nothing about the character of The Rock was premeditated. Oh, sure, you could make the argument that I had been preparing for his emergence for the better part of two decades, but I never made a conscious decision to create The Rock as you see him today. The quirks and peculiarities evolved organically. I never said, "Hmmm, I need a gimmick. I need an angle, I need ... I need ... *I need an eyebrow!* And then—I know!—I'll take the most basic maneuver in wrestling and turn it into the most electrifying move in wrestling, and I'll call it *The People's Elbow!* Yeah ... that's the plan!" It was nothing like that.

Opportunities don't come knocking all the time in the World Wrestling Federation. You have to be patient. Generally, if you've been wrestling for a while, you will get a chance to speak, to show what you can do with a microphone. But you have to make the most of that opportunity. It's almost like a screen test or an audition. They'll let you cut one or two promos, and if they don't see real potential, if there's nothing special about you or what you're saying, then that's it. You go back to being a man without a voice.

That might sound harsh, but it's the reality of doing business at the end of the millennium. The entertainment industry is extraordinarily competitive. We're competing not only with World Championship Wrestling but with everything else on the television dial. We have to put the best possible product out there because if we don't the viewer grabs the remote and zaps us into oblivion: *"Who is this goof?" Click!* On to the WCW's show . . . or to *Friends* . . . or a movie . . . or a basketball game. Whatever else might be on in that time slot. The options are practically limitless, and the viewer's attention span is short. We have to grab them and hold them. It's crucial that we don't put a guy in front of the camera who babbles and mumbles and stumbles over his words.

As Rocky Maivia, my interviews were all scripted for me. I was a babyface being introduced to the fans, and that was just the way it worked. The writers would hand me a few sheets of paper and say, "Here you go, Rocky. Memorize this." And I would do exactly as I was told, and the interview or the promo would be the absolute shits. Not because the material was bad, necessarily—I think our writers are sensational, and it's beyond me how they juggle so many story lines and produce so much material in such a short period of time—but simply because I was so stiff and formal. The audience knows when you're reading something, when you're not really into it. Not until I got my first opportunity to speak as The Rock did I begin to feel like a ten-year-old kid again. Now I'm given almost complete creative freedom when it comes to interviews and promos. I'll be given just a bare-bones outline: *Rock/Austin promo . . . WrestleMania . . . two weeks.* Something like that. And then I'll hang some flesh on the skeleton.

The preparation for a great promo or interview begins with the writing. I'm constantly writing ideas down. It happens all the time. I'll be sitting at the dinner table with Dany and all of a sudden I'll start laughing and say, "Hey, get me a piece of paper—quick!" If we're at restaurant, I might start scribbling on a napkin, and Dany will say, "Promo idea?"

"Uh-huh."

Usually I'll just stuff it into a pocket or a desk drawer for a few days, then I'll take it out and start working with it, expanding on it. I'll think about the parameters of the match, the opponent, his eccentricities and flaws—all of which are fair game when cutting a promo. For example . . .

Okay . . . I'm going into a Last-Man-Standing match against Mankind. He's one of the toughest guys around. Been in explosion matches, where you fall on something and the son of a bitch blows up. So, obviously, this isn't his first barbecue. What can I do to make this promo compelling? What can The Rock do to make it entertaining? I can poke fun at his physical characteristics— *"It looks like a monkey took a crap and out came Mankind!"*—which is the most common approach, or I can try to get *really* creative and incorporate current events and popular culture, as I did during a *Sunday Night Heat* telecast. I was at the announcer's table getting ready for a match against Mankind:

"Tonight The Rock is going to play movie director, and let you see firsthand the unedited, uncut version of The Rock's major motion picture, entitled Laying the Smack Down on Your Roody-Poo Candy Ass! *And when it's all said and done, and all the smoke has*

cleared, and the millions and the millions of The Rock's fans have finished chanting his name, the Titanic *will still be sunk, Monica Lewinsky will still love her cigars, and The Rock will have kicked the living piss out of Mankind!"*

To a degree, all of my promos are scripted, meaning there are certain lines and phrases I plan to include, and there's a general overall theme. But there also is a lot of improvisation. Generally I put together an outline that includes three major points: a strong opening, a concise and entertaining body, and an electrifying, super-strong go-home.

Start to finish, it looks (or sounds) something like this (what follows is one of my all-time favorite promos, which aired two weeks before *WrestleMania XV*, in March 1999):

"WrestleMania XV, *the Brahma Bull against the Rattlesnake. It does not get any better than that. Stone Cold Steve Austin, as far as The Rock is concerned, the greatest book ever written is titled* The Brahma Bull vs. The Rattlesnake. *And the beauty of this novel is that it has infinite chapters. Which means it never ends. It also means, for the rest of your natural life, The Rock will be kicking your monkey ass all over God's Green Earth.... And when it's all said and done, and the smoke has cleared, and the millions and the millions of The Rock's fans have finished chanting his name...and you and The Rock float up to that big World Wrestling Federation ring in the sky, and you extend your hand and say, 'Hey, Rock, thanks for the memories...' don't be surprised if The Rock looks at you, raises The People's Eyebrow, shakes your hand right back, and says, 'No, Stone Cold...thank you for the memories.' And then, Stone Cold Steve Austin,*

The Rock will take his other hand and slap the taste right out of your mouth for being the biggest piece of trailer-park trash walking God's Blue Heaven!"

Here's an excerpt from another of my favorites, this one directed at the Undertaker:

"Undertaker, do you think you impress The Rock by coming out here with your little Undertaker symbol and claiming to steal the souls of all these poor jabronis in the World Wrestling Federation? Do you think you impress The Rock by making your eyes roll up into the back in your head? Well . . . The Rock says . . . you come to King of the Ring. And you try to sacrifice The People's Champ. But instead of taking your eyes and rolling them up into the back of your head, The Rock says take your entire thirty-three-pound head, spin it around backwards like The Exorcist, *have it roll down your back, and catch it with your hands. And then, Undertaker, take your own head, turn that sumbitch sideways . . . and stick it straight up your candy ass!"*

One of the most enjoyable aspects of putting together a killer promo is seeing and hearing the reaction of the fans. They hang on to every word, knowing they're going to be entertained, and they respond by chanting my name or erupting in applause. For the most part, anyone who watches The Rock knows they're in for something different. My opponent can be out there talking about The Rock, challenging The Rock, but as soon as the music hits—*"If you smell what The Rock is cooking"*—the crowd is like, "Oh, shit! We're gonna get our money's worth now!" because they know The Rock is going to say some wild stuff and whip them into a frenzy.

I put a lot of time into my promos—more time

than just about anyone else, I'd say. And I think it shows. No matter what the other guys say, I'm confident my response will be entertaining.

For example, a few of the Undertaker's promos have focused on The Rock's age. Well, as The Rock's popularity has risen, his youth has become a badge of honor. So when the Undertaker insinuates The Rock is too young to hold such a lofty position in the World Wrestling Federation, he's just asking for trouble. On one occasion the Undertaker opened his promo by saying, "Listen, young man . . . and I do mean *young*." And his go-home line was, "I am going to take you to the learning tree!" I thought that was kind of cute, but a few days later, on *Raw*, The Rock did what he does best: He used the Undertaker's own words as fodder for one of his promos:

"Undertaker, you run your mouth about how you'rer going to take The Rock to the learning tree. Well, you're not going to have to drag The Rock to the learning tree. The Rock will gladly go to the learning tree with you. And then he'll pause once we get there. He'll reach up and break off a branch. And he'll pick each and every leaf off that branch. Then he'll turn it sideways and stick it straight up your candy ass!"

The crowd went wild, as they almost always do when The Rock cuts a promo.

SHINE IT UP REAL NICE
TURN THAT SUMBITCH SIDEWAYS
AND
STICK IT STRAIGHT UP
YOUR CANDY ASS!

KNOW YOUR ROLE, JABRONI!

To me, one of the coolest things about The Rock is the way wrestling fans have embraced so many of his catchphrases. I can't believe that a word like "jabroni" has entered the lexicon of popular culture. Most wrestling fans think it's a word The Rock invented. Sorry, but that's just not the case. *Jabroni* is a word that has been around this industry for a long time. It was an insider word, typically referring to someone in an unflattering manner, as in, "That guy is a real jabroni . . . a nobody." My dad used it all the time when I was growing up. When I started wrestling I thought, *Hell, I like that word. I'm gonna use it.* So there I was one night, cutting a promo, looking into the camera and saying, "Ken Shamrock, you little jabroni!" Remarkably enough, it just kind of stuck.

The same was true of "Do you smell what The Rock is cooking?" I heard that years ago, while I was playing football at Miami, and I thought it was a great expression. It's sort of like, "If you know what I mean." *Wink-wink.* I first thought about incorporating it into a character about three months after I joined the World Wrestling Federation. I was talking to someone backstage before a show, and, right out of the blue, I said, "Yeah ... if you smell what I'm cooking." It got a nice laugh, and I remember thinking, *Hmmmm ... that's a pretty good line.* I could use that. Then, nearly two years later, I'm sitting with Gennifer Flowers before *WrestleMania XIV*, and it just comes out. It wasn't planned at all. But the reaction was incredible. I knew right away that I was onto something.

Fans are incredibly sharp that way. They will instantly let you know whether something works. I'll say, "You're gonna get a double Rock Burger with cheese!" and the next time we go on TV, there are thirty signs in the arena saying, "I want a Rock Burger!" I always check out the signs, because they let me know when something is clicking. It's like I said— this is a collaborative business. None of us works in a vacuum. You learn from your coworkers, and you learn from your fans.

It would be easy at this point for me to go out there and say the same things night after night, to rely on nothing but the popular catchphrases. But there's no challenge in that, and there's no opportunity for growth. Any act gets old without periodic fine-tuning. The Rock has been a unique presence in the sports-entertainment industry, and I won't allow him to get stale. I choose to be creative and innovative and entertaining. That's what makes it interesting for me and enjoyable for the fans. There's no better feeling than getting a standing ovation from fifteen thousand people the minute I touch the microphone. But I understand that the response—and the popularity of the character—is due not only to the audience's desire to be in on the game but to the fact that there is always the potential for the unexpected. For example, when the fans started chanting, "If you smell what The Rock is cooking," I could have done what most other wrestlers would do—what they've always done: revel in it. But I didn't. I decided it would be more interesting . . . more fun . . . to have The Rock get pissed off at the audience, to shout, "HEY! THIS AIN'T SING-ALONG WITH THE ROCK! YOU KEEP YOUR MOUTHS SHUT!" The very first time I did that, nobody booed, nobody screamed, "Go to Hell!" They just laughed and applauded.

That's when we all knew we were on to something big with The Rock. I remember sitting with Vince McMahon after the show, drenched in sweat, having worked my ass off to entertain a crowd in true heel fashion, and saying, "Vince, man, I don't get it. I'm doing all I can to shit on these people."

Vince threw up his hands and smiled. "They appreciate creativity, Rock. And they're just letting you know it."

chapter 15

WRESTLEMANIA!
LEMANIA!

IT'S FRIDAY NIGHT, March 26, *when we arrive at the Doubletree Hotel in Philadelphia. We drive around the back, where a team of eight security guards is waiting for us. "You're the last one in," one of them says with a smile. "Follow us." Our bags are taken, the car is whisked away, and we're quickly escorted to our room. Then we're escorted to the restaurant, which has been kept open specifically for us. The restaurant is on the second floor, overlooking the lobby. From below I can hear a buzz, the humming of hundreds of people talking at once, drinking, laughing, having a good time. Periodically a specific word or phrase cuts through the din and makes itself known.*

"*The Rock is up there!*"

"*The Rock is eating!*"

They can't see me, but they know I'm here. Word has gotten out.

"*Whip Stone Cold's ASS!*"

"*Austin is a roody-poo!*"

"*DO YOU SMELL WHAT THE ROCK IS COOKING?!!*"

Dany and I have grown accustomed to this sort of reaction, but Dany's brother, Hiram, who is with us on this night, is absolutely amazed. The next morning, bright and early, I do a personal appearance at a sporting-goods store. Dany and Hiram tag along. While I'm signing autographs, the manager of the store tells Dany and Hiram that they're welcome to do a little shopping—at no charge. The store is theirs. Dany is very conservative about these things, so she picks out just one or two little items. But Hiram . . . he's twenty-two years old, and his eyes are jumping out of his head. Like a kid cut loose in a candy store, he starts loading up: shoes, sweats, T-shirts . . . as much stuff as he can carry.

When Hiram's arms get tired we return to the hotel. We enter through the back, through the kitchen, accompanied by a small battalion of security guards. As we exit the elevator and begin walking down the hall, I can see a maid coming out of our room. There is a little boy by her side, perhaps seven years old. He has a camera in his hand. They are both smiling as they pass us.

"*Get all the pictures you needed?*" I say. But there is no response. I turn to one of the security guards and say, not in an angry tone, but in a tone that I hope conveys seriousness, "I want you to take care of that."

I'm reasonably sure the maid meant no harm, but then again . . . who knows? Dany and I have our personal belongings in that room, and someone has been in there taking pictures, doing God knows what else.

"It's a huge invasion of privacy," I say to the security guard, who by now is talking into a cellular phone, asking for an audience with the manager of the hotel. A few minutes later our bags have been stacked on a cart and moved to a new room, a beautiful suite overlooking the Philadelphia skyline.

Better, The Rock would say. Much better.

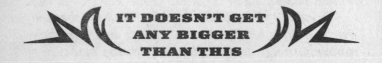

IT DOESN'T GET
ANY BIGGER
THAN THIS

WrestleMania is the granddaddy of them all, the biggest event in sports-entertainment. Dating back to 1985 and *WrestleMania I*, which featured Hulk Hogan and Mr. T, as well as guest appearances by an eclectic group that included Liberace and Muhammad Ali, every edition of *WrestleMania* has been a wildly spectacular gala event. It's like the Super Bowl and the Academy Awards rolled into one.

WrestleMania XV promised to be the biggest of them all. I say that in part because, of course, I was the headliner, along with Stone Cold Steve Austin. But I'm also speaking objectively. Tickets for *WrestleMania XV*, at the First Union Center, had gone on sale six months earlier, and all twenty-one thousand seats had been gobbled up in ninety minutes. The Pay-Per-View audience was sure to be the largest in *WrestleMania* history.

The night before the event itself I attended *WrestleMania Rage*, a party for five thousand people broadcast live by the USA Network. It was basically a celebration of *WrestleMania*, a way to acknowledge its mushrooming popularity and success. Isaac Hayes, the R&B singer of *Shaft* fame (and who more recently has been reborn as the voice of "Chef" on *South Park*), was master of ceremonies, which was kind of cool. And, of course, the party wouldn't have been a party without The Rock cutting a killer promo, which is what he did.

"Stone Cold Steve Austin ... The Rock knows how much you like to drink. So The Rock is offering you a couple of drinks tonight. The drinks are on The Great One. But here's a stipulation, Austin: The Rock says don't get drunk and pass out, or else you'll wake up with The Rock's fist in your mouth, and his foot up your ass!"

That was it ... short and simple. Steve wound up cutting a promo later in the show, but behind the scenes, off camera, it was a different kind of atmosphere, very laid back, enjoyable. All the guys were there with their wives or girlfriends, so it was a rare opportunity for everyone to get together and kick it, enjoy the party, just hang out. It was the calm before the storm.

When we got back to the hotel, I had trouble falling asleep, which I had expected to happen. I didn't want to disturb Dany with my tossing and turning, so once she drifted off, I moved to the living-room area of the suite and just kind of sat there in silence, looking out at the city, thinking about the next night, the biggest night of my life. Different scenarios ran through my mind, different moves and spots that I thought would work. I tried to visualize the entire evening. At this point I hadn't had any concrete discussions with Steve. All we really knew was that I would be doing the honors for him. By the time the main event of *WrestleMania* came to a close—Austin vs. The Rock—I would have put him over clean and given him the World Wrestling Federation title. The torch would have been passed again. That much we knew. Beyond that most basic of outlines, though, there was mainly blank space.

Far from being upset about dropping the belt, I felt a sense of pride. I was happy to be doing this for Steve, not only professionally, but personally. Steve is, quite simply, a good son of a bitch, and one of my closest friends in the business. I wanted to do this right, not only for myself and our fans, but for him. In the weeks leading up to the match we had talked periodically, but only in bits and snatches. I'd see him in the hallway and say, "Steve, I've got an idea," and then run it by him quickly. He'd say, "Yeah, I like that. As a matter of fact, not only can we do that, but what do you think of this . . . ?" And then he'd make a suggestion. Unfortunately, we hadn't really had a chance to speak that night, so the actual planning of the match, the intricate choreography, would have to take place the next day, in the hours leading up to the match. I wasn't particularly nervous about that, though, because I'd worked so often and so well with Steve in the past. I trusted him and he trusted me. We were a team, and there was no way we weren't going to put on one hell of a show.

GAME FACE

I woke around eight, which means I'd logged about five hours of sleep—not bad considering how wired I'd been the night before. I sat around on the living room couch for a while and listened to some gospel music on the radio. Then I got dressed. It was Game Day, so my typical morning road uniform (shorts, tank top, and basketball shoes) was not an option. On this day it was Rock Wear only. By the time Dany and I went downstairs for breakfast, around 11:30, I looked like a star. I looked like The Rock.

After breakfast I took a limo to the First Union Center. My dad accompanied me on the ride—Dany and Hiram, as well as my mom and Dany's father, would arrive at the arena several hours later. We arrived at the First Union Center at around 1:30 and walked together to my dressing room through a pha-lanx of well-wishers: ushers, security guards, vendors, World Wrestling Federation front-office personnel, other wrestlers. At around 1:45 I dumped my gear off in my locker room and said good-bye to my dad. He wanted to hang out with some of the other old-timers who were there, and I had work to do. It wasn't an emotional scene or anything ... probably for a couple reasons. One, we knew we'd be hooking up again later, before the show, and two, that's just not my dad's style.

"I'm going to go grab a coffee," he said.

"Okay, I'm going to go get something to eat."

"See ya."

"See ya."

In the catering area I met up with Pat Patterson, the agent in charge of The Rock's match with Stone Cold Steve Austin. Pat has an unbelievable mind for our business. He's considered one of the best psychologists in the industry, and he has an incredible knack for coming up with creative finishes to matches. That's why he'd been assigned to the main event at *WrestleMania XV.* It was his job to help us formulate the kind of climax this match deserved. Obviously we couldn't just go out there and go . . . *Stone Cold Stunner! One-two-three!* We had to take twenty-one thousand fans on an emotional roller-coaster, and no one was better at that than Pat Patterson. So we threw some ideas back and forth. We were just starting to get rolling when Steve Austin stopped by our table.

"You eat yet, Steve?" I said.

"Already did."

"How about if I meet you in the ring in fifteen minutes?"

"I'll see you out there."

We walked into the arena to the sight of the *Wrestle-Mania XV* banner being unfurled and the sound of preproduction: hammering, drilling, pyrotechnic tests every few minutes: *"Fire in the hole!" BOOM!* We met in the ring, The Rock wearing his $500 shirt and $200 shoes, Steve in his typical Stone Cold outfit:

Stone Cold Steve Austin T-shirt, Stone Cold Steve Austin hat, shorts, and Magnum boots. Pat was there, too, tossing out suggestions, helping us work through the details of the biggest match of our lives. We had roughly thirty minutes of ring time to fill. As always, we worked in reverse—from finish to beginning. It's easiest that way. If you know how the match is going to end—if you can see it—then everything leading up to that point flows naturally.

We started talking about the climactic spot. Since this was the biggest *WrestleMania* ever, and our match had the potential to be remembered as one of the most entertaining matches in history, I decided we should go for broke. So I proposed something truly special.

"What I'd like to do, Steve, is kick out of the Stone Cold Stunner." This was not a minor suggestion. The Stunner, of course, was Steve's signature move, and arguably the most famous move in wrestling. No one had ever kicked out of the Stone Cold Stunner. It was a move that always ended matches and brought the house down. What I was proposing was so bold, and so obviously favored The Rock, that a *quid pro quo* was implicitly required. "And not only that," I added, "but I'd like you to kick out of The Rock Bottom." That was fair enough, since The Rock Bottom had proven equally inescapable over the years.

"What do you think?" I asked.

Steve smiled. "Hell, yeah."

Coming up with that piece of the puzzle was crucial, because I thought it was a vital part of the match that would propel both of us to another level . . . and we'd take the crowd along for the ride. We were conducting business in the ring, negotiating the arc of the match, and Steve's gracious acceptance of my proposal made everything else easier. We now had the biggest hook of the match, the exchange that would leave the audience breathless and lead naturally to the conclusion.

We also talked about how the referee would be incorporated into the match. Originally Paul Wight was scheduled to be the referee. I was against that, not because I have anything personal against Paul, but simply because I felt his presence in the ring might detract from the match. Paul is seven feet tall and weighs five hundred pounds—he's the biggest professional athlete in the world. I think it's been proven that any time you have a special guest referee, people get distracted. They have a tendency to hold back their emotions and wait for the big surprise: *What's the ref going to do?* Conversely, if you have a referee who's five ten, 160 pounds, the audience knows he's strictly a supporting character, and they focus on the two combatants. At some point in the last day or two it was decided that Paul would not referee our match, so that freed us up creatively. We talked about the possibility of starting with three referees and eventually ending up with one. Maybe I'd evict one of the refs with a Rock Bottom, and Steve would belt another with a chair . . . or he'd use the Stunner.

The ideas and suggestions flowed freely as we hung out against the ropes. At one point Vince McMahon walked out, saw what we were doing, and nodded. He didn't come over and crack jokes or anything like that. This was Game Day, and it was the game of the year. Vince is typically very respectful of situations like that. Unless he has a point to make, he leaves us alone in the hours leading up to a match. By 3:30 we had the foundation for a pretty good script.

"Let me mull all of this over for a little while and then we'll get back together," I said to Steve.

"Okay."

I went back to catering and had another small meal: chicken breast, baked potato, broccoli. A steady stream of people stopped by the table to wish me luck. Not as in, *"Good luck, Rock, I hope you beat Stone Cold Steve Austin,"* because obviously we all knew how it was going to turn out. They were simply offering encouragement—*"Have a great one, man"*—the way you would to an actor who is about to perform the biggest role of his life.

Throughout the day my pager kept going off as friends and family members from all over the country called to wish me well. My grandmother left about seven messages. Around 5:30 I had to stop responding. The doors were about open and the building would soon be filled to capacity. I walked over to Steve's dressing room for a bit more rehearsal. When I walked in he was on the phone, and clearly upset. Steve was going through a real hard time with his personal life that spring, and now he was obviously trying to cope long-distance with a family crisis—just a few short hours before the most important show of his career.

"If there's anything I can do to help, just let me know," I said when he got off the phone. "If at any time tonight we get out there and you forget something, you just let me know. I'll be there for you. I promise."

"Thanks," Steve said. "I'm all right."

I knew he would be. Steve is a complete professional, which is why he's reached a level of stardom not attained by any other wrestler.

We started going over the match again, this time in greater detail. We walked through things in the locker room. It's hard to explain, but when you know someone well and you enjoy working with him, there's a chemistry that kicks in during this phase of the process. You can feel a synergy in the room. It's electric! Pretty soon the ideas were flowing. We were talking faster, completing each other's sentences:

"How about if you—"

"Shoot you off the ropes?"

"Yeah . . ."

"Great! And then you hit me with your swinging neck-breaker . . ."

"Damn! That's exactly what I was thinking! And then we can try this . . ."

Before long the adrenaline was pumping and we had a first-class match. The excitement was building, so much that we were no longer just talking, but shouting:

"This is going to be a motherfucker of a match!"

"Yeah, and wait until we do this (pretending to be the announcer): 'One . . . two . . . and Austin kicks out!!'"

"Oh, these people are in for a night."

"You know it!"

After a while there was a knock on the dressing-room door. It was Jim Ross, who would be broadcasting the event that night. Jim wanted to listen to our blueprint so that he would know what to expect and be able to prepare sufficiently. This was a testa-

ment to Jim's commitment to the business. He's been
around long enough, and he's sharp enough, to call a
match with virtually no advance scouting. But he
wouldn't do that. Jim is the best play-by-play
announcer the business has ever seen, and he wanted
to make sure that his performance on the mike would
be equal to the performance in the ring. Pat Patterson
came by, too, as well as Earl Hebner, one of the referees. After watching us do another walk-through,
everyone agreed it would be a hell of a match. I
thanked Pat, Earl, and Jim for stopping by, and then
I slapped hands with Steve.

"See ya in a few," I said.

"I'll come find you."

We would meet again in a couple hours, right
before the match, to go over everything one more
time. For now, though, we went our separate ways.
Dany and my mom were waiting for me outside, so I
went to see them for a little while. Dany had brought
me one last prematch meal: chicken and pasta. They
both wished me good luck, I told them how much I
loved them, and then I went to my locker room. I
couldn't get dressed yet, though, because I knew I was
scheduled to cut a promo at the end of *Sunday Night
Heat*, the live network television show leading into
WrestleMania XV. The promo was in the form of an
interview conducted backstage, and it was broadcast
live on a giant screen to the audience at the First
Union Center, so I could hear the reaction outside.

"Rock, this is your biggest title defense. What are
you going to do to prepare?"

He put the microphone in my face, and I made a
motion with my hand, like I was going to slap him.

He, of course, jumped, and as soon as he moved, I could hear—feel—21,000 people laughing and cheering. *"The Rock says ... hold that microphone up to The Rock's mouth, jabroni, before The Rock slaps the taste out of your mouth ... The Rock says, Stone Cold Steve Austin, tonight is the night that you go one-on-one with The Great One. And your monkey ass is going to be made famous, compliments of The Rock. You run your mouth about how The Rock comes out here and recites his little nursery rhymes? Well The Rock has prepared a little nursery rhyme specifically for you, and it goes like this: Mary had a little lamb. . . . Then again, piss on the lamb, piss on Mary, and piss on YOU! The Rock is going to go out there tonight and do what he does best, and that's lay the smack down on your ... roody-poo candy ass!"* And as I started to say those words, I could hear the audience saying "roody-poo candy ass" right along with me.

"No! No! No!" I shouted into the microphone, admonishing the audience. *"Don't do that!"* Silence. *"Stone Cold Steve Austin, after all is said and done, the millions ..."* I paused, took a deep breath ... and heard twenty thousand people complete the sentence for me: "... and the millions of The Rock's fans ..." I paused again, looked pissed off, and went on ... *"The millions and the millions of The Rock's fans are going to realize that The Rock is, without a shadow of a doubt, the most electrifying man in sports-entertainment, and the best damn World Wrestling Federation Champion there ever was! If you smell ..."* The arena began to rumble ...

"WHAT THE ROCK ... IS COOKING!!!"

"Hey, Philly, this ain't sing-along with The Rock! The Great One says it by himself!" The entire building shook with laughter. I said it again, this time alone: *"If you smell ... what The Rock ..."* I paused, very theatrically, lifted a hand to my face, pushed my chin down, turned my head to the side, and cocked The People's Eyebrow ...

"... is cooking!"

A lot of people told me afterward that they had never seen a better promo. Certainly it was the first fan interactive promo. Regardless, it was a promo that really got me excited about getting out there and putting on a terrific show.

READY TO RUMBLE

The show began at eight o'clock with a stirring rendition of "America the Beautiful" by Philadelphia's own Boyz II Men. There were thirty or forty of us gathered around a big television monitor in the back, listening and watching. As the song came to an end, and the band's gorgeous, rich harmonies filled the arena, I looked over at Steve. He looked back at me,

nodded, and tapped his bare forearm, which was covered with goose bumps.

I smiled and held up my arm. *Me, too.*

We went to our respective dressing rooms and put on our uniforms. As I pulled on my kneepads, my boots, my trunks, I kept visualizing spots. I tried to commit to memory every detail of the match. I threw on a Rock T-shirt and walked over to Steve's locker room one last time, just to make sure everything was in order. We stayed together for a little while and watched some of the preliminary events, starting with the Brawl for All, a legitimate boxing match between a World Wrestling Federation guy, Bart Gunn, and Butterbean, a rotund professional boxer with a deceptively strong punch.

"I'll tell you what," Steve said. "I'll bet you right now Bart knocks that sumbitch out."

I laughed. "I don't know, man. Butterbean is a real boxer. He can throw some heavy punches ... but Bart's a brawler, too."

The bell rang, and within the first forty-five seconds Butterbean threw a big uppercut that damn near decapitated Bart. Just lifted him off the ground and knocked him unconscious.

"Jesus Christ almighty!"

Steve and I jumped to our feet simultaneously. It was so bad that we were honestly concerned for Bart's safety, because people have been known to die from a punch like that. But within a few minutes he was sitting up and talking.

"Good thing you didn't bet real money on that match," I said to Steve. He just laughed. We walked through the match one more time and agreed that we had it down.

"Holler at me later," I said before leaving.

"I'll find you," Steve said.

The main event was scheduled for 10:30. By now it was 10:15. The only person in the locker room with me was my father. Although I believe he was just as excited as I was, he didn't say much. He just stood there quietly while I splashed water on my face, rubbed baby oil on my skin, and cranked out a few sets of push-ups.

"Are you ready?" he finally asked.

"Yeah . . . damn right I'm ready."

"How much time do you guys have in the ring?"

"About thirty, thirty-five minutes."

Dad nodded. "That's great . . . great. You've got everything down?"

"Uh-huh."

He was formal, but I could tell he was welling up with emotion. My father had seen me perform at *WrestleMania* before. He wouldn't say much to me afterward, but my mother would always report that he had spent the entire night bragging about his son.

I took my World Wrestling Federation title belt out of a bag and slung it over my shoulder. "Okay, Dad. It's time."

"Okay," he said. "Do what you do best: kick ass! Good luck . . . do great."

Then we hugged.

"I love you, Dad."

"I love you, too."

At the gorilla position I put my belt down in front of Bruce Prichard. Vince McMahon was there, as were Gerry Brisco, Pat Patterson, Jack Lanza, and all three referees. And Steve, of course.

"How much time before we go out?" I asked Bruce.

"You've got about six minutes."

I started jumping around, doing some push-ups, trying to keep my sweat going. Steve was running in place. While warming up we talked some more about the match. We were calling things back and forth to each other, shouting out various moves and spots, testing each other's knowledge of the script. Just beyond the curtain I could hear the noise rising and falling as the crowd anticipated the main event. My heart was pumping furiously. I grabbed a bottle of water and washed off my hands. At the exact same time, Steve and I looked at each other and held out two fingers: *two times!* That had been the signal for the Rock/Austin handshake from the very beginning. We slapped hands twice, pointed at each other, and slapped hands a third time.

"See you out there," we said in unison. "Let's do it!"

I poured some water over my head and grabbed the title belt. Outside there was an interlude of silence, a moment of utter quiet as the crowd waited for something to happen. And then my music hit.

"DO YOU SMELL WHAT THE ROCK IS COOKING?"

"THE ROCK SAYS ... THE ROCK SAYS ..."

I heard someone yell "Go get 'em, Rock!" as I stepped through the first set of black curtains. Three more steps and I was through a second and final set of curtains ... into the arena ... into ... *madness!*

The First Union Center erupted! Flashbulbs popped and blinked. I could hear almost nothing, not

even my music. The noise was deafening. Doing the
infamous, arrogant Rock strut—spitting, snorting,
snotting all over the place, holding The People's Title
high, for all to see—I made my way down the aisle
and into the ring. By this time I was completely in
character. Dwayne Johnson had melted away, and in
his place was . . . The Rock!

THE ROCK SAYS . . . IT'S ONE HELL OF A MATCH!

As The Rock is sauntering around The People's Ring, his music ends and the crowd gets real quiet. Suddenly the sound of breaking glass roars through the sound system, and the crowd goes nuts. Stone Cold Steve Austin is on his way. But that's okay because The Rock is waiting. He locks eyes with Austin and makes a gesture with both hands, as if to say, "Bring your ass, you piece of shit!" So Austin comes into the ring, and as he steps through the ropes, he tries to make an ascent up the first turnbuckle. But The Rock is right there, in his face, meeting Stone Cold Steve Austin, screaming at him: "Where in the living fuck do you think you're going?" No one has ever had the balls to challenge Stone Cold like this. Every other wrestler gives the Rattlesnake his space, for fear of getting bitten. But not The Rock. This is what The Rock does best, going back to the days when The Rock was intimidating sumbitches in the Orange Bowl, employing that age-old Rock adage: *Hit, stick, and bust dick! And talk shit!* Stone Cold goes up to the second turnbuckle, and now he's trying for the third. But The Rock stands directly in front of this jabroni and says, "You ain't ready for The Rock." Stone Cold starts jabbering back at The Rock, acting like he's actually saying something that's half-ass intimidating to The Rock. He tries to go around The Rock again, but like the man and a half that he is, The Rock takes a step to his right, cutting Austin off.

"You ain't going nowhere . . . and The Rock means nowhere!" Stone Cold pretends to ignore The Great One and tries to go around The Rock again. But The Rock isn't about to let Stone Cold pass. He blocks Austin's path again. "Didn't The Rock just say you ain't going nowhere . . . you piece of shit?!"

And then, like the cheater he is, like the piece of trash that everyone knows he is, Stone Cold hauls off and nails The Rock. The Rock nails him right back, and now the fight is on. The crowd is going crazy. It's *WrestleMania XV*, Austin and The Rock, one Great One, one piece of trash, toe-to-toe in the middle of the ring, going at it like two gladiators in the best damn match there ever was.

For ten minutes . . . fifteen minutes . . . Stone Cold Steve Austin and The Rock try to tear each other apart. The action spills outside the ring, as The Rock proceeds to kick Austin's monkey ass all over the First Union Center—through the sea of The People's Champ's fans . . . up and down The People's Aisles. Stone Cold is a tough piece of trailer-park trash, though. He fights back. As they climb back into the ring, Austin is getting the better of The Rock. But Austin doesn't understand the immensity of the athlete he's facing. He gets sloppy, and now The Rock is there to greet him with The Rock Bottom . . . *WHAM!* Right in the middle of the ring! Stone Cold Steve Austin goes down. This could be it. The Rock covers—*one . . . two . . .*

Ohhhhhh! Stone Cold Steve Austin does the impossible—he kicks out of The Rock Bottom! No one has ever done that before. It's the biggest shock of The Rock's career. But, true to form, The Rock comes back even stronger. Now he's furious. Now he's going to do some serious damage to Austin's candy ass.

This guy is kicking out of The Rock's big finish? He's trying to embarrass The Rock? The Rock doesn't think so. . . .

The Rock decides to teach Stone Cold a lesson. He leaves The People's Ring and grabs a chair. Then he throws that chair into the ring. The Rock is getting ready to whack Stone Cold with the chair when Stone Cold surprises The Rock with a kick. The chair falls to the mat. The Rock is hurt. Stone Cold Steve Austin grabs the chair and prepares to nail The People's Champ in the face. Austin wants to hurt the millions and the millions of The Rock's fans. He wants to rid them of The People's Eyebrow. But as Stone Cold swings that chair like Hank Aaron, The Rock reaches up and grabs that jabroni of a referee, whose name is Mike Chioda, by the belt and pulls him down ... right in front of The Rock's face. *WHAM!* The ref is eating steel!

Stone Cold hesitates when he realizes what he's done, and that gives The Rock time to do what he does best: kick ass! The Rock pummels Stone Cold Steve Austin, drives that jabroni right to the mat. Now that there's no referee, it's time for The Rock to win at all costs. The Rock grabs that steel chair and starts talking shit to Austin: "Get up, you piece of monkey crap! Get your ass off that floor because you're about to have a Rockwich. You're about to have a Rock Burger with extra cheese. Only in this case, the cheese is made out of ... *steel!" WHACK!* The Rock creases Austin's forehead with the chair. Stone Cold is really stone cold now. He's out colder than a block of ice.

Now, there just happens to be a second referee, Timmy White, in the ring, and this jabroni is checking on the first referee, who is still taking a nap, courtesy of The Rock. So The Rock yells at Timmy White, "Hey! Get your fat ass in here and make the count!" With all the confidence in the world, The Rock practically lounges on Stone Cold as the referee begins to count:

"One ..."

The entire crowd is counting along, yelling at the top of their lungs ...

"Two ..."

It's almost over. ... Ohhhhhh! Once again that son of a bitch kicks out. Now The Rock is really pissed, and the one thing you don't want to do is piss off The Rock. A lot of unfortunate people have found that out in a very personal, physical way. Stone Cold has kicked out of The Rock Bottom. He's kicked out of a chair shot from The People's Champ. So now The Rock grabs this jabroni of a referee and he plants him with The Rock Bottom, leaving the match, once again, without a referee. See, if the refs aren't going to be competent, then The Rock would just as soon not have a referee. But as soon as The Rock turns around, there's Stone Cold Steve Austin . . . with a big surprise: a boot to the gut! Followed by a Stone Cold Stunner! The fucking place goes bananas! Stone Cold rushes to cover. This is his big finish. The third referee, Earl Hebner, is running down the aisle. He slides into the ring as the fans chant in unison, in time with his hand, "ONE . . . TWO . . ."

OHHHHHHHHHH . . . The Rock lifts his shoulder! He kicks out of the Stone Cold Stunner, something that no one—and The Rock . . . means . . . no one—has ever done! Not only is there a hush in the arena, there is a sense of *Oh, my God! What can possibly happen next?*

The answer isn't long in coming. As The Rock kicks out of the Stone Cold Stunner, Vince McMahon, the chairman and CEO of World Wrestling Federation Entertainment, Inc., comes strolling down the aisle and belts Earl Hebner. This naturally distracts Stone Cold Steve Austin, and pretty soon The Rock is making like Ali. Forget the butterfly crap, though. The Rock goes straight to the "sting like a bee" part. He nails Stone Cold with an uppercut to the nuts. OWWWW! The Rock actually hears Stone Cold say, "Oh, my God, you just made me into a woman!" Stone Cold goes down. He's writhing in pain, and The Rock thinks he hears Stone Cold saying something else. It sounds like . . . it sounds like . . . *"I quit!"* Or is it . . . *"Please, Rock . . . no more?"* The Rock thinks about taking pity on poor Stone Cold, but hey, there's no referee, and The Rock can't ring the bell because The Rock isn't an official. Guess Stone Cold is out of luck.

So The Rock and Vince McMahon start doing a little tap dance on Austin's bald head. But as The Rock is putting the boots to Stone Cold, he hears something, something that sounds like applause. And then he hears cheering, the sound of twenty-one thousand fans going wild. The Rock starts to wonder, *What in the hell is going on here?* He turns around and what does he see? That 280-pound lump of gorilla shit, Mankind! And Mankind is wearing a ridiculous tie-dyed referee T-shirt, like he thinks he's going to be in charge of this match. Mankind jumps into the ring and decks Vince McMahon. The Rock looks at Mankind with astonishment. "What in the living hell are you doing?" The Rock says. "Do you want The Rock to layeth the smack down on your candy ass?" While formulating an answer, that goof starts staring at his watch, like he's going to tell The Rock what time it is again. His idiocy distracts The Rock, and suddenly Stone Cold Austin charges at The Rock from behind. He rolls up The Rock. Mankind hits the mat as fast as he can and begins to count: "one ... two ..."

OHHHHHH . . . The Rock kicks out again! Come on, Stone Cold . . . you don't beat The Rock with an amateur move like that . . . with a "schoolboy"!? You're looking at the teacher, for Christ's sake. You're looking at the principal ... the superintendent ... the goddamn secretary of education! You'll have to do better than that.

The Rock proceeds to hammer Stone Cold Steve Austin with another Rock Bottom. But The Rock is a highly intelligent man, so he doesn't settle for an ordinary Rock Bottom. He gives Austin the *WrestleMania* Rock Bottom Special! As Austin is lying on the mat helpless and dazed after absorbing The Rock Bottom, The Rock stands over Stone Cold and looks at him with disdain, like the piece of Texas trailer-park trash that he is. The people are going wild! Despite all the hatred they feel for The Rock, they still want him to deliver the most electrifying move in sports-entertainment: The People's Elbow. So The Rock slowly removes his elbow pad from his right arm and tosses it into the crowd. He takes off to the left, hits one set of ropes, jumps over that big

pile of garbage—and it is a big pile . . . good thing The Rock has a great vertical leap—comes back around, and prepares to drop. The leg shimmies, the flashbulbs explode, and The Rock throws all his weight into The People's Elbow and falls earthward. This . . . is . . . it!

OHHHHHH . . . Stone Cold Steve Austin slides out of the way. The Rock hits the mat with a tremendous *CRASH!* He bounces up, holding his arm. The Rock is howling. He's dislocated his elbow. And now Stone Cold Steve Austin is kicking The Rock, treating him like he's just some roody-poo standing on the corner of Know Your Role Boulevard and Jabroni Drive. The crowd senses that the end is near. But The Rock is a man and a half—at least! With his left hand he catches Austin's boot in the middle of a kick to the gut. Then The Rock takes his right hand and he flips Stone Cold the bird, right square in his face: "You go fuck yourself, you piece of shit!"

The Rock spins Stone Cold around, hooks him for The Rock Bottom again. But Stone Cold delivers three quick elbows to The Rock's skull and gets out of The Rock Bottom. The Rock does a three-sixty, and he's met with another boot to the midsection. The Rock is doubled over! He's in pain! He takes another Stone Cold Stunner . . . he takes it spectacularly, doing a backflip in the air, as only The Rock can. Stone Cold hooks the leg. The crowd begins to chant . . .

"ONE . . . TWO . . . THREE!"

And with that, the roof blows off the First Union Center. Although The Rock is still dazed from the Stone Cold Stunner, he realizes it's the loudest noise he's ever heard. Did Stone Cold beat The Man? Did he beat The Rock? Well, The Rock will always call a spade a spade, so . . . you're damn right he beat The Rock. Did Stone Cold Steve Austin give The Rock all he could handle? You're damn right he did. Did The Rock give Stone Cold all *he* could handle . . . and then some? You're damn right he did! It took two Stunners to beat The Rock, and Stone Cold was one People's

Elbow away from getting beat by The People's Champ. So remember this: One way or another, come hell or high water, you can bet that The Rock will one day recapture the title. And he will go down in history as the best damn World Wrestling Federation Champ there ever was!

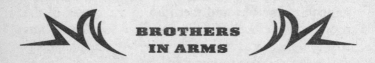

BROTHERS
IN ARMS

As I walked back up the aisle, I could hear Steve's music playing. I knew he was celebrating in the ring, popping cans of Budweiser and spraying the audience, toasting a victory as only he can. I was so happy for him, and for us, and for what we had accomplished. But I had to stay in character. I had to keep scowling and spitting and snorting, at least until I passed through the curtains.

Backstage I was mobbed by everyone: Vince McMahon, Shane McMahon, the agents and staff, some of the boys.

"Great job, Rock!"

"That was one of the best ever!"

"Fantastic!"

"Thank you," I kept saying. "Thank you very much."

My father was there, too. He wrapped me in a hug and told me how proud he was. After about three or four minutes I made my way back to Steve's locker room. I fell into a couch and tried to relax, but my heart was still pounding. I was drenched with sweat. An odd blend of euphoria and exhaustion enveloped me. I kept thanking God under my breath—thanking

Him for blessing me with the strength and the ability to reach this point.

The door flew open and in walked Steve Austin. He tossed the belt—*his belt, now*—onto the couch. I jumped to my feet and met him in the center of the room, and we hugged for a good ten seconds. It was strong hug, a real fucking brotherly embrace reflecting a tacit understanding that we had just shared something remarkable.

"Thank you," Steve said.

"Thank *you*. It was my pleasure."

As we released our hug, we both fell into the couch, completely spent. Other people started pouring into the room. One of them was Jim Ross, who came over and started hugging both of us, shaking our hands.

"What did you think, J. R.?" I said.

"Oh, God, man . . . that was one of the best, if not the best match I have ever called." I could see that he was in tears. It was an emotional night for Jim. Three months earlier, while calling a match in England, he had gotten word that his mother had passed away. That very night Jim began suffering from Bell's Palsy, which can be provoked by stress. Jim was taken off the air after that match. *WrestleMania XV* was his first night back behind the microphone, and he was just so happy to be home again, and to have called such a great match, that he was overcome with emotion. I was proud of J. R.'s return that night; quite frankly, had he not called the match, it would not have been the same.

"It was an honor to have you call it, J. R.," I said. "Thanks."

People kept flowing into the room until it took on the air of a party. Eventually Mark Yeaton, the bell ringer and timekeeper for our match, walked in, his body straining beneath the weight of a big blue cooler.

"Beer time, boys!" he shouted.

"All right, Mark!"

We all cracked open beers and started talking about the night.

"Now that was the marquee match *WrestleMania* needed," Steve said. "Rock versus Austin—it does not get any bigger or better than that."

"Hell, yeah!" J. R. said. "And you guys are gonna get paid for it, too."

The whole room cracked up. A dozen grown men convulsed with the kind of true and hard-earned laughter that comes only with victory. I lifted my beer into the air and shouted over the noise . . . "Well, hell! I'll drink to that!"

chapter 16 OWEN

I MET OWEN HART in Corpus Christi, Texas, in March of 1996, on the night of my very first World Wrestling Federation match. We sat around for more than an hour, sharing memories of family and friends and the business. For both of us, the business was family. We had grown up in it. And, in fact, the branches of our respective family trees had intertwined on occasion. When I was a little boy, living in Hawaii, Owen's older brother, Dean, lived there, too. Dean Hart used to help my grandparents when they were preparing for a show. He would help set up the ring and the venue . . . sometimes he'd even work as a referee. I liked Dean a lot. I was an only child and kind of looked at him as a big brother. I used to chase him around, pester him to play with me. He was a grown man, and I can imagine what was going through his mind—*Will somebody get this little brat the hell away from me?*—but he was always friendly and accessible. Just like Owen.

I shared with Owen whatever memories I had of Dean, who has since passed away, and he shared his memories of visiting Hawaii with his older brothers, who wrestled for my grandparents. He remembered getting caught up in a hail of fists at ringside in one match because the Hart tag team was wrestling a local Samoan team.

"It was crazy," Owen said. "I was in the middle of all these six-foot, three-hundred-pound bodies . . . and the men were even bigger." That was typical of his skewed view on life and the business. Owen saw humor in everything. He had a big, easy laugh, and an even bigger heart. When I arrived in the World Wrestling Federation, Owen and Bret Hart were stars, and yet they never treated me (or anyone else) with disrespect. It just wasn't their nature.

On May 23, 1999, at a Pay-Per-View show in Kansas City, Missouri, my good friend Owen Hart died. He fell ninety feet while being lowered into the ring before a match. I do not know what happened, what caused this terrible accident, and I have no intention of ascribing any blame. I only know that I was backstage in the dressing room, going over the details of my upcoming match with Triple H and Chyna. We were talking, moving around, trying to figure out how to make the match memorable, when Sergeant Slaughter walked into the room and said, "Owen is hurt." I looked at Hunter, then I looked at Sarge and said, "God, come on. Are you serious or are you ribbing?" Owen was known for his pranks, and I thought maybe this was just another example of his twisted sense of humor.

"No," Sarge said. "It looks pretty bad. They're working on him in the middle of the ring."

My heart sank. And then it almost seemed to stop beating for a moment. I got up, walked down the hall as fast as I could, and went straight to the curtain. As I reached the gorilla position, where everyone was gathered, I could see the shock on their faces, the disbelief. People were crying, hugging. And then it hit me: *This is real.* I walked up to the curtain and looked out. The EMTs were working on Owen in the middle of the ring, giving him CPR. The crowd was on its feet, absolutely silent. *My God . . . that's my friend. I have to go out there.*

I turned around. Vince McMahon was standing there, watching everything on the monitors. He was in shock, just like the rest of us. "Vince," I said, "I want to go out there—what do you think?"

Vince just stared at me, with a look on his face that seemed to say, *Rock, that's entirely up to you.* After a few moments, though, Vince spoke. "If you go out there, Rock, those people are really going to react to you." I thought about it. I was in full uniform. I was The Rock. What would happen if I charged out into the arena, full of emotion? "They may think this whole thing is a work," Vince said.

We were thinking exactly the same thing. "You're right. I don't want to demean what's happening out there right now."

So I waited anxiously, helplessly by the curtain, until they wheeled Owen through on a stretcher. One of the EMTs was still straddling Owen, pumping his chest, desperately administering CPR. I walked alongside them and said a prayer as I looked at Owen's face. Then I helped load the stretcher into the ambulance. I climbed into the passenger side of the vehicle and looked into the back, where they were still working furiously on Owen. I kept praying that God would save my friend's life . . . praying that God would bless Owen in any way if he was not to make it.

After the ambulance drove off, we were all in shock. There was a lot of crying and hugging. I felt completely numb. And now, somehow, we had to deal with the task of going out there and performing. Triple H and I talked about the rest of our match, tried to finish putting things together, but it was almost impossible because we were so worried about Owen. Two minutes before we were scheduled to hit the stage, we were told that Owen had died. I immediately said another prayer, right there in the locker room. I thanked God for having enriched my life by letting me get to know Owen. I said a prayer for his family. Then—and I know this sounds strange—I started to think about the performance, the show. I thought . . . *Can I really go out there right now?* Not *should* I go out there . . . but *can* I? *Am I capable of performing?* I could not remember anything about the match we had designed. My mind was a blank. Everything seemed . . . *pointless.*

But as quickly as I asked myself that question— *Can I go out there now?*—the answer came. I envisioned Owen saying, "D. J., you have to go out there."

It was, of course, one of those situations where you're damned if you do, damned if you don't. If you go on with the show, you're going be criticized by people who feel you're being insensitive or disrespectful. And if you cancel the show ... well, you've got a packed arena and 500,000 people across the country who have paid forty or fifty bucks for the Pay-Per-View. And some of those people are going to be pissed. That's just the way it is. Either way, all of the blame is going to be placed on Vince McMahon rather than on The Rock or Triple H or the Undertaker or Stone Cold Steve Austin. That's unfortunate, because we each made a conscious decision to go out there and continue with the show. I personally felt comfortable with going on because I knew Owen, and I believe Owen would have wanted that.

After my match I called Dany. Then I called Owen's brother, Bret. His machine picked up: "Bret, this is probably one of a hundred messages you're going to receive," I said. "I just want to tell you I'm sorry. And if there's anything I can do, please call me."

The next night on *Raw* we scrapped all story lines and dedicated the show to Owen. We all felt—and by "we" I mean talent, technicians, and front-office personnel—that somehow it would have been inappropriate to simply go out and do our regular show as if nothing had happened. It wasn't that we were worried about being disrespectful. It was more a matter of feeling that this was an opportunity to say good-bye to Owen, to let him and his family know how we felt.

So we put everything on hold, and the entire evening became a tribute to Owen Hart. None of the matches meant anything. If you wanted to work, you could come out and wrestle and say something about Owen. If you didn't want to work, then you didn't have to work. It was entirely up to each individual. But the *show* belonged to Owen. I chose to wrestle

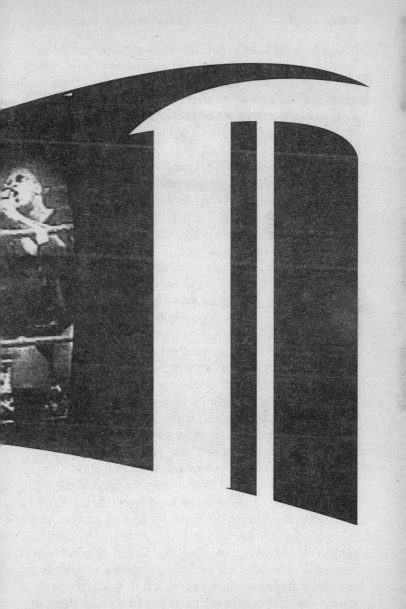

and get on the microphone as I usually do, and do my little bit. I chose to stay in character when I got on the mike—to speak as The Rock and dedicate everything I was saying, as well as everything I was going to do, to Owen. I think he would have appreciated that.

Again, though, we took a lot of heat for the way we handled that situation. *Damned if you do, damned if you don't.* We would have been damned as a company if we had simply put up a little video tribute to Owen saying, "Thanks for the memories," and then continued with our story lines. But at the same time, we as a company, and especially as Owen's fellow wrestlers and entertainers . . . we were damned for going out there and dedicating the show to him. That pissed me off! I mean, there were a lot of people . . . critics . . . who said they couldn't believe how insincere and callous the show seemed; how we used Owen's death to propel our ratings. I heard accusations that none of the wrestlers meant what they were saying, that all of the material was scripted. How dare you say that! How dare you say that about me . . . or my coworkers! Every single guy who worked that night damn near broke down in tears. The emotion and the work that we put into that evening were genuine.

I will say for the record that I am extremely proud of that show. I'm proud of the way everybody handled it, and I'm proud of the way the guys went out there and busted their asses for Owen. Every single one of them—putting on boots for Owen, and putting on tights for Owen, and going out there and cutting promos for Owen . . . *working* for Owen. When I hear that cynical bullshit about how disgusting it was, that the entire show was just a gimmick to boost the audience . . . well, it makes me sick. Because I was there in the locker room that night, when we all cried together and talked about all the good things that Owen had brought us, and all the strange and funny things he had done to make us laugh, and how much we all were going to miss him.

The following Monday Owen Hart was laid to rest. Dany and I flew to Calgary for the funeral and paid our respects to Owen and his family. Not surprisingly, there was a huge turnout, hundreds of people in the church and literally thousands more waiting outside in the rain. It was a testament to Owen's popularity. He had touched so many lives. The hardest part, for me, was seeing Owen in the casket. He was such a strong man, so full of life and energy and warmth. Now he was gone. That's an image I will never shake. But at the same time, it won't outweigh the memories I have of Owen, the good times we shared, and the smile he always put on my face.

chapter 17

GOTTA WEAR SHADES

A KEY TO SUCCESS in our industry is listening to the crowd. I was taught that at a very young age. In listening to the fans at *WrestleMania XV*, we knew that we would be lucky to get one more Pay-Per-View event out of the Austin-Rock rivalry. The original plan had been for *WrestleMania* to be the first of four blockbuster events. The story line would stretch out over several months, and The Rock and Stone Cold Steve Austin would kick the living crap out of each other on a regular basis.

That arc simply wouldn't work now. With their support of The Rock in Philadelphia, with their singing and chanting and laughing, the fans had cast their vote: *"We like The Rock ... even if he is an ass-*

hole." It's not impossible to have two babyfaces at the top of the ladder, fighting each other for titles and the fans' affection. Hulk Hogan and the Ultimate Warrior pulled it off in the 1980s. But the feeling in our company was that it would be counterproductive. Regardless of what people say and how the industry has evolved, I think there are some basic tenets to which you must adhere. One of them is this: People want to boo somebody, and people want to cheer somebody. It's that simple. And it was becoming increasingly clear that when The Rock met Stone Cold Steve Austin, the fans were spending all of their time cheering.

Rather than allow the act to grow stale, we decided to have just one more Rock-Austin Pay-Per-View—at *Backlash* in April. In that match, once again, I put Steve over in the middle of the ring—*one-two-three!* He held on to the World Wrestling Federation title with a clean victory. But that was only one function of the match. Equally important was The Rock's continued slide toward babyface-dom. I had been having talks with the writers and the office about how to handle this transition. To me, it was vital that The Rock remain The Rock. I was completely opposed to a 180-degree turn from heel to babyface. It had to be gradual, subtle, genuine. And in the end, even a babyface version of The Rock had to exhibit all, or at least most, of the vile characteristics that made the heel version of The Rock so compelling.

For starters, we brought The Rock's relationship with the Corporation to a violent and thrilling conclusion. Shane McMahon had hit The Rock with a chair during *Backlash*, setting up the denouement. So, on the next *Raw,* The Rock cut a promo in which he told the crowd, *"Hey, this still isn't sing-along with The Rock, and he still doesn't care if you boo or cheer. But The Rock has one big problem, and that's a pile of steaming, stinking monkey crap named Shane McMahon!"* The crowd, of course, went nuts. This was the showdown they'd been waiting for. In this scenario, it was easy to root for The Rock; compared to Shane McMahon, he really was a babyface.

The Rock went on with his promo . . . feeding the frenzy with style and flair. *"Shane McMahon, you are three seconds away—"* And before I could finish, fifteen thousand people were shouting, "AND THE ROCK MEANS THREE SECONDS!"—*"before The Rock lays the smack down on your candy ass!"* I held my hand up and began counting: *"One . . . two . . . THREE!"* That was it. The Rock proceeded to nail Shane McMahon and the rest of the Corporation flunkies. He beat Shane McMahon's ass exactly as the fans expected. Rock Bottom, People's Elbow . . . everything. It was electrifying.

Now The Rock's babyface fuse had been lit. But it was still important that we not overdo it. We didn't want The Rock to suddenly start fighting only heels. We didn't want him to make a dramatic entrance side by side with Stone Cold Steve Austin. And we sure as hell didn't want him walking out, grabbing the microphone, and shouting, *"All right everyone! It's sing-along with The Rock!"* The Rock was too cool for that. Instead, he began directing his promos, his venom, more directly at his opponents and less at the crowd. As a babyface The Rock would no longer come out and say. *"There are twenty thousand pieces of trailer-park trash here tonight!"* That wouldn't work. At the same time, he wasn't about to undergo a personality change. We weren't about to forget what brought The Rock to the dance: his ability to talk, his ability to work, and his attitude. The Rock was a colossal asshole. That wouldn't change. But as a babyface it was like . . . *Yeah, but he's a cool asshole.* Would you see The Rock in a tag-team match with Stone Cold Steve Austin against two top heels? Absolutely. But The Rock would stay in character. He'd say, *"The Rock would just as soon slap you in the face as slap your hand to tag you in. You'll never get a Christmas card from The Rock. Then again, The Rock is a highly intelligent man, and to beat these two jabronis . . . sure, he'll use you for all your worth. But after the match, you're on your way!"*

THE SKY'S
THE LIMIT

A lot of accomplished wrestlers, both current and retired, have advised me to belly up to the trough while it's full. "Get it while you can," they tell me. "Just ride this wave and then get out." Well, to me that's not the right attitude. I have been fortunate to accomplish a tremendous amount in a relatively short period of time. And I've been blessed in that I have a beautiful family with whom I can share my success. Quite frankly, without Dany and my parents and my grandmother, everything else would be insignificant. But I can't help feeling as though I've just begun to lay the foundation for my career. I'm only twenty-seven years old. There's so much more I want to do. I'm committed to making sure that each match is better than the one before it, that every interview/promo is more creative and entertaining than the last. I am not merely passing through here. I grew up in this industry. My roots are deep. It's extremely important to me that when all is said and done, Dwayne Johnson— aka The Rock—will be remembered as one of the biggest stars, if not the biggest star, professional wrestling has ever seen. *Ride the wave and get out?* I don't think so. In some form or fashion, I'll be involved in this business for the rest of my life because

I absolutely love what I do. I have a passion for this business and a never-ending desire to be the best.

Does that mean I wouldn't consider branching out and accepting other challenges? Absolutely not. I've done some TV work and I've received numerous motion-picture offers. Most of the scripts I've seen haven't been worth consideration, but when the right opportunity comes along, I'll probably take the plunge. We've all worked very hard to place The Rock at a certain level, and we just want to make sure that his first movie is a good movie. Will The Rock be the next James Dean or Cary Grant or James Stewart? I don't think so. But he could be the next Arnold Schwarzenegger . . . only better looking.

The Rock's ascent has been so meteoric that I still find it somewhat remarkable to have these options. I still get a huge kick out of meeting celebrities and having them compliment my work. Nicolas Cage (whose son loves wrestling) once told me that The Rock is his absolute favorite. That completely blew me away! I mean, this is an Academy Award winner, and he's talking about The Rock's charisma, The Rock's talent. Incredible! Luther Vandross, Mike Tyson, Shaquille O'Neal—they're all big fans of The Rock. One of my best buddies is Michael Clark Duncan, who starred in *Armageddon* with Bruce Willis and *The Green Mile* with Tom Hanks. Michael is the world's number one Rock fan. Sometimes I think he'd rather have a spot on the *WrestleMania* card than win an Oscar. I had an opportunity to meet Jack Nicholson at the Emmy Awards. He looked me right in the eye and said, "Rock, you're doing a great job. Keep up the great work." To me, that is just so humbling.

It's also reflective of the rising popularity of professional wrestling. Our industry has experienced nothing less than a renaissance in recent years. Our audience has mushroomed and evolved. "Rasslin'" is out and "sports-entertainment" is in, and with that change has come a completely different attitude— both on the part of the people within our industry and the fans who support us. There was a time when a lot of wrestling fans hid their devotion. They followed the business and watched our television shows, but when they went to work in the morning, they kept their fetish to themselves. Not anymore. Wrestling has come out of the closet. From Middle America to Manhattan, from Silicon Valley to South Dakota, professional wrestling is embraced and supported with a fervor usually reserved for World Cup soccer matches. At the dawn of a new millennium, our typical adult fan is as likely as not to have a college degree and a household income in excess of $50,000. Our television ratings have been soaring and World Wrestling Federation stock is now traded on Wall Street.

With this success, of course, has come a fair amount of criticism, most of which is either unfounded or misdirected. It's funny . . . I don't recall Brian DePalma getting this much heat when he directed *Scarface*. I don't recall hearing anyone jump all over Steven Spielberg for the violence in *Saving Private Ryan*. I'm not saying the World Wrestling Federation is artistically equivalent to those films, but I do think it's important to recognize exactly what we're doing. We're making little movies . . . every week . . . every month. With a live audience and no laugh track. We're producing a live play, a highly

physical, male-oriented soap opera, and Vince McMahon is our director. You have to look at it and judge it in that context.

We are an edgy program, and our industry has become racy and sexual. I can't deny that. But we really are tame in comparison to a lot of network television. No one gets raped on our show. No one has sex on our show. Regardless of what the media says, and sometimes the comments are hilarious, there is no racism on our show. And the violence is of the comic-book, action-adventure variety. People get hit in the face with chairs on our show. They get kicked in the balls. But no one gets shot. And everyone comes back to fight another day.

Is it appropriate for an eight-year-old to watch *Raw Is War*? Probably not. Our primary audience is adult males, ages eighteen to thirty-four. That's why we run a parental advisory before the show. That's why it airs from 9:00 P.M. to 11:00 P.M. And that's why we have a kid-friendly show on the weekend, with the sexual content and most of the violence edited out. Children who are up at ten or eleven at night watching *Raw* should be mature enough to know the difference between reality and fantasy. And if they're not, then they shouldn't be watching. But it's up to the parents to monitor their own children. The Rock should not be held responsible for your children's viewing habits; nor should Vince McMahon.

That said, I acknowledge that we are responsible for the product we put out there, and that's why I'm always very conscious of the things I'm doing . . . the things The Rock is doing. I am immensely proud of our show and its success. Our writing staff is among the most creative in the entertainment business, and certainly the most tireless. Thanks to their innovative, byzantine story lines, and the talented, devoted troupe of players who bring them to life, professional wrestling has achieved mainstream acceptance, something that was almost unimaginable when I was a boy ... when Rocky Johnson, the Magnificent Muraco, Jimmy "Superfly" Snuka, and other titans of their time ruled the ring.

I think they'd be happy. I think they'd be proud.
I know they would.

 ## KING OF
THE RING

June 27, 1999 (Greensboro, NC)—The lights dim and twenty thousand leather-lunged fans at the Greensboro Coliseum begin chanting his name: "ROCKY! ROCKY! ROCKY!" Once again The Rock is fighting for the World Wrestling Federation title. Once again The Rock is about to make some candy-ass jabroni famous. This time it's the Undertaker, the reigning Federation champ. As usual, in his customary Rock style, The Rock cuts a devastating promo. Then he beats the Undertaker's dead ass, from pillar to post, for thirty minutes. Does The Rock win the Federation title? Absolutely not! Does it take three men to beat The Rock? You're damn right it does! So make no mistake about it . . . The Rock walks out of the Greensboro Coliseum without a belt, but he walks out to raucous cheers, still The People's Champion. World Wrestling Federation title or no World Wrestling Federation title, The Rock is still, without a shadow of a doubt, the number one man in this business.

Does The Rock care whether you shout his name? Does he care whether you hold up signs proclaiming your love and respect? Hell, no! The Rock never has and never will ask for the adulation of the fans. But The Rock knows that the fans can and always will appreciate the fact that The Rock has a single, solitary intention, and that is to go out every night and do what The Rock does best: entertain the people. The Rock says he is not only the best on the microphone and the best in the ring, but the most charismatic, the most compelling, the most talented . . . simply put, the most electrifying man in sports-entertainment . . .

. . . IF YOU SMELL WHAT THE ROCK IS COOKING!

BONUS CHAPTER

Filming the video for "Know Your Role"
by Method Man, from the
World Wrestling Federation *Aggression* CD.

Signing the #1 bestseller in New York City.

Some of the millions . . . outside Tower Records.

The most electrifying move in sports-entertainment:
the People's Elbow.

The Rock vs. Big Show at *No Way Out*.

Co-hosting *Much Music* in Toronto, Canada.

Triple H hitting Rock bottom!

Filming *Smackdown* video game commercial,
Miami, Florida.

Trying to decapitate D-Von Dudley.
In a loving way, of course!

Hosting *Saturday Night Live* with cast members
Will Ferrell and Horatio Sanz.

Giving the People's Elbow to Stephanie McMahon
at *Wrestlemania XVI*.

Layin' the smack down on Triple H
in a match I'm very proud of, the
"Iron Man" match at *Judgement Day*.

The Rock vs. Christian on *Smackdown*,
Tacoma, Washington.

The Rock: The best damn
WWF champion there ever was!

The Rock hosting MTV's *Total Request Live*.

Just bring it!

Welcoming Mick Foley back from retirement.
The Rock 'n' Sock connection one more time.

ACKNOWLEDGMENTS

This book came to fruition through the hard work of many talented people. I would first like to give my thanks to the Lord for all the countless blessings he has given me. I know his eyes are always open. I would like to thank my wife, Dany, my tag-team partner in life. Without her love, patience, input, and support I would not be where I am today. Special thanks to the talented Joe Layden, who is not only an extremely creative writer but has the unique ability to understand exactly what thoughts I am trying to convey. A very special thank you to my mother and father: my father for his love, support and guidance, and for being years ahead of his time in the business. He has inspired me and helped me to have a true understanding of the psychology needed to succeed in this business. My mother for being the backbone of our family; she is the kindest and warmest person I have ever known. A special acknowledgment goes out to my grandmother Leah Maivia; she has been a pioneer in this business and a source of tremendous love and support. To my grandfather in heaven, the High Chief, I love you and miss you. You have helped pave the way for my future and I know you are watching from above. I also want to thank my new family in Miami: my in-laws, Hiram and Dani Garcia, and my new special grandparents John and Chela Quintana. Much love goes out to my sister-in-law Marlo, her husband, Jorge Perez, and my partner in crime in Miami, "The People's Brother-in-law," Hiram Garcia. You have all become very important people in my life. To my family who live all over the world: the Bowles, my Uncle Jay, Curtis and family, the Maiavas, and of course Uncle Neff who has been a tremendously strong limb on my family tree. To the Anoais—my Uncle Afa and his family have been an important part of my family's life. I also want to acknowledge the Snukas, especially my Aunt Sharon, who was carved from the same rock as my mother. To the Fafitas, the Fitisemanus, the Iopus, the Fanenes, and the Faleautos; thank you all for your love and support. To my friends Al and Bruce Rosen, my little buddy, Milton, to Sunny and Linda Baker.

Thanks to Judith Regan of ReganBooks for seeing the enormous potential in this project, and to Jeremie Ruby-Strauss for his editorial guidance. Thanks, also, to Frank Weimann of The Literary Group.

A very special thank you goes to Vince, Linda, Shane, Marissa, and Stephanie McMahon. They are the individuals who give me a weekly platform on which I am allowed to entertain the millions and the millions. Their guidance and belief in my abilities have brought me to the level I am at today, and for that I am grateful.

To all the warriors I work with every night: they are the most talented and dedicated sports-entertainers in the business today! Much love goes to Steve Austin, the Undertaker, Triple H, and Mankind. I admire and learn from all of them daily.

A tremendous thank you goes to the entire World

Wrestling Federation team, from the Stamford offices (the first floor to the fourth floor), and to all those at the television production studios; from the New York crew to the agents; from talent relations to marketing and all those who are on the road nightly with The Rock. Each individual who works for this company is an integral part of my career and I want to thank them all. THEY ARE THE MOST ELECTRIFYING TEAM IN AMERICA.

PHOTO CREDITS

P. 119 "CAN YOU SMELL WHAT THE ROCK IS COOKING? AT THE UNIVERSITY OF MIAMI ON GRADUATION DAY, 1995." (COURTESY OF AUTHOR'S PHOTO COLLECTION.)

P. 120 "MY DAD WITH TERRY FUNK, BEFORE THEIR NWA WORLD TITLE MATCH." (COURTESY OF AUTHOR'S PHOTO COLLECTION.)

P. 124 © 2000 WORLD WRESTLING FEDERATION ENTERTAINMENT, INC. ALL RIGHTS RESERVED.

P. 131 "DANY AND ME IN HAWAII WITH ALL MY SAMOAN BOYS." (COURTESY AUTHOR'S PHOTO COLLECTION.)

P. 143 THE ROCK WITH VINCE MCMAHON. LEXINGTON, KENTUCKY, NOVEMBER 16, 1998. (PHOTOGRAPHER: RICH FREEDA) © 2000 WORLD WRESTLING FEDERATION ENTERTAINMENT, INC. ALL RIGHTS RESERVED.

P. 144 "THE FIRST MATCH: THE ROCK VS. THE BROOKLYN BRAWLER, MARCH 1996, IN CORPUS CHRISTI, TEXAS." (COURTESY OF AUTHOR'S PHOTO COLLECTION.)

P. 152 "THE ROCK'S FAVORITE PASTIME." (COURTESY OF AUTHOR'S PHOTO COLLECTION.)

P. 160 THE ROCK, LAFAYETTE, LOUISIANA, JANUARY 21, 1997. (PHOTOGRAPHER: RICH FREEDA) © 2000 WORLD WRESTLING FEDERATION ENTERTAINMENT, INC. ALL RIGHTS RESERVED.

P. 164 THE ROCK. © 2000 WORLD WRESTLING FEDERATION ENTERTAINMENT, INC. ALL RIGHTS RESERVED.

P. 172 FANS IN CHARLOTTE, NORTH CAROLINA, JUNE 28, 1999. (PHOTOGRAPHER: DAVID MCLAIN) © 2000 WORLD WRESTLING FEDERATION ENTERTAINMENT, INC. ALL RIGHTS RESERVED.

P. 174–175 "INDUCTING MY DAD INTO THE CAULIFLOWER ALLEY CLUB IN 1996 WITH NICK BOCKWINKLE (LEFT) AND PAT PATTERSON." (COURTESY OF AUTHOR'S PHOTO COLLECTION.)

P. 182 THE ROCK VS. THE BROOKLYN BRAWLER. CORPUS CHRISTI, TEXAS, MARCH 10, 1996. (PHOTOGRAPHER: RICH FREEDA) © 2000 WORLD WRESTLING FEDERATION ENTERTAINMENT, INC. ALL RIGHTS RESERVED.

P. 191   THE ROCK VS. GOLDUST AT *SURVIVOR SERIES.* NOVEMBER 17, 1996. (PHOTOGRAPHER: JIM SULLEY) © 2000 WORLD WRESTLING FEDERATION ENTERTAINMENT, INC. ALL RIGHTS RESERVED.

P. 200–201 THE ROCK, BROOKLYN, NEW YORK, AUGUST 28, 1999. (PHOTOGRAPHER: RICH FREEDA) © 2000 WORLD WRESTLING FEDERATION ENTERTAINMENT, INC. ALL RIGHTS RESERVED.

P. 202   THE ROCK. MAY 25, 1999. (PHOTOGRAPHER: RICH FREEDA) © 2000 WORLD WRESTLING FEDERATION ENTERTAINMENT, INC. ALL RIGHTS RESERVED.

P. 208–209 THE ROCK VS. STONE COLD STEVE AUSTIN. LEXINGTON, KENTUCKY, NOVEMBER 16, 1998. (PHOTOGRAPHER: RICH FREEDA) © 2000 WORLD WRESTLING FEDERATION ENTERTAINMENT, INC. ALL RIGHTS RESERVED.

P. 216   "THE ROCK'S WEDDING DAY, MAY 3, 1997." (COURTESY OF AUTHOR'S PHOTO COLLECTION.)

P. 219   "MY TWENTY-SEVENTH BIRTHDAY WITH DANY AND MY SISTER-IN-LAW, MARLO." (COURTESY OF AUTHOR'S PHOTO COLLECTION.)

P. 228   FANS IN SAN DIEGO, CALIFORNIA, MAY 2, 1999. (PHOTOGRAPHER: TOM BUCHANAN) © 2000 WORLD WRESTLING FEDERATION ENTERTAINMENT, INC. ALL RIGHTS RESERVED.

P. 233   KANSAS CITY, MISSOURI, AUGUST 24, 1999. (PHOTOGRAPHER: DAVID MCLAIN) © 2000 WORLD WRESTLING FEDERATION ENTERTAINMENT, INC. ALL RIGHTS RESERVED.

P. 240   THE ROCK IN THE NATION OF DOMINATION WITH KAMA MUSTAFA (THE GODFATHER) AND D'LO BROWN. PENN STATE UNIVERSITY, PENNSYLVANIA, JANUARY 12, 1998. (PHOTOGRAPHER: TOM BUCHANAN) © 2000 WORLD WRESTLING FEDERATION ENTERTAINMENT, INC. ALL RIGHTS RESERVED.

P. 246   THE ROCK. © 2000 WORLD WRESTLING FEDERATION ENTERTAINMENT, INC. ALL RIGHTS RESERVED.

P. 247   THE ROCK HITTING KEN SHAMROCK WITH A CHAIR (ALSO WITH FAAROOQ). EVANSVILLE, INDIANA, FEBRUARY 3, 1998.

(PHOTOGRAPHER: DAVID MCLAIN) © 2000 WORLD WRESTLING FEDERATION ENTERTAINMENT, INC. ALL RIGHTS RESERVED.

P. 250   THE ROCK VS. MANKIND IN THE "I QUIT MATCH" AT ROYAL RUMBLE. ANAHEIM, CALIFORNIA, JANUARY 24, 1999. (PHOTOGRAPHER: RICH FREEDA) © 2000 WORLD WRESTLING FEDERATION ENTERTAINMENT, INC. ALL RIGHTS RESERVED.

P. 253   THE ROCK VS. KEN SHAMROCK. © 2000 WORLD WRESTLING FEDERATION ENTERTAINMENT, INC. ALL RIGHTS RESERVED.

P. 254   "PRESENTING AT THE 1999 EMMY AWARDS. MOMENTS LATER, JACK NICHOLSON WOULD COMPLIMENT 'THE ROCK'S WORK.'" (COURTESY OF AUTHOR'S PHOTO COLLECTION.)

P. 255   THE ROCK. © 2000 WORLD WRESTLING FEDERATION ENTERTAINMENT, INC. ALL RIGHTS RESERVED.

P. 257   "MYSELF AND MY BEAUTIFUL NIECES IN HAWAII." (COURTESY OF AUTHOR'S PHOTO COLLECTION.)

P. 258   FAN IN ST. LOUIS, MISSOURI, NOVEMBER 15, 1998. (PHOTOGRAPHER: TOM BUCHANAN) © 2000 WORLD WRESTLING FEDERATION ENTERTAINMENT, INC. ALL RIGHTS RESERVED.

P. 259   THE ROCK. © 2000 WORLD WRESTLING FEDERATION ENTERTAINMENT, INC. ALL RIGHTS RESERVED.

P. 268   "THE ROCK WITH BOYZ II MEN, *WRESTLEMANIA XV*" (COURTESY OF AUTHOR'S PHOTO COLLECTION.)

P. 272–273 THE ROCK ON CAMERA. NEW HAVEN, CONNECTICUT, APRIL 27, 1999. (PHOTOGRAPHER: TOM BUCHANAN) © 2000 WORLD WRESTLING FEDERATION ENTERTAINMENT, INC. ALL RIGHTS RESERVED.

P. 277   THE ROCK. NASSAU COLISEUM, NEW YORK, DECEMBER 29, 1997. (PHOTOGRAPHER: RICH FREEDA) © 2000 WORLD WRESTLING FEDERATION ENTERTAINMENT, INC. ALL RIGHTS RESERVED.

P. 278   THE ROCK. © 2000 WORLD WRESTLING FEDERATION ENTERTAINMENT, INC. ALL RIGHTS RESERVED.

P. 281   THE ROCK GIVING THE PEOPLE'S EYEBROW. DETROIT,

PHOTO CREDITS

 **COLOR INSERT**